Topics in Astrology

Bob Makransky

Copyright © Bob Makransky 2015, 2020

Dear Brutus Press

ISBN-13: 978-0-9677315-5-1

Acknowledgements

The chapters on "Transiting Changes of Station", "Lunations", "Willie & Maud", "Politics of Relationship", "Day of Reckoning", "Picking Winning Lottery Numbers", and "Transits to Angles" ©1993, 1995, 2001, 2002, 2010, 2011, 2012 by *Dell Horoscope Magazine*. Reprinted with permission. Special thanks to Ronnie Grishman for this use.

The chapters on "Mayan Astrology" and "Theodore Roosevelt's Secondary Progressions" originally appeared in *Diamond Fire* magazine. Special thanks are due to Joseph Polansky for this use.

The chapters on "Mental Chemistry", "Interpretation of Transits", and "The Chance of a Lifetime!" originally appeared in *The Mountain Astrologer*. Special thanks to Nan Geary for this use.

"Poem in October" by Dylan Thomas, from THE POEMS OF DYLAN THOMAS, copyright ©1945 by The Trustees for the Copyrights of Dylan Thomas, first published in POETRY. Reprinted by permission of New Directions Publishing Corp.

Special thanks to Gene Vikutan of AstroApp.com for providing the Sunshine House System horoscope charts.

This book is dedicated to the memory of Flora Urquhart of Oakland, who blew my mind so bad that I started studying astrology; and to the memory of my teacher don Abel Yat Saquib, who blew my mind so bad that I gave it up.

Contents:

Acknowledgements 3

A Note on References 6

Natal Astrology:
Intuition in Astrology 7
The Sunshine House System 13
The Mantle 24
Astrolocality 37
Mental Chemistry 43
Ira Einhorn 50
The Nodes in the Houses 59
The Slave of Duty 64

Relationships:
The Politics of Relationship 66
Assessing Partnership Compatibility 73
Sexual Significators in Synastry 82
How to Compare Two People's Horoscopes 85
Willie and Maud – a Spiritual Marriage 104

Transits:
Interpretation of Transits 117
Mutual Transits 130
Transiting Synodic Cycles of Venus and Mercury 153
Transits to the Angles 163
Turning Points 178
A Day of Reckoning 185
Lunations 191
The Chance of a Lifetime! 199
Saturn Return Readings 209

Progressions and Directions:
Archie Goodwin's Horoscope 217
Theodore Roosevelt's Secondary Progressions 220
Primary Directions for Beginners 233
Why Directions Sometimes Fail 239

Horary and Electional Astrology:
La Noche Triste 242
Nixon's Question 244
The *Titanic* 251
Picking Winning Lottery Numbers 256

Mundane Astrology:
A Baffling Problem 270
Thatcher's Comet 273

Mayan Astrology... 276

Theory:
On the Domification Problem 294
The Celestial Hourglass 299
Geodetic Equivalents 306
What Do We Mean by "Strength"? 311

Tables:
Table of Favorable and Unfavorable Planetary
  Combinations 88
Table of Keywords for the Transiting and Natal Planets 118

Books by Bob Makransky................................. 315

A Note on References:

Chart data (unless otherwise specified) is taken from AstroDatabank (http://www.astro.com/astro-databank/Main_Page).

References to the life of Theodore Roosevelt are embedded in the main text in superscript [brackets]. These are taken from the following sources:

(from 10/27/1858 to 9/13/1901):
The Rise of Theodore Roosevelt by Edmund Morris, Ballantine Books NYC 1979
(from 9/14/1901 to 3/4/1909):
Theodore Rex by Edmund Morris, Random House NYC 2001
(from 3/9/1909 to 1/18/1919):
T.R – The Last Romantic by H.W. Brands, Basic Books NYC 1997
(else):
(*Autobio*) = *Autobiography* by Theodore Roosevelt, 1913, Project Gutenberg ebook 2002

References to the life of William Butler Yeats are embedded in the main text in superscripts as follows:

◇ page references are:
from 1865-1914 = R. F. Foster, *W.B. Yeats: A Life, I: The Apprentice Mage*, Oxford U. Press 1997;
from 1915-1939 = R. F. Foster, *W.B. Yeats: A Life II: The Arch Poet*, Oxford U. Press 2003
{} page references = W. B. Yeats, *Memoirs* (and *Journal*), ed. by Denis Donoghue, Macmillan NYC 1973
[] page references = W. B. Yeats, *Autobiographies*, ed. by William H. O'Donnell and Douglas N. Archibald, Scribner NYC 1965
^^ page references = Maud Gonne and W.B. Yeats, *The Gonne – Yeats Letters 1893 – 1938*, ed. by Anna MacBride White and A. Norman Jeffares, Syracuse U. Press 1994
page references = W. B. Yeats, *A Vision*, NYC: Collier, 1966.

Intuition in Astrology

Astrology is not just an intellectual enterprise (although it does depend on concepts); rather, it is a training ground for intuition, or what one might call "direct knowing". This is why a beginning astrologer with psychic ability will generally give more correct information to a client than a non-psychic astrologer who has been studying the subject for a lifetime. Although the study of astrology does require much left-brain activity (learning what different symbols and combinations of symbols mean), true comprehension and application of astrology is more a matter of opening up our intuitive channels, of letting go of our ego defenses, intellectual belief systems, and doubts, and of learning to respect and respond to our gut feelings.

This was easier to do for astrologers in centuries past than it is now, because the trend in our modern society has been toward rationalistic and materialistic solutions to problems. We are taught to rely upon so-called objective thinking, and to distrust our own feelings, which cannot be corroborated and therefore leave us standing alone. Indeed, the modern trend in astrology has been to move away from intuition.

One trend in this direction is represented by humanistic astrology, which eschews prediction and opts instead for a Gestalt approach, relying upon psychological mumbo-jumbo instead of telling people what's really happening, and probably going to happen, in their lives. Humanistic astrology has something of a sour grapes flavor to it; beyond that, it can do a disservice to clients who are not (usually) as interested in a holistic analysis of their human potential as they are in solid information about their love lives, finances, health, etc.

Another trend has been towards materialistic astrology which seeks to recast astrology in terms which would be acceptable to academic science. Astrologers of this school try to find statistical proof for the verities of astrology, which – as Michel Gauquelin after a lifetime of effort has shown – is impossible except for the tiniest little bits here and there. These astrologers attempt to remove from astrology anything that smacks of superstition or mysticism. Thus most astrologers of the materialistic school reject the use of "unscientific" signs and houses, even though there is no more statistical proof of the validity of midpoints than there is for signs and houses. In their toadying to the scientific establishment (which rejects them anyway, as it rejected Gauquelin) materialistic astrologers risk being led into intellectual dishonesty.

Such trends notwithstanding, astrology is still one of the last strongholds of spiritual truth in our society. Most of what we do nowadays is done on the basis of logic, conditioning, immutable schedules, what other people expect from us or would approve of, rather than on the basis of what *feels right*. In other words, we do what we think we ought to do instead of doing what our hearts tell us to do. And while this is a viable strategy for success in materialistic society, you can't do astrology this way.

To be an intuitive astrologer, it helps to have the sign Aquarius emphasized in your natal horoscope. But even if you're not a "natural", it is still possible to emulate those Aquarian qualities which facilitate relating to other people on an intuitive level: democracy, seeing other people as your equals, being willing to relate to people from all walks of life and stations of society without shame, superiority, or false humility. If you are not capable of seeing others as your equals, then you are defending yourself against them; and whatever you are doing to defend yourself against them will prevent you from psychically attuning yourself to them.

To get your intuition flowing you must be willing to fly with your hunches. If it's important to you that you always be right, then you'll never make it as an intuitive astrologer. The channel through which insight flows is blocked by the door of worrying about whether you're right or wrong. Only the courage to be wrong can open you enough to feel what's going on, what the real needs of the client are, and what his or her chart is trying to tell you. Once you're no longer afraid of looking foolish, you just say the first thing that pops into your mind.

Everyone who visits an astrologer does so because some question is weighing on them. Even when they claim to be consulting you out of mere curiosity, in truth there is some problem bugging them, or else they wouldn't have come to you. It's your job as an astrologer to elicit and address their problem. This is not done by questioning them, but by examining their horoscopes and by staying open to their feelings; and this can be done even when the clients are not physically present.

In everyday life we tend to block the feelings which other people send our way. We're usually more concerned with maintaining our own self-image, with impressing people, with winning their approval, than we are with listening to them and understanding where they are coming from. When interpreting charts it is necessary to put aside your own attitudes and prejudices and see the clients and their problems from their own point of view, without any judgments or criticism. You have to go into an interpretation without a point of view of your own.

One good way of doing this is to begin every horoscope interpretation with an invocation. You do this silently: take a moment to ask for divine guidance in helping your clients to find the answers they are seeking. If you are a Christian you can call upon Jesus for this help; if not, you can call upon the spirit guardians of astrological wisdom to guide you to the correct judgments. The point is that by beginning your interpretation session with a prayer you wipe the ego slate clean by the symbolic act of surrendering your own will (desire to look good) and letting the powers of the universe take over.

The best training ground for intuitive astrologers is horary astrology. In horary you use little pieces of the chart (the planets and houses which govern the particular question being asked) and ignore everything else, which helps to focus your attention. One thing that tends to overwhelm neophyte astrologers is the sheer mountain of information in a birth chart, since they have not yet learned what to focus on and what to ignore. Beyond that, a horary horoscope is completely centered in the now moment, is less encumbered by personal history (yours or the clients'), and is usually prompted by a strong desire for an answer; which makes it easier to tune into than a natal chart, where there are all sorts of themes and crosscurrents of emotion going on which have to be sorted out.

The flux of the universe is constant – and movement is extremely fast. What was a correct prediction a moment ago may not be valid now. A horary chart erected tomorrow may give a completely different message than one erected to answer the same question today. This is why it's best, when you are using horary astrology for your own guidance, not to go to the oracle on your own, but rather to wait until some outside event happens (which bears on the question) and to erect the horary chart for the moment of that event. Such charts are always readable, even if they contain strictures – such as a void-of-course moon – which normally defeat interpretation (in such cases the answer is usually "no" or "not yet".)

Another reason why horary astrology is a better training ground for intuition than natal astrology is because it's more symbolic, less rational. A typical horary textbook consists of a quick set of rules designed to suggest answers, and then long lists of symbols for each horoscope factor. For example, a list (Simmonite's) of places ruled by Saturn might read: "deserts, woods, obscure valleys, ... dens, ... church yards, ruinous buildings, ... sinks, wells, muddy, dirty, stinking places." When you've memorized – or better yet, gotten a feel for – what each symbol means (in this case, Saturn-type places), you find that in the moment of interpretation one particular item pops into your mind. You don't have to rack your brains to figure out the correct interpretation from the smorgasbord of possibilities; if you know what the symbol means (how it *feels),* then you'll always be led to the correct interpretation of that symbol in this instance.

Thus, horary astrology is more of a "symbol bank" than natal astrology: there's less of an intellectual system to it, and what system there is, is more abstract (such as the ring-around-the-rosy technique for locating questions in houses; e.g., the father's brother's income being shown by the second from the third from the fourth = the seventh house).

Horary astrology is more like dreaming, where natal astrology is more like being awake. Things are more symbolical in horary, hence closer to true feeling (what's really going on). Just as we can learn more about our true state of feeling – what's really making us happy or unhappy – by studying our dreams rather than by constantly examining and re-examining our waking lives, so too can we get sharper, clearer answers from horary astrology than from natal. Indeed, natal astrology becomes increasingly effective as we are able to integrate horary techniques into it.

The other day I was interpreting the chart of a young man who is leaving the service and trying to decide what he should do next. He had Mercury in Pisces opposing (and mutual reception) Jupiter in Virgo across the 9th – 3rd house axis. I got a strong impression that he should study and go for a professional degree in some humanistic field. He asked if he should study in his native

Puerto Rico or go abroad, to the States; I got the impression that he should go abroad – further abroad than the U.S. The word "France" popped into my mind, which made him chuckle when I told him because he doesn't speak French, doesn't have money to travel, and the whole idea seemed off the wall to him. Nonetheless I suggested that he look into it, to see what opportunities to study in France are available.

And that's that. That was my job as an astrologer. It doesn't matter if he never goes to France; it doesn't even matter if he's crossing the street tomorrow and gets run over by a truck. Whether my prediction is right or not has nothing to do with how well I did my job as an astrologer. There is a Zen story about the most celebrated archer in all of Japan, who has never once succeeded in hitting the bulls-eye. In astrology, as in Zen archery, the concern has to be for the process, not for the result. Because of a mysterious law of nature, that's the *only way to get good results.*

Now the prediction about going to France obviously has nothing to do with the horoscope feature which prompted that prediction. Neither Mercury, nor Pisces, nor Jupiter, nor Virgo, nor their combination, specifically carry the meaning "France". How "France" came out of that, I don't know. In someone else's chart that identical planetary configuration might have an altogether different meaning. And at another point in my client's life, when some other problem is bothering him, that same configuration might have a different interpretation also. Horoscope factors only mean something with respect to a particular client at a particular moment in time. Although we learn astrology inductively – we learn what, for example, Mars square Saturn means by studying the lives and characters of the natives we know who have Mars square Saturn – we cannot interpret charts inductively.

This is why most statistical studies of astrology are doomed to failure. Astrology is a wavelength we can tune into, not a dead specimen we can dissect and expect to learn anything from. We can learn to *feel* what Mars square Saturn means by studying its effects in a hundred cases; but we cannot arrive at a correct interpretation in the hundred-and-first case by extrapolating from a preconceived list of concepts or likely possibilities. There are just too many possibilities.

Nor can we gain anything by adding more and more points to the horoscope (hypothetical planets, midpoints, asteroids, etc.); all that does is muddy the waters. As Dr. Marc Edmund Jones pointed out, astrology should not be more complex than life itself. Rather, astrology should be a means of simplifying, of cutting across complexities and arriving at clear-cut answers. And this can only be done by bypassing the level of conscious, thinking mind.

We need to study what Mars square Saturn has meant in order to tune in to a certain feeling – the feeling of Mars square Saturn. Then when we run into a chart containing Mars square Saturn, we pick up this feeling and let it lead us to the correct interpretation. We do need a grounding in the basics – an intuitive feel for what the different horoscope factors symbolize – and this implies study. There are intuitive astrologers who can come up with the correct interpretation just by touching a chart (without even looking at it); but most of us are not blessed with such extraordinary ESP. Nonetheless, we can each develop our intuition by studying what all the different horoscope elements mean (how they each feel). The study of astrology itself serves to open our intuitive channels.

To be an intuitive astrologer requires humility. This doesn't mean false humility: not taking complete responsibility for what you're doing. It means not going into an interpretation with preconceived ideas, points to defend, a know-it-all attitude. Being an astrologer, even a beginning one, means that people are going to believe what you say. This is a *big* responsibility. There is a natural tendency to cop out of this responsibility by being either overly serious (playing the mountebank) or not serious enough (playing the dilettante). To be humble means to respect the client, to respect yourself as an astrologer, and to respect the craft of astrology. You have to go into each interpretation as if it were the first one you have ever done, and yet with the confidence that you will be guided to the correct interpretation. Then it all just happens by itself.

The Sunshine House System

Most of us astrologers have at one time or another wondered why astrology doesn't work as well as it's "supposed" to. Although adamant in defense of astrology when confronted by skeptics, we nonetheless agonize in our innermost souls as to whether the ancient astrologers were lying; or whether astrology just doesn't function as well in this decadent age; or whether– horror of horrors! – we may just be *fooling ourselves.*

No, no, it can't be that. After all, that prediction we made about cousin Tillie's boyfriend was right on the button! So why then, if astrology *does* work so well sometimes, do we find it so hard to make it work consistently? Where does the fault lie, dear Brutus – with astrology, or with ourselves?

Actually, the problem is not with astrology per se, but with how we modern, western astrologers have been practicing it (or better said: conceptualizing it) for the past several centuries. Ever since astrology and astronomy parted company 300 years ago, both branches of the Uranian science have gone astray. They've lost contact with their true roots – the astrology spirits who, from time immemorial, have guided astrologers and helped them to make accurate judgments.

The Hindu astrologers never lost contact with the astrology spirits, and hence they haven't gone through the crisis of confidence experienced in the west. The Hindu astrologers respect the astrology spirits (heed their counsel); they respect their craft; they respect themselves; and therefore they are respected in turn by their community. We occidental astrologers – in our endeavor to turn astrology into a "reasonable" and "rational" (hence "respectable") science (which it isn't) – have turned our backs on the astrology spirits, have prostituted our craft and ourselves, and thus justly deserve the opprobrium which mainstream society heaps upon us. If we were delivering up accurate predictions, you can be sure they'd be singing a different tune.

To the astrology spirits, all statistical research is hooey. It may be interesting and even illuminating, but even if it *did* score little points before the Rationalist-Materialistic Inquisition (which it doesn't), it has nothing whatsoever to do with astrology. Astrology is not a matter of mind nor of logic.

The aphorisms of the ancient astrologers were not meant to be taken as *rules* in the modern sense, but rather as examples of how to interpret charts by the Spirit (by intuition). We western astrologers have our rules – e.g. that moon in the 2nd house means such-and-such, or that Mars square Saturn means thus-and-so, etc. – and then we try to deduce meanings by using logical deduction (reasoning).

Rather, the thing should be done by *feeling,* not by thinking. The ancient astrologers and the Hindus did it that way. We don't need astrology spirits to interpret horoscopes; we can do that with our own feelings once we've learned how to get our intuition flowing. What the spirits want to do at this time is to teach (or reteach) us western astrologers HOW: give us concrete tools to work with.

Of course, there are some astrologers out there right now who are already doing this as a matter of course; and practically every astrologer has done it now and again: made an astoundingly accurate prediction without knowing quite how he or she did it. What the spirits want to do is to show us how to do it all the time – consistently give our clients specific, exact information rather than vague generalities such as those which are cranked out by computers.

To start with, the astrology spirits recommend changing the manner in which we calculate horoscopes. This is not because there's anything wrong with traditional house systems per se; after all, the ancient astrologers got good results from them. Rather, by misusing these horoscopes – by treating astrology and its guardians with disrespect – we western astrologers have put bad vibes over these horoscopes, and so have rendered them inoperative.

The spirits recommend abandoning all current house systems and using instead a system of 24 half-houses which are precisely analogous to the planetary hours. (see the Appendix of my book *Planetary Hours*). The exact details on how horoscopes should be interpreted in this system have yet to be worked out.

In the meantime the spirits recommend using a system of 12 houses in which the houses have the usual meanings (1st = personality, 2nd = money, etc.), but which are calculated as follows:

To obtain the houses above the horizon (7 – 12) the Sun's diurnal (declination) arc (the length of time from sunrise to sunset) is divided into six parts; to obtain the houses beneath the horizon (1 – 6) the Sun's nocturnal arc (the length of time from sunset to sunrise) is divided into six parts. Then these 12 division points are projected onto the ecliptic with house circles (house circles are great circles on the celestial sphere which pass through the north and south points on the horizon. The Campanus and Regiomontanus systems also project with house circles, but the former divides the prime vertical into 12 parts, and the latter divides the celestial equator into 12 parts).

Because this new house system results from a division of the sun's diurnal circle, we call it the *Sunshine House System.* Although we are trying to get away from logic, a moment's reflection will show that the sun's diurnal circle is indeed the most logical circle to divide to produce mundane houses. If the houses are to be considered analogous to the signs; and if the signs result from a division of the sun's yearly path (the ecliptic); then it follows that the houses should result from a division of the sun's daily path – its diurnal or declination circle; i.e., the small circle parallel to the celestial equator which passes through the natal sun.

Since the analogy requires that the angles be house cusps (or in any event, the spirits require it), projection of these 12 division points must needs be with house circles, since only a projection with house circles retains both the Ascendant and Midheaven as house cusps.

The Sunshine House System has two unusual features:

    1) Three parameters (Sidereal Time, Latitude, and Declination of natal sun) are required to compute house cusps, rather than only two (ST and Latitude) required by all other house systems. This feature precludes a table of houses for the Sunshine House System, but in this age of computers this is not really a problem.

    2) Opposite house cusps (except for the four angles: ASC, IC, DESC, and MC) do not lie opposite in the zodiac. In fact, it is common to find intercepted pairs of signs which do not lie opposite in the zodiac. This is an odd feature, but certainly not an objectionable one.

When I began recalculating the horoscopes in my files using the Sunshine House System, the first experiment I tried was secondary progressions to intermediate house cusps. I had always regarded secondary progressions to intermediate house cusps to be the acid test of proof for a house system (transits, because of retrogradation, are too uncertain to use as a test for timing). I had never seen secondary progressions to intermediate house cusps work in any of the half-dozen other house systems in which I'd tried them.

I found that – like most astrological techniques – progressions to the intermediate Sunshine House cusps work better in some charts than others; but when they do work, they are amazingly accurate. For example, in my own horoscope:

P SU 11th	began dairy farm (2 months later)
P SU 12th	beginning huge lawsuit (one month later; dragged on for next decade)
P ME 11th	birth of first child (3 months later)
P ME 12th	ex-wife informed me leaving with kids for another country (exact)
P VE 11th	middle of non-affair with K. (see "Why Directions Sometimes Fail")
P VE 12th	started blueberry farm; rapprochement with ex-wife (2 months later)
P MA 9th	graduated high school (exact) + entered college

However, my most interesting discovery occurred when I took a vacation and found myself in the (for me) unusual position of doing a lot of face-to-face natal consultations for complete strangers. I calculated all these new charts with the Sunshine House System, and I discovered the following:

Using the Sunshine House System and the traditional house symbolism (e.g. 7th = marriage, 8th = death, 9th = journeys / religion, etc.) I found that I obtained much clearer psychic impressions than I'd ever experienced in the 20 years I'd then been studying astrology. My astrology mysteriously reached an altogether new level. I'd be looking at some feature in a chart, and then suddenly I'd just *know*, beyond a shadow of a doubt, precisely what happened to that guy at age 6; or what he'll be doing in 20 years; or what's bothering him right now.

When I use the Sunshine House System, it sometimes happens that an actual picture pops up before my mind's eye; but more often it's just a feeling of something known – like reaching out for a memory of something which you know, but can't quite put your finger on – which horoscope symbols help you pin down or express in words. The impressions definitely come from the native, not the horoscope. Nonetheless the horoscope is intrinsic to the process. All feelings take off from symbols in the horoscope; and also the horoscope serves as a focus or way of conceptualizing feelings which are in the air. It can't be done without the horoscope (at least I can't do it without the horoscope).

Although you can use intuition with everyone, the clearest impressions come from natives who are themselves psychic, or who are at least open-hearted and straightforward people. The guy who sits there with his arms crossed and with an "I dare you!" look on his face can effectively block any attempts to psychically probe him. You have to break down such a native's screen of thought forms (penetrate his defenses) before you can give him his money's worth. I can usually get an antagonistic or dubious client to loosen up by starting (in a friendly and easy manner) with his or her current progressions and transits. I get clients used to the sound of my voice; I let them know that I'm not threatening nor judging them; and then, when they're relaxed, I can start pulling impressions out of them. The point is that if you're going to be an intuitive astrologer, you have to be open to the native (rather than defending some sort of ego trip of your own). This means respecting the native, and also respecting yourself; it means giving the person emotional space, and at the same time, not permitting him or her to encroach upon yours.

There is really no other way of being able to give specific information to a client except through intuition. That's the only way to cut through all the innumerable possibilities of what the symbols *could* mean logically, to arrive at what they do mean in a particular case. The materialistic astrologers who believe that astrology should be based upon reason rather than intuition are only promulgating an astrology of distrust: distrust in the Spirit, distrust in their own abundant inner knowledge, and distrust in the craft of astrology. We are not advocating "blind faith" in astrology here; we're talking about concrete results that we can each validate for ourselves in our own practice.

The Sunshine House System is a link, given to us by the astrology spirits, to help us activate and utilize our latent intuition. If you use a house-based astrology in your practice, I highly recommend your giving the Sunshine House System a whirl. I think you will be surprised and gratified to find how such a simple adjustment as changing the house system you use can produce such an amazing difference in the specificity and accuracy of your predictions.

You can obtain free Sunshine House cusp calculations from https://astroapp.com or http://www.astro.com/cgi/genchart.cgi (specify that you want Sunshine House System charts – on astro.com it's at the bottom of the house system drop-down list). Or, better yet, download the excellent free software from https://www.jcremers.com/ or https://www.astrolog.org/astrolog.htm.

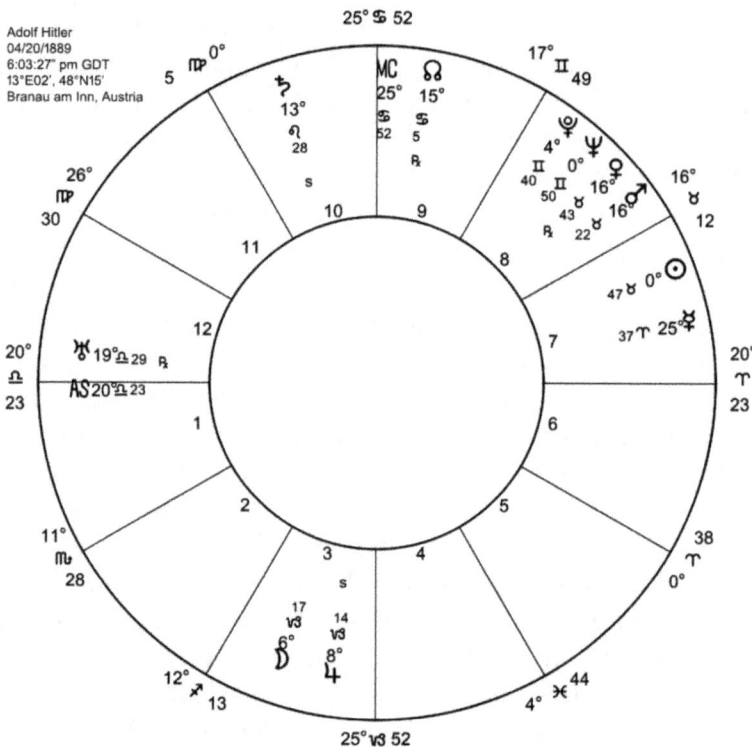

A good place to begin trying the Sunshine House System out is by looking at the Charubel symbols for the zodiacal degrees occupied by the Sunshine House cusps. Of the various systems of (usually channeled) symbols for the 360 zodiacal degrees which are available, I have found in practice that the Charubel symbols work the best most of the time, with the Sabian symbols (Dr. Marc Edmund Jones' version – *not* Dane Rudhyar's version) also suggestive and worth looking into. You can download Charubel's book *The Degrees of the Zodiac Symbolized* for free from any number of online sources. The story on degree symbols is like the story of the little girl who had a little curl right in the middle of her forehead: when they're good, they're very, very good; and when they're bad, they're horrid (in which case you just don't use them – but that may be a reason to suspect the birth time / ascending degree). When they do work they can provide a check on a rectification obtained by other means (e.g. primary and secondary directions to angles), or help to decide which is the correct one between two adjacent rising degrees.

Generally speaking, the symbol for the rising degree (ASC) describes who the person is; and the symbol for the culminating degree (MC) describes what they do, and how they do it. The other (ten) degree symbols don't always relate directly to the particular houses to which they correspond; rather, taken together they often "tell a little story" or describe the tone of the person's life. I've found that in my own case – and those of people whom I know well whose birth times I have rectified exactly by other means – the Charubel symbols for the Sunshine House cusps are often remarkable in the depth and exactitude with which they pinpoint major issues, attitudes, strengths, difficulties, talents, areas of denial, etc. in people's lives. In my own horoscope this set of symbols has been both a comfort to me, and also a source of hope and guidance.

Here we will use Adolf Hitler's horoscope as the example (see endnote for birth information). Most of Hitler's Sunshine House cusp Charubel symbols are pretty nasty; but they do tend to run to a type. This is often the case: that the collection of Charubel symbols for the Sunshine House cusps of a horoscope, as a group, evoke a consistent mood or flavor which describes how the people make their way in the world (for example, by being hard and mean, or gentle and wistful, or direct and forthright, or visionary and spiritual, or confused and clueless, or whatever). Although most of the Charubel symbols for Hitler's Sunshine house cusps are of the hard and mean variety, a few are indicative of his tremendous personal charm (having Venus sole dispositor) which endeared him to his intimates, such as his best friend Ernst Röhm, his niece and true love Geli Raubal, and his mistress Eva Braun (at least until he murdered them). Note the striking symbolism of Hitler's rising degree; and consider that the Charubel symbols were first published in 1898, long before the swastika assumed its present sinister import:

Table of Charubel Symbols for Adolf Hitler's Sunshine House Cusps

ASC 20°LI 23'	**A cross formed of darts, that is, having a barbed termination to each arm.**	A very positive character. A person of strong will. He will never allow anyone to impose on him. He is ever on the defensive; one with magical abilities.
2nd 11°SC 28'	**A bull pawing up the earth.**	Denotes a person who will have his own way; his anger is lasting.
3rd 12°SG 13'	**Death, with a scythe in one hand, and a bag of money in the other.**	A miser; one who will starve himself for gain; and one who would delight in slaughter and carnage if it would prove of some monetary advantage to himself.
IC 25°CP 52'	**Too revolting to be given.**	Whoever thou art who mayest have this degree on thy ascendant, keep out of bad company. Indulge not in stimulants; keep clear of the gambling hells, and seek to develop thy higher nature; by such a course thou mayest save thyself.

5th 4°PI 44'	A black pall suspended, and a man in a gloomy enclosure looking at it despairingly; finally he musters courage to lift the pall, and enters a dark passage, which, however, finally conducts him into the light of a glorious day.	Whosoever thou art with this degree on thy ascendant, be prepared for trials, but don't give up in despair; for ere thy fortieth year shall have expired, thy day will have dawned [*Nb. This actually occurred in Hitler's 44th year, with T Uranus opposition its natal position*].
6th 0°AR 38'	A man ploughing in the midst of a boundless plain.	This denotes one possessing a great amount of individuality and originality; ambitious of being the first in everything. Very jealous of a rival; not an agreeable companion.
DESC 20°AR 23'	A shovel standing near an open grave, in which I see a man digging.	This degree points to one who will be a sexton, an undertaker, or otherwise will have to do with the dead.
8th 16°TA 12'	A very small cottage at the base of a very high mountain, where jutting rocks appear to overhang the cottage perpetually threatening its destruction.	A truly good person; one who has Implicit faith in the Most High.
9th 17°GE 49'	The number 6 rules this degree.	Denotes a purely mercurial person; an expert in all mercurial employments.

MC 25°CN 52'	**A gentleman with a number of ladies in a carriage.**	This denotes a good and kindly disposition; a person very liberal with his presents, in - whose nature benevolence bubbles, lacking in circumspection, a veritable "Timon of Athens."
11th 0°VI 05'	**A wolf carrying away a lamb.**	Denotes deception, cunning, avarice, and cruelty. Such a degree, unless there be much to counteract it, would render the native liable to become a great criminal.
12th 26° VI 30'	**I see nothing but sunshine; all is bright – a cloudless sky.**	Denotes a prosperous person; he is truly happy, being born under most favorable conditions.

Note: per the horoscope for Adolf Hitler calculated by Wilhelm Wulff (Heinrich Himmler's personal astrologer) shown below, Hitler was born at 6:03:53" pm GDT (5:56:01" pm LMT) on April 20, 1889 in Branau am Inn, Austria (13°E02', 48°N15'); which here was rectified by Dr. Rumen Kolev to 6:03:27" pm via the primary direction Saturn conjunct MC mundane direct (Cardanus key = 59'12" / year) = 12/21/1907, the date of his mother's death, and two months before he failed the entrance examination for the Academy of Fine Arts in Vienna, which destroyed his ambition to become an architect. See Rumen Kolev's *Primary Directions I*, Astro-Research Center Zenith, Varna Bulgaria 1996 (available from http://www.babylonianastrology.com) for details. Anyone who wishes to delve into the house division question is advised to read my book on primary directions and celestial sphere geometry (and the mathematical basis of the Sunshine House System), available as a free download from:

https://www.dropbox.com/l/scl/AADAM79RJoyiAuaiL1cBL7iiXTx4ZKfBvBw
https://www.dropbox.com/l/scl/AACqoT8RC-qRUQB14ztImNgetUqX3-TGrdU
https://www.dropbox.com/l/scl/AACzLtDlnnPfTuFtJU7zOHnGk8zeXi11aNo

Secondary progressions to Sunshine house cusps in Hitler's chart aren't very revealing; there are only three, two of which occurred in his youth (before biographers tracked him), and the last one (P MA 9th = spring 1934) occurred the year after he assumed dictatorship of Germany, while he was in the midst of consolidating his power (and eliminating rivals).

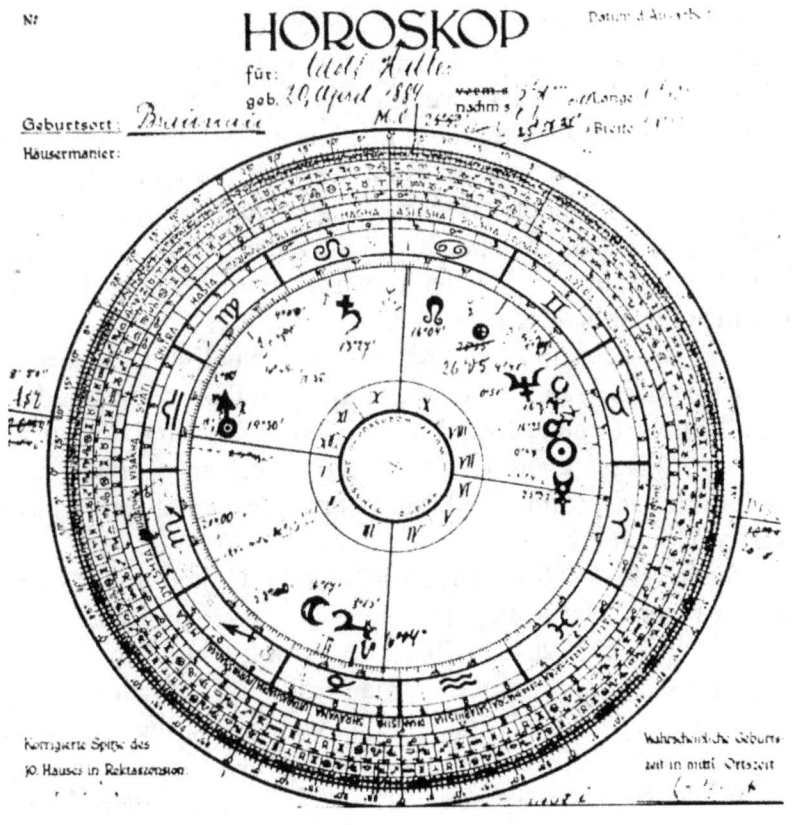

The Mantle

And it shall come to pass that I, the Lord God, will send one mighty and strong, holding the sceptre of power in his hand, clothed with light for a covering, to set in order the house of God.
— Joseph Smith[1]

The God of the polygamists is the God of the Old Testament. When God revived the ancient priesthood of Melchizedek, Abraham, and Moses in 1830 and appointed Joseph Smith as His Prophet, He revealed to Joseph Smith that the highest exaltation in the eternal world would accrue to those who sealed His new covenant with the Old Testament practice of polygamy (plural marriage). Polygamy was to be the outward sign of God's chosen people, the Mormons, setting them apart from the gentile tribes around them.

One of the first men in the new Mormon Church whom Joseph Smith told of God's revelation about polygamy was his friend and business manager, Benjamin Johnson. Johnson accepted the revelation as the true will of God; he gave two of his sisters in marriage to the Prophet as plural wives; and Joseph Smith later adopted him as his son. A special charge and order of priesthood was conferred upon him by Joseph Smith that became known, to Benjamin Johnson's descendants, as The Mantle.

The persecution of the Mormons — usually on the pretext of their practice of polygamy — drove them from their homes in the east, through Illinois (where Joseph Smith was murdered by an armed mob in 1844), and eventually to Utah where they finally settled. Joseph Smith had prophesized that his people would find a haven in the Rocky Mountains.

During the 1860's through 1880's the United States Congress passed stringent anti-polygamy laws aimed specifically at the Mormons, until in 1890 the official Mormon Church bowed to the political pressure and issued a manifesto condemning polygamy (thereby assuring Utah of statehood as well as the legitimacy of the Mormon Church in the eyes of the government).

While many Mormons acceded to the official line, a substantial minority of "Fundamentalists" regarded it as the betrayal of one of the most sacred principles of Mormonism, for which the early Saints had suffered persecution, and Joseph Smith martyrdom, to uphold. Many disaffected Fundamentalists continued to practice polygamy in secret, like Benjamin Johnson's grandson Dayer LeBaron (1886-1951), establishing themselves in polygamist colonies in Mexico.

Just before Benjamin Johnson died he conferred The Mantle he had received from Joseph Smith upon his grandson Dayer, with the words, "When I die my Mantle will fall upon you as the Mantle of Elijah fell upon Elisha."[2] He explained to his grandson that in the fullness of time God's purpose as predicted by Joseph Smith – to raise up One Mighty and Strong to set in order the house of God – would be fulfilled by the bearer of The Mantle.

After the old man's death, Dayer LeBaron wrestled in his conscience with the meaning of this responsibility until one day he had a vision in which he saw his grandfather seated on a beautiful throne, clothed in white robes, holding the golden scepter of the priesthood in his hand, and crowned with seven shining stars (which Dayer interpreted to symbolize his grandfather's seven wives); and out of the heavens came the voice of God which said to him, "This shall be your destiny if you abide my law."[3]

After this vision Dayer put all his doubts aside and accepted the law of plural marriage and the responsibility of The Mantle. Like most Fundamentalists, Dayer believed that the United States ("Babylon") would soon be destroyed due to its refusal to acknowledge God's latter day prophets; and his visions and inspirations led him to establish a colony of polygamists in Chihuahua, Mexico, where his thirteen children by his first wife and his six children by his second wife were raised.

Shortly before Dayer's death in 1951 he passed The Mantle on to Joel LeBaron (1923-1972), his fourth son by his first wife, using the same words his grandfather had used in conferring The Mantle upon him. Ultimately the weight of The Mantel would crush Joel and destroy him: two of his brothers would claim The Mantle from him; and a third brother would kill him for it.

Benjamin LeBaron, Dayer's oldest son by his first wife, was born on May 2nd, 1913 (Benjamin's birthtime is unknown – only Joel's time is known). Benjamin was a bright young man, a good student and the president of his high school class. However, at age 22 he suffered a nervous breakdown after being jilted by his fiancee, and from that time on he was in and out of mental hospitals for the rest of his life.

After his first nervous breakdown he began to hear voices which guided him, and he claimed to be a prophet of God. Because in his rational moments he had lost none of his old brilliance and articulateness, he succeeded in convincing (for a while at least) a number of converts, including his younger brother Ervil, that he was in fact a prophet of destiny. But over time his aspirations grew more and more grotesque: "I am the Prophet Mighty and Strong... I am God, the third; the Holy Ghost; or the third member of the Trinity since Adam went to Mars nearly three hundred years ago, leaving Jesus and Joseph Smith and myself in charge."[4] In spite of his delusions, Benjamin had a sharp mind and was said to be a gentle, kind-hearted, good-humored man.

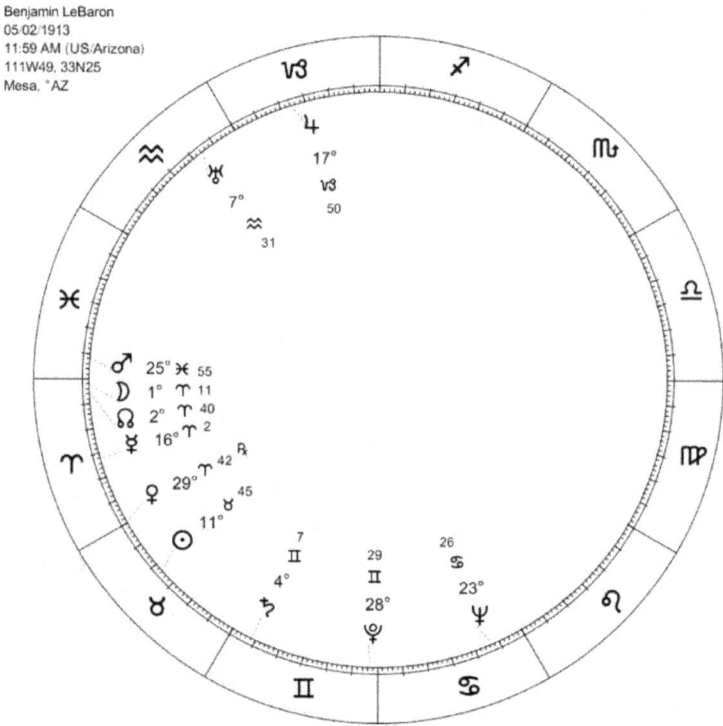

The backbone of Benjamin's solar horoscope is the T-Cross (Jupiter opposition Neptune, mutually square Mercury). A T-Cross shows a state of inner restlessness leading to a powerful outward drive and ambition. However, the T-Cross native tends to trip himself up (by means of whatever is symbolized by the short leg planet – in Benjamin's case, by Mercury = Mind), so that much of his energy goes into seething frustration rather than positive accomplishment. Jupiter opposition Neptune means, in the words of Charles Carter: "revolutionary tendencies of an ungoverned kind... tends much to religion in many forms... sometimes religious enthusiasm and unbalance due to emotionalism; often some form of deception, and a strong tendency to believe in wild 'cults'."[5]

Since Mercury is the short leg of the T-Cross, Benjamin's frustrated sense of destiny manifested as mental confusion, grandiose delusions with (because of the Jupiter – Neptune influence) a religious orientation. The sun square Uranus is another testimony to erratic behavior: "Self-will is likely to be extreme and the judgment is perverse, refusing to take account of the most patent and important facts."[6]

That Benjamin was able to obtain followers at all (at least initially, before his madness became obvious), is due to the conjunction of the moon (public) with the North Node (inspiration), which gives a natural, unpretentious manner that wins popularity with its outspokenness and sincerity.

Wesley LeBaron (born November 16th, 1914), Dayer's third son by his first wife, was a go-getter, a champion athlete in high school, and a very ambitious young man all around. He was intellectually brilliant – many who knew him thought him a genius – and he had various inventions patented and marketed. He had a calm, thoughtful temperament and was a lover of nature (especially animals).

When Dayer was an old man, Wesley had several dreams and visions which he claimed were inspired by God; and he tried unsuccessfully to convince his father to bestow The Mantle upon him in order to fulfill God's will. After Dayer's death Wesley claimed that he – not Joel – was in fact the recipient of The Mantle and the prophesized One Mighty and Strong. Over the next several years Wesley established his own church based on his own revelations, and obtained a moderate but intensely loyal following among non-LeBaron family polygamists.

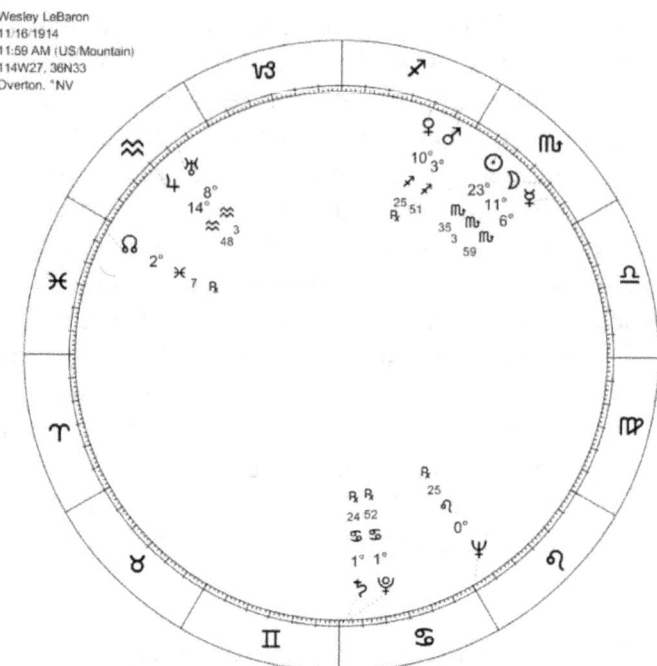

Note that Wesley's horoscope, like Benjamin's, contains a T-Cross, the indicator of dynamic albeit self-frustrating ambition. Here the Uranus opposition Neptune is square Mercury and the moon. According to Carter, Uranus opposition Neptune shows "high motives and ideals, but apt to go to extremes. Highly strung, intense, sensitive, and easily upset. Self-will is marked, and the native will not readily be thwarted or persuaded. The emotional force may be discharged in some such form as religious or pseudo-religious devotion."[7]

Here again Mercury is the short leg of the T-Cross, showing that the native trips himself up via the Mind (grandiose self-images); but here (as opposed to Benjamin's chart) Mercury is stationary (highly strengthened), so the tendency towards mental unbalance is alleviated. Mercury stationary knows exactly what it is doing. The moon is also found near Mercury, which adds some emotional volatility (wishful thinking) to the mental volatility (grandiosity) of Mercury. Moon - Mercury is good, however, for communicating with the public (makes the native quick and adroit, able to pick up the mood of the moment and communicate it forcefully). This is what brought him loyal converts outside his family.

Note how the planets in Wesley's chart tend to pair up in conjunctions: moon - Mercury (understanding, imaginative, agile); Venus - Mars (roguish or boyish charm); Jupiter - Uranus (fervent, inventive, unconventional); and Saturn - Pluto (intense, unyielding, dogged). According to Dr. Marc Edmund Jones, the tendency for the planets in a chart to agglomerate in Close Pairs indicates "an unusual capacity for applying or refining any skills or talents, and for developing a versatility that can win wide approbation."[8] That is, it shows cleverness, originality, resourcefulness, and practicality, which wins other people over to its own way of thinking. However, although Wesley obtained followers outside his family, he never succeeded in convincing his brothers of his claim to the Mantle.

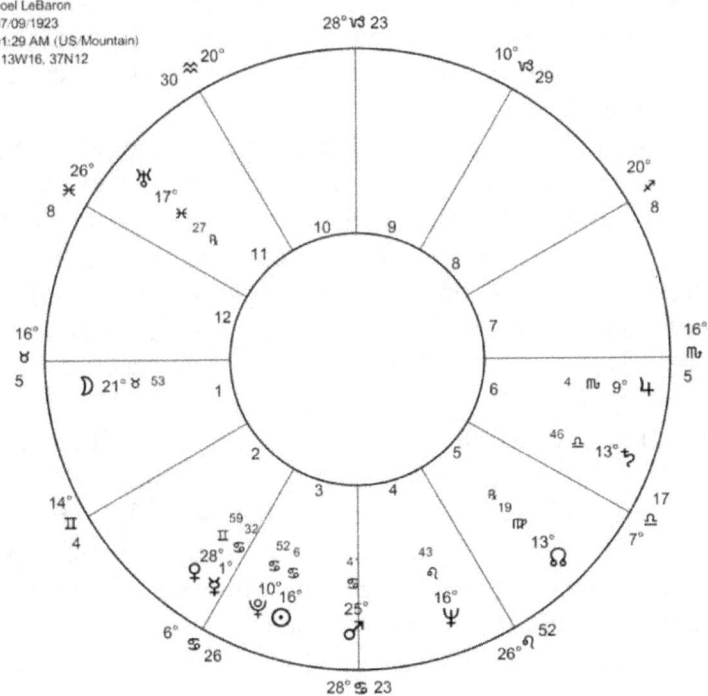

Joel and Ervil LeBaron were Dayer's fourth and fifth sons by his first wife. They were near in age and were inseparable companions throughout their childhood and adolescence. Together they served as dedicated missionaries in the Mormon Church, and with their younger brethren they worked ranches at the colony their father had established in Chihuahua.

When Benjamin began to preach that he was the predicted One Mighty and Strong, Ervil believed and followed him, which led Joel and Ervil to part company for several years.

Everyone who knew Joel considered him to be honest and honorable; staunch and upright; a natural, earthy, unsophisticated man and a dedicated Mormon. He was humble, polite and gentlemanly, gracious and understanding, a true friend. Note that in Joel's chart, the only LeBaron brother's chart for which a birthtime is known[9], no less than three planets are angular, which is a testimony to exceptional social success. Moon conjunct ASC shows tenderness, sweetness, and vulnerability which brings out the gentle and sympathetic instincts in others. Jupiter conjunct DESC shows benevolence and generosity – an avuncular appeal to others such as brings out their trust (not to mention success in marriage). Mars conjunct IC shows concentration, assiduousness and dedication, such as inspires commitment in others.

According to Dr. Marc Edmund Jones' Principle of Negative Indication, whenever all but one of a set of horoscope factors are present in a chart, the emphasis falls on the missing factor, but with a twist of the symbolism (like a parody of what it should mean). In Joel's horoscope planets conjoin all the angles except the MC; hence the emphasis falls on the MC (leadership, authority over others) but in an exaggerated, ineffectual way. Joel – although claiming divine authority and revelation – was a terrible leader. With his grand trine in water signs (true touch with the divine and spiritual; childlike innocence and vulnerability) he was far too soft and indecisive to be an effective leader and organizer. Nor was he an effective businessman: he gave out credit and loans indiscriminately, piled up huge debts, and eventually went bankrupt in every business he tried (trucking, gardening, sawmill, cattle ranch),

While Joel was the brother who received The Mantle from Dayer LeBaron, he never discussed the subject with his brothers. Suddenly one day in September 1955 they received word that Joel, on a trip to Utah, had incorporated his own church – the Church of the First-Born of the Fullness of Times – and declared himself to be the predicted One Mighty and Strong: "Thus saith the Lord: I have called my servant Joel F. LeBaron out of the lands of Mexico, even as I called my servant Moses that through him I might deliver my people from bondage, through him whom I have appointed unto this power to hold the fullness of the Melchizedek Priesthood."[10] Joel claimed that he had received a revelation directly from God about the exact pattern to use to set God's house in order.

Joel's brothers were shocked. The LeBaron family had long been the object of derision among polygamous Mormons because of the activities of Benjamin and Wesley; and now here came the "level-headed" and "sober-minded" LeBaron brother making the same claim!

On Joel's return to Mexico it was apparent to his younger brothers that he was indeed a changed man – that he was truly inspired. Since everyone who knew Joel considered him a man of utmost principle and probity, many of them – after the initial shock – tried to examine his claims objectively. Little by little his brothers and many of his polygamous friends put their doubts aside and, remembering that Dayer LeBaron had indeed given The Mantle to Joel, they accepted Joel as their Prophet and were baptized into his church.

Note that Joel's horoscope also contains a T-Cross (self-defeating ambition and drive). The wide moon opposition Jupiter indicates, according to Carter: "Kindliness and generosity, but restless and combative... an extremist either for or against religion. In his attitude to money and business affairs the native is not as a rule balanced... indifference and carelessness... imprudent... may cause the native to 'let things slide' to his or her detriment."[11]

Here the short leg of the T-Cross is Neptune, showing that the native trips himself up via his ideals and illusions – he tends to be a visionary and a frustrated dreamer. It is significant that progressed sun had conjoined Joel's natal Neptune in July 1955, two months before he declared he was the predicted One Mighty and Strong; and progressed Mars conjoined natal Neptune the following spring, at the time Joel actually organized his church and appointed apostles and counselors.

Of Joel's younger brothers, his most faithful and devoted follower was Ervil (born February 22nd, 1925), who had been his inseparable friend in childhood, and whom he now appointed Patriarch of the new church, second only to the Prophet (Joel) in priestly authority.

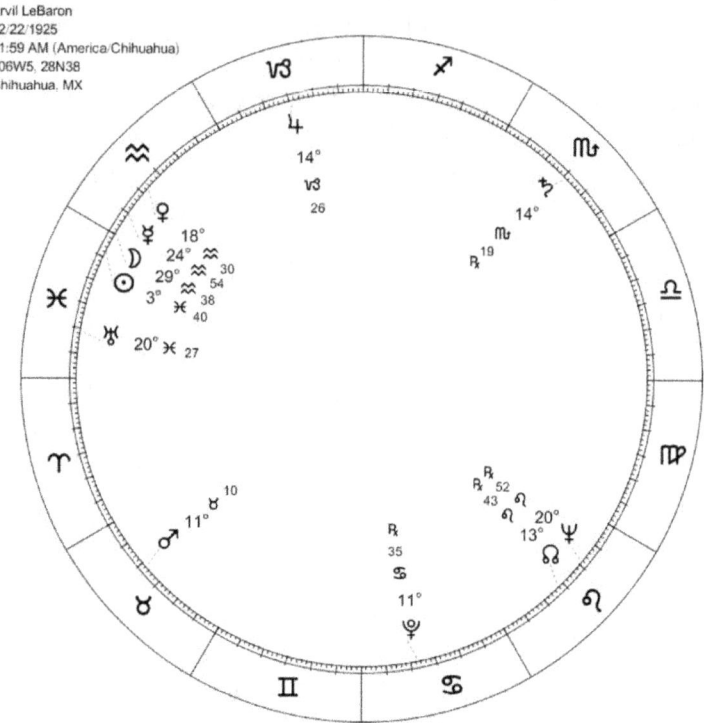

Ervil was the tallest (6' 4") and broadest in a family of tall men. He had previously been a disciple of his brother Benjamin (at first, before Benjamin's lunacy was apparent); and now he became an even more fervent follower of Joel. As Patriarch Ervil directed all missionary activities for the new church, and his tireless dedication, sincerity, and confidence in the truth of Joel's gospel brought many, many new converts to the fold.

Ervil's chart contains a Grand Square in fixed signs – a relatively rare configuration. The Grand Square native appears outwardly to be poised, friendly, outgoing – even saucy and mischievous (makes a sun-in-Aquarius impression); but inwardly he is torn apart by self-doubt and desperately needs other people's validation and approval to maintain his own self-esteem. Where the T-Cross at least has an outlet (the short leg) to vent its frustration and discontent, the Grand Square keeps its feelings bottled up and keeps its energy under tight (albeit superficially grinning) control, which is projected as a need to control others. Behind the native's blithe, self-assured, playful, exterior he is an intense, driven, self-obsessed control freak. Saturn (one point of the Grand Square) is stationary (greatly strengthened), showing shrewdness, cunning, and facility in manipulating people (especially since it is in the sign Scorpio). Mars opposition Saturn signifies, according to Carter, "hardness or sternness ... selfishness or egoism ... impatience with those who do not readily agree."[12] Carter states that the traditional "brutality, cruelty and blood-lust" interpretation of Mars opposition Saturn is "by no means invariably the case."

The other diagonal of the Grand Square is Venus / South Node opposition Neptune / North Node (note that Neptune, the planet of religion as well as illusion, is part of all the brothers' T-Crosses or Grand Square). Carter says of Venus opposition Neptune: "Divine discontent, and a constant restless seeking for an ideal which is not easily realizable on earth ... persistent dissatisfaction both with things and persons, varying from a petulant or peevish attitude, to a noble aspiration and persistent endeavor to seek for a fuller realization of inner visions... confused and deceptive conditions, uncertainty, treachery and instability."[13]

As the years went by and he took on more patriarchal duties, observers of Ervil noted a change in him. He gradually became less friendly and more dictatorial. He began taking special privileges – where Joel dressed in work clothes and drove a beat-up truck, Ervil started wearing tailored clothes and driving new and expensive cars. He appointed a huge church salary for himself. He interfered more and more in the lives of church members, decreeing who should marry or divorce whom, irrespective of the feelings of the people involved; and in this way gathered more and more plural wives unto himself.

Joel was of a forgiving nature and was disinclined to act on complaints he began receiving about Ervil's behavior, hoping that Ervil would straighten out on his own. Moreover Joel was away from the Chihuahua colony much of the time, establishing missions and a new colony in Baja California, thus leaving Ervil in charge of the church. In Joel's absence Ervil – who was now attracting supporters of his own – issued arbitrary orders and openly began to vie with Joel for power and influence. Ervil's thoroughly convincing salesmanship – his instinct for manipulating people by exploiting their weaknesses, flattering them shamelessly or bullying them with scarcely veiled threats – swayed many church members to his way of thinking. Once, when Joel was away, Ervil visited his home and (temporarily) convinced two of Joel's wives that he – not Joel – was the true Prophet of God.

As Ervil's support grew – completely unopposed by Joel – he started calling Joel a fallen prophet who had also failed in his financial endeavors and was leading the church to ruin. Finally Joel was forced to act, and with great sorrow in his heart he fired Ervil as Patriarch and stopped his lavish church salary.

Ervil, enraged, retaliated by claiming that the Patriarch was higher than the Prophet; that Joel was a false prophet in any case; and that he, Ervil LeBaron, was the One Mighty and Strong who had received The Mantel from their father.

Ervil's preaching and writings became more and more paranoiac until he was openly advocating the murder of all who opposed him and his Church of the Lamb of God. He trained a secret commando army to carry out his death sentences. Ervil's followers were kept in line by the promise of eternal glory if they died in carrying out their murderous missions, and with "hot lead and cold steel" if they should fail, or voice any dissenting opinion against God's True Prophet.

On August 20th, 1972 a hit team sent by Ervil ambushed Joel and killed him in cold blood. The assassins had previously been Joel's good friends and disciples (Uranus conjunct South Node in Joel's 11th house shows sudden treachery by friends; Joel's converse secondary South Node conjoined natal Uranus all of 1972, and his progressed moon conjoined the Uranus / South Node midpoint a week after his murder). Because Ervil's birthtime is unknown his progressions can only be approximated, but sometime during the year previous to Joel's murder Ervil's converse Mercury changed direction, signifying (according to Dr. Marc Edmund Jones) a "critical regrasp of experience" – that is, something "snaps", priorities are reordered, obstacles are swept aside. Also Ervil's progressed sun trined natal Neptune now – an odd aspect for a murder, but from Ervil's point of view this was a happy and spiritual event: his undisputed inheritance of The Mantle.

Joel and Ervil's mother was stricken with agony at the news that one of her sons had murdered another; and the members of Joel's church were shocked and frightened. Besides having lost their beloved Prophet and friend, they were all under threat of death commanded by Ervil.

Ervil surrendered to Mexican police in December 1972, protesting his innocence all the while. Although he was sentenced in November 1973 to twelve years' imprisonment, his followers bribed the Mexican authorities to release him a month later (his converse sun was approximately conjunct Jupiter and sextile Saturn at the time of his release).

Now Ervil burned for vengeance: he declared that God had sent him as a special servant, and "all those who should not hear the word of the Lord that this servant would bring forth would be destroyed."[14]

On December 26th, 1974 a band of Ervil's followers attacked Joel's new colony in Baja California, burning homes, wounding thirteen people (including two pregnant women) with high-powered rifle fire, and killing two young men.

On January 1st, 1975 a young woman follower of Ervil who had disagreed with him was kidnapped and murdered by two of Ervil's female hit squad members. Now prominent disciples of Joel were followed and threatened; homes were fired into.

On January 24th, 1975 witnesses to the Baja California attack were fired upon by shotgun blasts as they entered the courthouse to give testimony.

In April 1975 Ervil's hit squad abducted and murdered a Utah polygamist leader who was not a member of Joel's church. Ervil now issued threats against all Mormon and Fundamentalist leaders (as well as Joel's disciples), causing a panic in the Utah Mormon community. Security for the president of the official Mormon church was redoubled.

In June 1975 another of Ervil's disaffected followers was found shot to death.

On March 6th, 1976 Ervil was arrested in Mexico for having ordered the Baja California attack. From his Mexican cell he continued to direct his followers and issue new revelations (such as condemning the president of the United States to death for treason; and that he, Ervil LeBaron, was immune from death and would never be replaced by a successor). Again his followers were able to bribe Mexican authorities, and he was released on November 11th, 1976, at which time (approximately) progressed sun was sextile natal Mercury, converse sun trine natal Mars, progressed Mars sextile natal Node, and converse Venus trine natal Node.

On May 10th, 1977 another Utah polygamist leader – a greatly beloved doctor and friend (though not a follower) of Joel's – was murdered by Ervil's female hit squad. Also, about this time, Ervil ordered the death by strangulation of his own daughter – eighteen years old and pregnant with her second child – because she had become disaffected with his teachings. Now the FBI and Mexican government came down hard on Ervil and his followers. He was arrested in Mexico City on May 31st, 1979 (with transiting Mars exactly conjunct natal Mars) and immediately deported to the US.

On May 28th, 1980 (with transiting Saturn opposition natal Uranus) he was convicted of murder and sentenced to life in prison, where he died of a heart attack two years later. The church that Joel founded – although racked by dissension after his death and Ervil's war against it – still exists in Northern Mexico with some thousand polygamist members, working to set in order the house of God.

Notes

[1] Quoted in Verlan M. LeBaron's *The LeBaron Story*, Keele &Co. 1981, p.119.
[2] ibid. page 4.
[3] ibid. page 41.
[4] ibid, page 61.
[5] Carter, Charles E. O., *The Astrological Aspects*, London: Fowler,1930. Page 148.
[6] ibid, page 45.
[7] ibid, page 159.
[8] Jones, Marc Edmund, *The Essentials of Astrological Analysis*, Sabian 1970, page 298.
[9] Source: LeBaron, op. cit.
[10] LeBaron, op. cit., page 123.
[11] Carter, op. cit. page 66.
[12] ibid, page 126.
[13] ibid, page 119.
[14] LeBaron, op.cit., page 247.

Astrolocality

Of the few modern astrological techniques which seem to work quite well, astrolocality mapping is without question one of the most useful. The basic idea is to erect a horoscope for the same Universal Time (Greenwich Mean Time) as the birth chart, but for the location on the earth where the native lives (or plans to travel) at the present time. Thus the planetary positions in celestial longitude remain the same as in the birth chart, but the angles (ASC and MC) differ. The essential point is to observe what planets conjoin or aspect the angles for the new location.

One way to calculate the relocated angles using standard astrological software is to erect a chart for the UT (or GMT) of birth, but for the intended location. It is also possible to project the loci of points where a given planet conjoins or aspects the horizon or meridian onto a world map (but this requires special software). What emerges is a map with horizon (sinusoidal) lines running across it; and meridian (due north and south) lines running straight up and down. The idea is that these lines show favorable or unfavorable places on the earth. And in fact, they often do.

Note first of all that one must use very narrow orbs of inexactitude, which implies a very exact time of birth. Commercial astrolocality services and software providers downplay this most important point, since so few people know (or have rectified) their birth times to within a minute. A difference of one minute in the time of birth throws the planetary lines out by about fifteen miles on the earth; so if the birth time is not accurately known, the technique is largely useless. On the other hand, astrolocality mapping of places where a native has lived or had extraordinary experiences can provide a useful check on the accuracy of a trial rectification. As a matter of fact, I have yet to see an exactly rectified horoscope that doesn't yield at least one partile conjunction or opposition in longitude between a natal planet or angle in the birth horoscope, and a place on earth where the native has lived for any amount of time; with apropos astrological symbolism (consider e.g. the examples from my own horoscope, mentioned below, which have very close orbs). It really is necessary to use tight orbs – say, half a degree of longitude in measuring aspects to angles; or 30 miles on earth – at the outside, when considering favorable places to which to relocate or vacation. The astrological effect falls off rapidly beyond this orb.

It is important to use astrolocality software which computes all multiple-of-thirty degree aspects, since these can be very significant in astrolocality work (even though I only use Ptolemaic aspects in natal and predictive work). Not only that, but the cardinal points (0° Aries, Cancer, Libra, and Capricorn) and even the other sign cusps can be significant. Take a look at the critical degrees too: the ASC of the astrolocality chart cast for the place where I have lived for the past 43 years has no horizon aspects to any natal planets in my chart; but it is exactly (within 1' orb) conjunct a critical degree.

There doesn't seem to be a great deal of difference between horizon and meridian lines insofar as interpretation is concerned; but I term the horizon lines "karma" lines and the meridian lines "success" lines, because the former do seem to relate more to subjective, emotional experiences – life lessons; and the latter tend to relate to outward, societal issues: success – or lack of same.

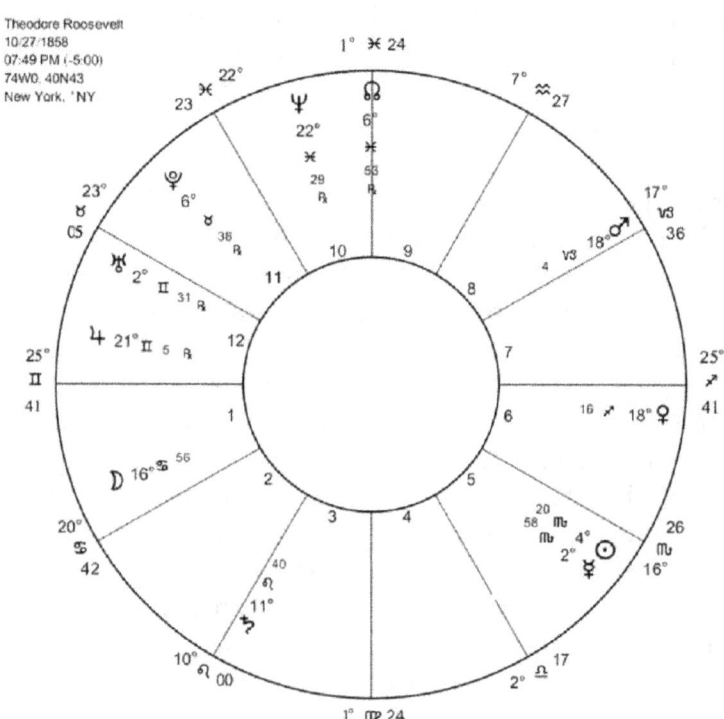

As an example, consider Theodore Roosevelt's chart relocated for Medora, ND, where TR went into the ranching business; had some great adventures; and eventually lost his shirt when a devastating winter killed all his cattle. The MC for Medora is 2° AQ 38', trine natal Uranus at 2° GE 31' (which is but 2 ½° from ASC), and square natal Mercury (which is combust and opposition Pluto) at 2° SC 58'.

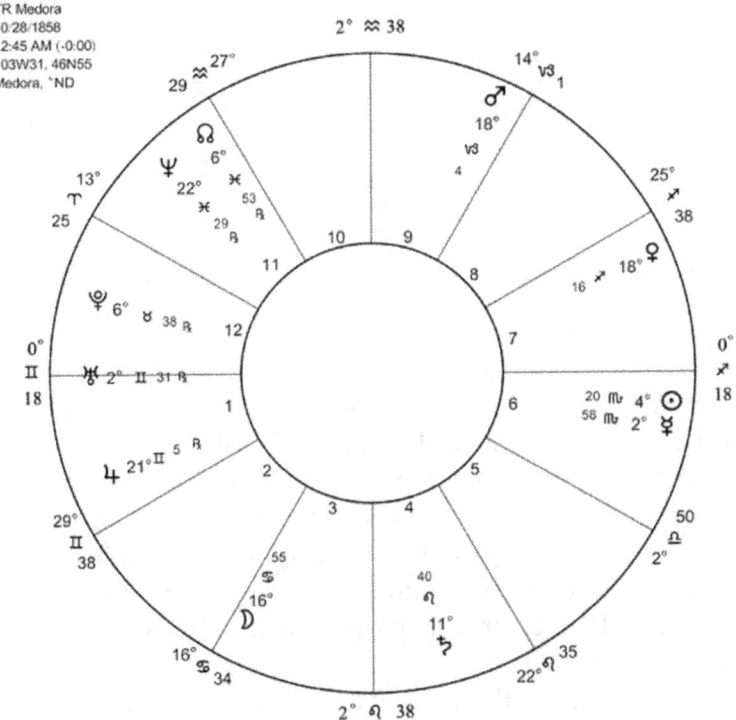

TR's chart relocated for the Battle of San Juan Hill, Cuba – which he termed the greatest day of his life – has 11° GE 42' rising, sextile natal Saturn at 11° LE 40'.

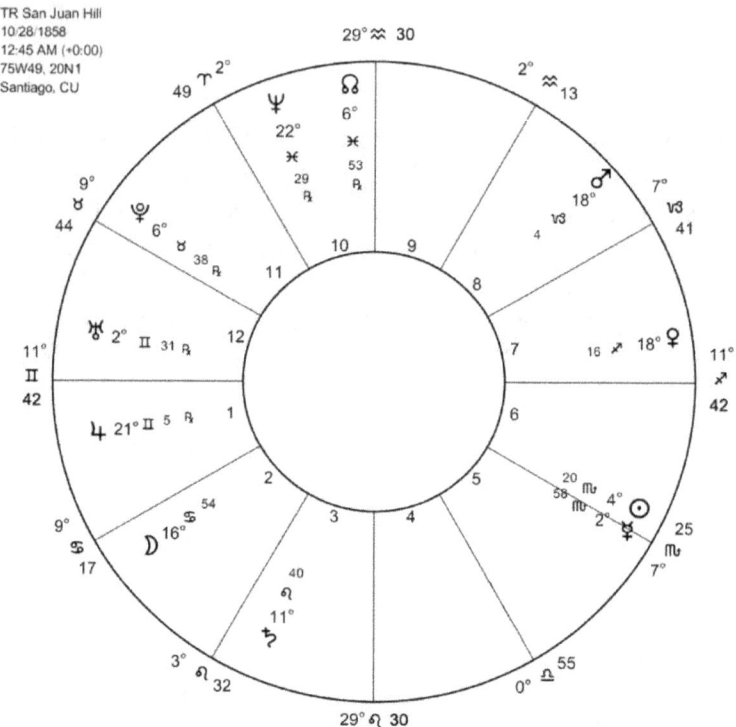

TR's chart relocated for Washington DC has 21° GE 23' on the ASC, conjunct his natal Jupiter in 21° GE 05'.

Another important point to remember is that planets which are strong in the natal chart – which are unaspected or well-aspected; or at the least strong by sign, angularity, conjunct a bright fixed star, etc. – will point to places which are fortunate for the native. Planets which are afflicted or otherwise weak will only bring pain or disappointment.

For example, the ASC where I went to college (Hartford) is located at 4° SC 34', square my natal moon in 4° AQ 38'. My natal moon opposes a Venus-sun-Saturn-Pluto conjunction on the MC, and trines Neptune. Now, I wasn't particularly happy at college; and in fact I never graduated (which fits the lunar symbolism). On the other hand, I got into psychedelic drugs (Neptune) and the hippie movement at college, which definitely changed my life for the better.

The ASC for Buffalo, where I spent a rather sad few months in my youth, is located at 29° LI 26', square my afflicted Venus at 29° CN 36'. I got busted coming into the US from Canada to visit an ex-girlfriend, and had to spend the winter freezing my butt off awaiting trial, and watching her screwing everyone in sight but me.

The MC where I spent a tough but liberating year and a half (Santa Rosa CA) – overworked, underpaid, and stressed-out; but at the same time disciplined and tough (have never been in such good physical shape before or since then) – is located at 24° GE 35', conjunct my natal Uranus at 24° GE 37' (Uranus forms a duet with Mars in the natal chart).

The DESC where I journeyed for 4 months to South America (to visit an old college buddy who'd gone off to live alone in the jungle and was about 87% nuts by the time I arrived) is located at 12°LE 35', conjunct my natal Pluto at 12° LE 50' and my natal Saturn at 11° LE 55'. It was a pretty intense and sobering experience (particularly once when I got lost in the jungle), but nowhere near as bad as I might have feared had I known that I was heading straight into the heart of my Saturn-Pluto conjunction.

Once I was driving across the country with a few pounds of marijuana under the front seat of my car, when I was stopped by cops in Albuquerque who asked for my license; and then suddenly they called six more police cars and surrounded me. After about 15 minutes of suspense the cops came to my car, returned my license, and told me to have a nice day. For me Albuquerque has an ASC of 8° CN 35', square my natal Neptune in 8° LI 31' (my natal Neptune mediates my sun – Moon opposition since it is the point of a wedge which trines moon and sextiles sun-Saturn-Pluto on the MC, so for me Neptune is highly favorable).

It might be asked why I haven't moved to a place which is more favorable to me. The answer is that I didn't discover astro-locality until I had already moved to my present abode, where I have lived for the past 43 years. Anyway, it's exactly on a semi-sextile Uranus meridian line (stressful), which is a good description of the course of my marriage here; and this place is also exactly conjunct a critical degree horizon line, which is bad for material things but good for spiritual things: I've gone bankrupt in two agricultural businesses I started here, but I've made some amazing spiritual connections with my Mayan neighbors. Moreover, the only really good aspect in my otherwise afflicted natal chart is the Mercury – Jupiter trine; and I guess I'm just not an Iowa, Missouri, Kansas, Oklahoma, or Texas kind of person (though I'm presently contemplating a move to a Jupiter line in central Mexico).

Remember the caveat about exact birth times: if you don't know your exact birth time (to within a minute) then the astrolocality technique is useless.

Mental Chemistry

Life is like body-surfing: most of the time you're just standing there waiting for the right wave to come; and then when it does come you have to hurl yourself into it at the precisely correct moment, and ride it in to shore. If you're a little too slow; or if you're a little too fast; or if it wasn't the *right* wave; then you're left standing right where you were.

In *The Essentials of Astrological Analysis*, Dr. Marc Edmund Jones described a simple technique which indicates whether a person is a little too slow, a little too fast, or just right in grabbing and riding the waves of life. He called it *mental chemistry*, and it is shown by the combination of two horoscope factors:

1) Whether the moon is relatively slow or fast in its daily travel; and

2) Whether Mercury rises before or after the sun.

The moon's relative speed shows a native's *perceptual* capabilities: how a person processes information, whether his or her perceptions are *alert* (fast moon) or *deliberate* (slow moon). Since the moon's daily travel – the difference between the moon's longitude at midnight (or noon) Universal Time before birth and its longitude at midnight (or noon) UT after birth – averages 13° 11' (13.18°) per day, we will define a native's perception to be alert if the moon was moving faster than this on the day of birth, and deliberate if the moon was moving slower.

In the words of Al H. Morrison[1]: "The 'fast' moon ... scans rapidly with a wide-open search pattern. If there is anything going on, anything new or unfamiliar, anything different from expectation, it is instantly perceived. In a complex environment, as most social environments are, there are so many details and processes to notice that the 'fast' moon native has his mind receiving an avalanche of input, fresh data." On the other hand, "Where the moon is slow in its apparent motion, the native's perceptual capabilities are focused, or directed toward observing whatever the native is motivated to seek, or has been conditioned to pay attention to, or whatever he fears. Other information is simply not perceived, not observed. This leaves the mind relatively lightly burdened, with minimal input of perceived data to process."

However, the moon's speed is not merely a symbol for how fast information is gathered and processed – it also has to do with how people gather themselves together and gird themselves for action. The natives whose perceptions are alert move quickly to get on top of a situation: their immediate impulse is to attack. They like things clear and definite and aboveboard, and they are nonplused by subtleties. When they have a bee in their bonnets they have no patience for any other point of view, nor interest in exploring possible consequences and ramifications – they don't even want to hear about them. They move by impulse and instinct, they make up their minds immediately, and thereafter they can't be budged or moved to reconsider. In conflict they try to take their opponents by a storm, to overwhelm them, to give them no space in which to move. Their actions and reactions are quick and decisive.

On the other hand, natives whose perceptions are deliberate move slowly and hesitatingly: their immediate impulse is to draw back. They get at things by indirection, by outflanking the situation, by bogging things down and operating under the cover of confusion. Where the alert types act like sharks, the deliberate types act like octopuses – hiding on the bottom and masking their intentions in a cloud of murk. In conflict they refuse to expose themselves but rather outwait their opponents, letting them be the ones to make the errors.

The other horoscope factor which makes up a person's mental chemistry is Mercury's position with regard to the sun at the moment of birth. If Mercury is located earlier than the sun in the zodiac, so that at dawn on the birthday Mercury had already risen (was in the 12th house), then the native's attitude is said to be *eager*; whereas if Mercury is located later than the sun in the zodiac, so that at dawn on the birthday Mercury was still beneath the horizon (in the 1st house), then the native's attitude is said to be *certain*. The difference here is in how people categorize information, interpret it, and fit it into preconceived patterns, whether these be individualistic (eager) or conventional (certain). This is a process of reason or self-consciousness rather than one of knee-jerk response.

In the words of Leyla Rael,[2] "The Epimethean (certain) Mercury type of person tends to react to life more cautiously and based on past experience (either his or her own personal experience or according to traditional, cultural patterns). But while such a person is at best thorough and objective, mentally free from many purely emotional prejudices, at worst he or she can cling almost obsessively to obsolescent ideologies or display a conservatism bordering on rigidity. The Promethean (eager) Mercury type of person tends to leap into life with his or her mental antennae fully extended to receive information. While such a person may be able to act based on a compelling inner vision of what is possible – and may at best be flexible, prophetic, and responsive to the needs of the moment – at worst he or she may be merely conniving, facile, and crafty, going this way or that according to his or her own advantage."

Another way of saying this is that the certain natives have to be sure of themselves before they act – they need to feel that their actions will garner the stamp of approval of their social milieu. Thus they are restrained and are oriented towards goals and purposes. They interpret the world in terms of a guiding philosophy of social responsibility in which each member must do his or her own share, and these natives are scrupulous in observing their part of the bargain. They play the game by the rules – whatever they conceive those rules to be. They are wary, dutiful, and put their faith in principle and obligation.

The eager natives, on the other hand, are unrestrained and experimentative. They don't need any social authority to sanction their actions, but rather follow their inclinations of the moment. They do what is expedient or convenient rather than what will be thought praiseworthy by others. They are optimistic and free-wheeling, and are able to bounce right back whenever life slaps them down.

Now, when there is a perceptive alertness combined with a rational certainty (fast moon and Mercury rising after the sun), then the native is quick to react but possesses a powerful governor on his or her impulses. An example of this alert-certain type is Abraham Lincoln. He was a shrewd and opportunistic politician, but his conscience and sense of responsibility for the consequences of his decisions made him a target for the radicals and extremists surrounding him.

Contrariwise, when there is a perceptive deliberation combined with a rational eagerness (slow moon and Mercury rising before the sun), then the native is slow to react but possesses a compensatory flexibility and adaptability. Andrew Johnson, who succeeded Lincoln as president, is a good example of this deliberate-eager type. He held fast to his principles in complete isolation but always managed to come out on top – first as the only Southerner to remain in the U.S. Senate after the secession of the Southern states, and later by successfully defending himself against a trumped-up impeachment.

In both of these cases there is considered to be a healthy balance between the perceptual and rational faculties, in the sense that these natives are able to resolutely hold their ground in the face of confusion and to marshal their resources effectively to deal with situations as they arise. They are able to grapple directly with the problems of life and to take things as they come – to recognize which waves are the *right* waves and to know when to hold back and when to jump forward.

But when perceptive alertness combines with rational eagerness (fast moon and Mercury rising before the sun), or when perceptive deliberation combines with rational certainty (slow moon and Mercury rising after the sun), then the perceptual and rational faculties are out of balance. Natives of these types are easily thrown off their stride or confounded by situations requiring quick decision. They don't really pay attention to what is going on around them, but rather only to their own reactions to what is going on around them. The alert-eager types become flustered and the deliberate-certain types become obstinate, but in either case these unbalanced natives tend to fall out of synchronization with the speed of their environment: alert-eager natives move too fast and deliberate-certain natives move too slow – their suggestions and actions are not apropos.

Where the balanced types have a self-control or instantaneous analysis which reacts to sudden changes by stiffening to attention, the unbalanced types tend to either overreact or underreact, alternating between overweening cockiness and fierce indignation, with no middle ground of calm discernment. Thus they tend to waste their energies in ineffectual posturing, more interested in proving something or in making an impression rather than in working with other people. These natives are too set in their manner of being, too wrapped up in their own self-images, too self-satisfied, to make allowances for changing conditions or for different types of people – i.e. they don't really know how to interact. Thus they tend to be escapists – to obsess over a niggling sense of personal privilege – rather than to effectively deal with the realities of the situations and relationships in which they find themselves.

In the words of Dr. Jones, "When the effective set of mind … shows the combination of rational eagerness and perceptive alertness the life is usually characterized by an altogether unnecessary impatience. The native is inclined to stumble over his own toes most of the time, and he is apt to end up with actions and associations that not only fail to fulfill their promise but often handicap him very seriously by exhausting every potentiality of his make-up."[3] Basically what happens is that these natives are overly intense and pushy. They tend to blow minor issues out of all proportion, and to trivialize matters of the greatest urgency and seriousness. They run around in circles and don't get anywhere. They set up a myriad of compulsive routines and are greatly annoyed whenever these are abrogated by circumstances. They have a fitful, flighty energy which is never comfortable or in repose but rather is constantly fluttering and fussing about, making this or that unnecessary adjustment to the environment, to arrange everything neatly so that they can finally relax – but of course they never do. They are constantly primping and preparing for some future that never comes.

An extreme example of the eager-alert type (Mercury 6 days from Greatest Western Elongation – which is as eager as it gets – and moon very fast: 15° 13' per day) is John Brown, the rabid abolitionist and author of the Pottawotami massacre in Kansas where numerous innocent people were killed; and then leader of an abortive attack on the federal arsenal at Harper's Ferry which aimed at fomenting a slave insurrection. Probably John Brown, more than any other single person, made any last-minute reconciliation between North and South impossible: he pushed an already strained situation beyond the point of no return: "The John Brown raid had jangled Southern nerves fatally. It started a chain of hysteria like the 'great fear' of 1789 in the French Revolution. Rumors of slave insurrection popped up on every side. … Extremists on both sides whipped up hostile sentiment between sections."[5] The eager-alert types aren't so much ignorant of consequences as they are contemptuous of them.

They shoot from the hip, push things to the limit, and stampede other people with their impatient absolutism.

According to Dr. Jones, "When the reason demands a continual certainty and the perceptivity tends to be deliberate, the individual is apt to withdraw within himself to an extent that hardly is to his interest and perhaps indeed to slip off into altogether abnormal practices and points of view."[5] These natives are perverse and contrary. They delight in phlegmatic wrong-headedness, in controlling things by being in no particular hurry. They make good diplomats, in the sense of being willing to spend years holding out for the precise shape of the conference table or order of seating around it. They are more concerned with form and decorum rather than with substantive issues. They tend to confuse indifference with disinterest; obduracy with strength; stodgy pride with nobility of spirit. They will not budge an inch from their inflated sense of dignity and righteousness until they are completely overwhelmed by events, and then their responses are usually too little, too late. They tend to be preoccupied with self-congratulations, gloating with smug pride over some past that never happened.

An extreme example of the certain-deliberate type (Mercury 3 days past Greatest Eastern Elongation – which is as certain as it gets – and moon very slow: 11° 47' per day) is William Jennings Bryan. Although remembered today principally as a thrice unsuccessful presidential candidate and the butt of defense attorney Clarence Darrow's ridicule during the famous Scopes monkey trial, Bryan championed many Populist causes which were later adopted. But in typical certain-deliberate style he tended to look back rather than forward. Although well-versed in the Bible, he was ignorant on most all other topics, particularly economics, his supposed specialty. In Theodore Roosevelt's words, Bryan represented "a kind of rural toryism, which wishes to attempt the impossible task of returning to the economic conditions that obtained sixty years ago."[6] Bryan's problem as a politician, as historian Richard Hofstadter points out, was that although Bryan was brilliant at focusing the popular sentiment of the times, he always followed behind his public rather than leading it.

What counsel to give these unbalanced natives? It's not that terrible an affliction, nor that uncommon (half of all horoscopes are unbalanced). These natives are quite content with exactly how they are. What they are seeking is respect rather than effectiveness or economy of action. The counsel is more for the other half of the population – on how to understand and deal with the unbalanced types. The alert-eager natives have to be indulged in their quirks; you have to tolerate their little obsessions and prerogatives – i.e. you have to be as alert as they are to avoid their tripwires.

Conversely, the deliberative-certain types require a lack of pother or hurry – a patience greater than their own – to prove to them that you mean business and to win them over. In either case, the way you get the unbalanced natives' attention and cooperation is by outdoing them at their own games: giving them the respect they need before they feel comfortable and can open up and relax into a situation or relationship. Dealing with the unbalanced types is a good spiritual lesson in flexibility and agility – exactly the qualities needed to catch life's waves and ride them rather than be thrashed about them.

Notes

[1] Al H. Morrison, "The Hankar Crystal," *The Astrological Review* vm. 44 no. 1 (Spring – Summer 1972).

[2] Leyla Rael, "Discover Your Problem-Solving Style," *Dell Horoscope Magazine,* December 1978, page 49.

[3] Dr. Marc Edmund Jones, *The Essentials of Astrological Analysis*, Sabian, Stanwood WA 1970, page 383

[4] Samuel Eliot Morison, *The Oxford History of the American People*, Oxford U. Press, NYC 1965, page 605.

[5] Dr. Marc Edmund Jones, op. cit.

[6] TR quoted by Samuel Eliot Morison, op. cit. page 812.

Ira Einhorn

Ira Einhorn was perhaps one of Philadelphia's best-known characters in the 1960's: hippie guru, environmental activist and organizer of the city's Earth Day celebration, media spokesperson for the counter-culture, parapsychology researcher, fellow in Harvard's Kennedy School of Government, and architect of a futurology information network funded by the Bell Telephone Company. He was brawny and athletic, with long, graying hair gathered in a pony tail, baggy shirt and pants, powerful, piercing blue eyes, a broad grin and exuberant personality.

He bowled people over with his driving energy and magnetism, and with his encyclopedic memory and fascinating conversation (he devoured a book every day). To quote from the *Philadelphia Inquirer*, "Through the years he has been known as the city's oldest hippie, a rebel, a free spirit, a social philosopher, a guru, a teacher, a counterculture poet, ladies' man extraordinaire, a freeloader, a writer, a lecturer, and none of the above."

This fond description of Ira was published on March 29th, 1979, as part of the newspaper's account of Ira's arrest for the murder of his ex-girlfriend, Holly Maddux, and the discovery of her mummified remains in a trunk in his apartment.

For there was another side to Ira Einhorn – one he carefully concealed from the executives, editors, scientists, professors, and beautiful young women whom he cultivated, and who cultivated him. Ira was a psychopath who on two previous occasions over the years had committed assault with intent to kill on his girlfriends of the moment; but these incidents, having occurred at exclusive eastern women's colleges, were hushed up at the times they occurred, and no charges against Ira were ever preferred. The two sides of Ira Einhorn are documented in the book *The Unicorn's Secret* by Steven Levy (Prentice Hall 1988 – the quotations in this article are taken from this book); and in the movie *The Hunt for the Unicorn Killer*.

Holly Maddux was a bright and talented woman of extraordinary, ethereal beauty. She had been a cheerleader in her high school in Tyler, Texas, and was voted most likely to succeed. She went to Bryn Mawr College near Philadelphia, where she was soon drawn into the political, sexual, and drug scene of the late 60's. It was there that she met Ira, and fell under his spell.

The couple lived together for five years. It was always a stormy relationship, marked by infidelity, violent arguments and frequent separations. Although Holly was very intelligent, hardworking, and dedicated, she had little self-esteem. She was overwhelmed by Ira's self-confidence and celebrity, and she let herself be wholly dominated by him, unable to break free of his overpowering personality. After each argument Ira would appear contrite and plead with her to return to him, and she would give in.

Finally Holly met a man in New York who loved her and who convinced her to cut loose for good. She intended never to see Ira again, but she had to return to Philadelphia to get her belongings, and Ira insisted on having one last talk with her.

That night, September 11th, 1977, the neighbors below heard a violent argument going on in Ira's apartment, which culminated in a crash. The next day Ira told his friends and mother that Holly had run away and left him, leaving no word on where she was going.

A month after Holly's disappearance, her concerned parents engaged a private detective to try to locate her. Ira's evasive answers to his questions aroused the detective's suspicions, and after a year of meticulous investigation – including reports by neighbors of a horrible stench that had issued from Ira's apartment for months – the detective gathered sufficient evidence to turn the case over to the Philadelphia police.

On March 28th, 1979, police officers knocked on Ira's door, showed him a warrant to search the apartment, and found Holly's withered body in a trunk in his closet. Examination showed that she had died as the result of being beaten over the head at least a dozen times.

Ira's friends couldn't believe it. A train of prominent Philadelphians – lawyers, university professors, corporate executives, ministers, economists, journalists – took the stand during Ira's bail hearing to testify to his excellent character and reputation. Ira steadfastly denied all knowledge of Holly's murder, or of how her body could have turned up in his closet. He claimed he had been framed, and most of his friends (at least initially) believed him.

However, as the months rolled by and more evidence against Ira piled up, he began to find himself increasingly shunned and isolated. Facing almost certain conviction, Ira decamped just before his trial in mid-January 1981.

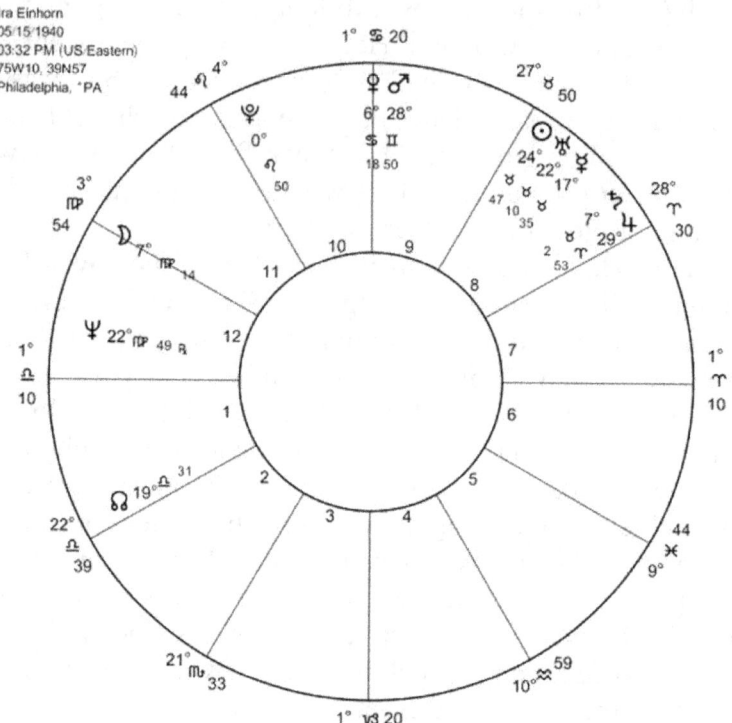

I knew Ira casually, back in the 60's (we lived in the same hippie slum apartment building in West Philadelphia's Powelton Village section). Among his other accomplishments, he was a competent astrologer; and his horoscope (birth data given by him personally) appears above. In this analysis we will pursue two themes: examining the horoscopic signatures of Ira's brilliance; and examining the signatures of his sociopathy. As is usually the case in astrology, these things are not shown in only one way, but rather by a number of different testimonies.

The first thing that strikes the eye is the stellium of planets in the 8th house of death, which indicates a powerful conscious or unconscious fascination with death and the astral world (8th house planets also denote psychic ability). A native with a concentration of planets in the 8th is drawn to death; either he has many near death experiences himself; or many experiences of the deaths of others; or he may have psychic experiences, interest in the occult, etc.

Ira was strongly attracted to psychic phenomena, and he worked closely with Andrija Puharich and Uri Geller to publicize ESP research. In short, 8th house planets often act to focus the native's attention on the death plane, though not necessarily in a morbid or violent manner (depending on the planets).

What inclines Ira's chart to a violent fascination with death is the fact that the stellium occurs in the early signs (Aries and Taurus), which makes for what Charles Carter, in *Some Principles of Horoscopic Delineation*, termed a primitive ego: "This does not necessarily imply criminality, but there is usually some crudeness and failure to appreciate intellectual and aesthetic values. At worst, there can be a violent criminality." While a stellium of planets in Aries-Taurus in the 8th doesn't necessarily indicate that the native is a killer, it does suggest a thrill-seeker, someone who likes having his adrenaline pumped up by ideas of death.

Other roots of Ira's psychopathy can be seen in the condition of Mercury, planet of the mind. Mercury approaches Superior Conjunction with the sun, which indicates a person who is outwardly sweet and friendly, but inwardly as hard as a diamond. As my book *Thought Forms* explains, the Mercury Superior Conjunction native seems to be soft and outgoing – a huggable, loveable teddy bear. He projects an "aw shucks" awkwardness and self-effacing bashfulness. But in more intimate relationship he shows himself to be a person who always has to be right, always has to win, never will admit he's to blame. This is one of several testimonies in Ira's chart to his repression of feelings of shame for wrongdoing – his refusal to consciously recognize his own dark motives when these contradict his exalted image of himself. As a woman friend of Ira's said, "He's an extremely controlled person, everything he did was thought out and calculated. He liked having the upper hand ... He was very, very closed."

Mercury conjunct sun is more a matter of character than intelligence. Although the native may be blind to his own motives and taken-for-granted assumptions, he nonetheless possesses keen critical faculties and powers of discrimination and analysis. In Ira's chart, Uranus is interposed between the sun and Mercury, which adds a wild-card element to his mentality: flamboyance, unpredictability, and a fierce independence of thought and action. Of the cases of Uranus interposed in a sun-Mercury conjunction from *Astro-*

Databank, there are many examples of natives noted for their keen analytical abilities and intellectual brilliance, such as Johannes Kepler, Sigmund Freud, and Margaret Mead; and also natives who were noted more for their emotional extremism and instability, such as French Symbolist poet Paul Verlaine, who went to prison for shooting his lover, Arthur Rimbaud; and Dutch Communist Marinus van der Lubbe, who was executed by the Nazis for burning down the Reichstag.

Since what we are examining here is Ira's public life, in the interpretation of his chart we will stick closely to his angular planets: Venus, Mars, and Neptune. Venus and Mars are widely conjunct; but this conjunction is brought together and emphasized by the Midheaven, which it flanks. Venus conjunct Mars gives a youthful, saucy, coquettish charm and a pixiesque good humor, which has a definite sexual basis. There is often a sense of androgyny with this aspect: the women are a trifle butch; the men are a trifle effeminate or else – as in Ira's case – exaggeratedly macho. Ira boasted of having seduced over 200 women while he was still in mid-career; and having observed him in action personally, I would regard this claim as modest.

The Venus-Mars conjunction straddles the Midheaven, so this part of Ira is the part the world knew and loved: the feisty, gutsy tilter at social windmills, who once lit up a joint during a live radio debate with the head of the city's narcotics squad; who greeted visitors at the door of his apartment stark naked; who dominated every group and conversation with his earnestness and élan. This is the Ira who captivated the professors, reporters, and CEO's who came forward to testify for him in court, saying things like, "He has the highest level of integrity. A man who goes out of his way to help people, a man who keeps his word, a man who in his feelings is compassionate and loving."

The most important testimony to Ira's personal (as opposed to intellectual) brilliance – his ability to fascinate a broad spectrum of people – is shown by the fact that the culminating Venus (ruler of the Ascendant) is at her greatest brilliancy. This often-overlooked horoscope factor is of great significance in those charts in which it occurs. Venus is at her greatest brilliancy about 36 days before and after inferior (retrograde) conjunction with the sun, when it is roughly 39° from the sun in longitude. Exact times are given in https://www.astro.com/swisseph/ae/venus1600.pdf. Allow an orb of plus or minus a week; in Ira's case, Venus attained greatest brilliancy five days after he was born.

Venus at greatest brilliancy endows its natives with a great poise and sang-froid under all conditions (for more information about the meaning of Venus greatest brilliancy in the natal horoscope, see my book *Planetary Strength*). These natives are fluid, able to adapt smoothly to changing circumstances with little pother or wasted motion. There is something real and reassuring about these people – they go right to the heart of matters. They are imperturbable, cool and collected, placid and unruffled; and thus their presence is soothing and relaxing. Their utter ease of manner and winning personalities make them the sort of people others instinctively trust. Some examples of natives with Venus at greatest brilliancy are: Will Rogers, Henry Fonda, Jimmy Stewart, Ricky Nelson, Dwight Eisenhower, Theodore Roosevelt, and W.B. Yeats. Venus at greatest brilliancy is utterly charming; and this charm is a strategic and wily charm: "Ira would take a position seated directly in front of you in a lotus posture, the eyes would just lock in, and the contact, the engagement, was complete."

Even after his arrest, most people who knew Ira refused to believe he could possibly be guilty. Arlen Specter, ex-District Attorney of Philadelphia, author of the Warren Commission report on the Kennedy assassination, and soon-to-be U.S. senator from Pennsylvania, agreed to be Ira's defense lawyer. To one and all, Ira swore his innocence, claiming he had been framed by the CIA to silence his work in psychic weaponry. "When challenged with the ultimate question – 'Did you do it, Ira?' – (he) would draw on what he knew was his most effective weapon: his belief in himself. Holding no grudge about being asked the question, he would coolly look his accuser in the eye and answer in the negative. It was a rare person who engaged Ira Einhorn's deep blue eyes in that exchange and walked away thinking that Ira was guilty."

Venus at her greatest brilliancy is Venus at her most powerful; and it must be borne in mind that although Venus is beautiful and seductive, her fundamental nature – as Dr. Marc Edmund Jones pointed out – is ruthlessness. Through complete vulnerability she achieves complete dominance.

In Ira's chart, the culminating Mars is six degrees past square with Neptune; and while this is by no means the closest aspect in the chart, it is brought to special prominence by the proximity of these planets to angles. Indeed, much of the story can be read from this one aspect.

Mars square Neptune is extremely idealistic and naïvely overreaching, and therefore easily hurt and disappointed. The native is inclined to close up, to keep a stiff upper lip, and to simmer inwardly (play the martyr) rather than to express openly what he's really feeling, or to take overt action to right matters. Mars square Neptune tends to let things slide, to play Mr. Nice Guy, until he's ready to explode. Charles Carter, in *The Astrological Aspects*, says of this contact: "The native is often slow to admit error. His abilities may fall short of his aspirations – indeed, they are sure to do so; hence there may be a poignant sense of failure, often due to some inner neurotic condition rather than to an outward and tangible obstacle. The contact often breeds irrational fears or phobias … perfectly level-headed on nearly all matters, yet is liable to lose his balance in respect of some."

Here we find Neptune rising in the 12th house of secrets and self-undoing. Ira knew that he was given to murderous attacks: on two previous occasions (it was learned later, after Ira had jumped bail) he had savagely attacked young women and nearly killed them. One he strangled and left on the floor unconscious; the other he beat over the head with a bottle. In both cases Ira had been the women's lover for some time, and he attacked them at the point when they were about to break up with him. In both cases the attacks were not emotional outbursts, but rather were deliberate and coldly methodical. Ira wrote in his journal after these two incidents: "To kill what you love when you can't have it seems so natural that strangling Rita last night seemed so right." And "Suddenly it happens. Bottle in hand I strike away at the head … In such violence there may be freedom."

So Ira knew of this flaw in his character – this hole in his heart. Yet he never sought help, but rather justified his shame to himself by glorifying it, by putting himself above human morality, and then by relegating the whole business to his subconscious (Neptune in the 12th hides things). A psychopath is a person who will not take responsibility for his acts, who will not act in good faith, who will never open his heart.

In Ira's case, because Mars square Neptune is angular, when the explosion came it had a public denouement: Ira wanted to be famous, and he's a lot more famous now than he was in the 60's; he wanted to be sought after, and he succeeded: he wanted to be a model – an object lesson – for other people, and he certainly succeeded at this. The angular square of Mars to Neptune is a very difficult aspect to integrate.

At the time Ira murdered Holly, his progressed Mars was exactly sextile natal Neptune (a progressed sextile is not "good" if the two planets involved afflict each other in the natal chart; in this case, the progressed sextile will trigger the underlying square configuration). What is more, on the very day he was arrested for murder, transiting Mars opposed natal Neptune.

Furthermore, when Ira jumped bail, transiting Neptune was but half a degree past square to natal Neptune. In a sense, the entire saga of Ira's murder of Holly, and his arrest for that murder, are symbolized by the angular square of Mars to Neptune.

It was not until 1997 – when that converse progressed sun squared natal Mars; and also converse progressed Saturn conjoined natal Jupiter – that Ira was discovered to be living in the French countryside with his wife, under the name Eugene Mallon. During his many years as a fugitive Einhorn was convicted in absentia for the Maddux murder, and the Maddux family had won a $907 million wrongful death judgment against him. Despite an extradition treaty between the United States and France, officials in France initially refused to return Einhorn, where he would serve life in prison without the possibility of parole.

In August of 2000 – six months after progressed Mars squared natal Saturn; and also progressed sun sextile natal Uranus (which it closely conjoined in the natal chart); also one-degree-per-year-in-longitude radix-directed Pluto crossed his Ascendant now – French Prime Minister Lionel Jospin finally signed the extradition order, but Einhorn appealed the extradition order and as of 2000 had not returned to the United States.

Ira litigated against the decree before the *Conseil d'État*, which ruled against him. He then attempted to slit his throat, and eventually litigated his case before the European Court of Human Rights, which also ruled against him. On July 20th, 2001, Ira was extradited to the United States. Interestingly enough, and contra-intuitive, is Jupiter's transit of Ira's natal Mars, Midheaven, and Venus at this time. One might have expected such a good transit – especially to the seat of authority, the Midheaven – by the benefic planet of judges, Jupiter, would have freed Ira; particularly since Jupiter sextiles these points in the natal chart. Also converse progressed Mercury sextile natal sun and superior conjunction progressed sun – the sun symbolizing authority – should surely have resulted in Ira's liberation, if we were trying to predict the thing in advance rather than analyze it post hoc. This is an example of a failure of an astrological interpretation. These things happen; predicted events don't always occur as predicted; the universe itself is not as predictable as we would like or tend to imagine. There is no need to apologize for astrology's occasional failures; much less lie about them. Perhaps there were other probable realities where Ira did it bring it off.

However, in this one, after only two hours of deliberation, a jury did not find Ira's testimony credible and affirmed his conviction on October 17th, 2002, with transiting Saturn conjoining his natal Mars. As of this writing, Ira is incarcerated in the state prison at Houtzdale in central Pennsylvania.

The Nodes in the Houses

In the birth horoscope, the clatter and bustle of everyday life – the ways in which we hook ourselves up to society's wheel of rewards and punishments – are shown by the planets (their aspects, house positions, etc). By contrast, our karmic agendas – the real lessons we are seeking to learn from our experience in this lifetime – are shown by the moon's Nodes (and their aspects and house positions). The moon's Nodes are the zodiacal points where the moon's orbit crosses the sun's orbit (the ecliptic), and they have a cycle of about 18 years (moving on average 3' of arc retrograde per day).

We look to the planets to see where we will be successful or failures; accepted or rejected; glorified or ashamed; but we must look to the Nodes to find the real key to our happiness and unhappiness. True happiness and fulfillment have nothing to do with success, acceptance, or glory; true happiness depends on stilling our restless minds and insatiable desires, rather than scurrying around making incessant adjustments to our environment.

The Nodes symbolize a hidden underside of everyday life. The North Node in your chart shows where you've got a good attitude, and things just click for you without any effort on your part. North Node shows where you relax and let things happen instead of making things happen. By contrast, the South Node shows where you've got a crummy attitude, where you refuse to let go of your images and expectations, where you bang your head against the wall in frustration and self-pity. South Node shows issues of control, inability to just relax and let go. It's your place of obsessive concern. In short, the North Node shows where you put your hopes, whereas the South Node shows where you put your expectations. Interpretations for the Nodes conjunct the planets are given in my book *Planetary Combination*.

North Node in 1st house and South Node in 7th house: You possess a plain-spoken, unabashed personal style which others find convincing and sincere. You have a winning personality – you are self-confident and able to handle yourself with purposefulness and élan – and your positive, non-judgmental attitude elicits the good will of others in turn. Because you come on to other people in wholly aboveboard fashion, you tend to ignore or deny your darker motives, ascribing them instead to your partner. This is not a good position for marriage as you tend to use partners (hide behind them or blame them) to cover your own shortcomings and unacknowledged motives.

North Node in 2nd house and South Node in 8th house: Money's not really a problem for you; whether you're rich or poor, you just don't let material concerns be a problem. You know you'll always have enough money for your own needs – and if not, then you'll just make do without; and this attitude in turn tends to attract good fortune to you. Because you have the material side of daily life under good control, you tend to ignore spiritual, abstract, "impractical" considerations. You are obsessively focused in the busyness of everyday living – meddlesome and finicky, overly reliant upon your own perspicacity and pluck – unwilling to let go and trust in the Spirit to sustain you.

North Node in 3rd house and South Node in 9th house: You are level-headed and practical, punctilious and well-organized. You possess mechanical aptitude, or else an attentiveness to details and a consideration for the sensibilities of others, which enables you to keep your everyday environment relatively smooth-running and hassle-free. On the other hand, you are inclined to routinize your life, to make things as convenient and superficially simple as possible, and hence easily become prejudiced, stuck in a rut, unable to see past the problem of the moment to take an objective, long-range view. You tend to rely upon pat answers rather than true ideals.

North Node in 4th house and South Node in 10th house: You are a private individual, very sensitive and emotionally vulnerable. Your unerring intuition enables you to act with complete assurance, authority, and finality. You succeed in carving out your own space (niche) in life by being both determined and unobtrusive. Because you prefer the freedom of solitude and have flimsy psychic defenses, you put up a screen of smug prissiness or wrong-headed contrariety when you are forced to deal with people in groups. You pull away from any group to go off on your own tangent, and your capricious, prima donna demands for special recognition and indulgence incline other people to leave you alone.

North Node in 5th house and South Node in 11th house: You have a buoyant, optimistic, hopeful outlook and take a childlike delight in the adventures of everyday living. You are playful and flirtatious – quite the lover boy (or girl). You are daring, impish, and preserve a true spirit of fun. Your focus upon enjoyment in the now moment often leads you to wishful thinking. You have a blind spot when it comes to planning for your future or seeing where your best long-term interests lie. This lack of perspective also colors your personal relationships: you may ignore (act cool or indifferent towards) your true friends and well-wishers in the pursuit of your beguiling companion of the moment.

North Node in 6th house and South Node in 12th house: You are dogged, cheerful in adversity, and willing to roll up your sleeves and get to work at whatever task is at hand. You are practical, clever, and down-to-earth: a model to others of patience, responsibility, and forbearance. Your moral courage and independent nature have the negative effect of making you rather narrow-minded and impervious – wholly tuned into your own wavelength. You are remote and aloof; hold other people at arm's length; and can be annoyingly deaf to reason in your strict insistence upon your own private space and prerogatives.

North Node in 7th house and South Node in 1st house: You are artless, spontaneous, and feel you have nothing to hide; hence you are able to get on a very personal and intimate basis with other people right away. Therefore you tend to attract partners who are serious about relationships and who are willing to commit themselves with you all the way. However, as you are quick to commit yourself emotionally (to "flash" on people), you are also quick to draw back from commitment. You have a vain, petty side which is impatient, unwilling to make allowances over the long haul, and quick to strike out on its own rather than become bogged down in compromise.

North Node in 8th house and South Node in 2nd house: You have open psychic channels and are clearly attuned to emotional nuances and messages from the world of the spirit. You have an unshakeable faith in the sustaining power of the universe, and are willing to follow your own star wherever it might lead you. Your expectant attitude tends to attract unexpected opportunities and the help of other people. On the other hand, your exalted vision can be used to justify complacency and dreamy-eyed laziness, since you regard yourself as above petty grubbing and striving. Your chintzy disdain for everyday realities willingly delegates to others all responsibility for practical matters and material concerns.

North Node in 9th house and South Node in 3rd house: You are clear-sighted and have the capacity to surmount stuffy, matter-of-fact thinking, take a broader perspective, and reach a deep understanding of people and their problems. Your sober judgment and unerring insight give you the potential for true wisdom. However, you can also become taken by your own cleverness and fall into a smug, know-it-all attitude. Your taking things for granted and lack of appreciation for the little things grate on people (such as siblings and co-workers), who are forced to deal with you and your self-superiority on an everyday basis.

North Node in 10th house and South Node in 4th house: You are dignified and noble, possessing a true sense of personal dedication, competence, and fitness. You may have some area of expertise in which you are capable of superlative performance; or else you personify some lofty moral ideal for your social group. Therefore, people naturally look up to you and entrust you with authority. On the other hand, you tend to be volatile – lacking in inner certainty and staying power – because you depend too much upon where you receive approval or deference from other people to determine what direction you will take in life, rather than rely upon your own gut-level feelings and instincts for your sense of stability and security.

North Node in 11th house and South Node in 5th house: You are forward-looking, optimistic, and cheerful. You are always able to turn aside from harshness and focus on the best in people and the silver lining in any situation. You attract true friends because you are friendly yourself – thoughtful, unassuming, and always hopeful for the future. On the other hand, you can be vague, woolly, and non-committal: too fixated on some idealized future in which everything is perfect to be truly relaxed in the now moment. You are perpetually in motion – fussing about, manipulative, unable to just let go and enjoy yourself.

North Node in 12th house and South Node in 6th house: You are shrewd and calculating, quite the canny operator. You are quick to pick up on subtleties, unspoken vibrations, and the real motives of other people. You have a wry sense of humor and offer an ironic commentary on the passing scene which enables you to serve as the detached voice of reason in any group. On the other hand, you are somewhat mannered or exaggerated, complaining, inclined to strut and strike poses rather than to deal with nitty-gritty issues or soil your hands with real work. You expect other people to serve you, wait on you, and indulge you.

The Slave of Duty

Frederic, the hero of Gilbert and Sullivan's *Pirates of Penzance*, was born 21 leap year days before 1940 – i.e. on February 29th, 1852 (recollect that 1900 was not a leap year). In his youth he had been accidentally apprenticed to a pirate when his nursemaid Ruth misunderstood his father's injunction to apprentice him to a *pilot*. Although he hated piracy, Frederic's deep-felt sense of duty made him stick with it until he was finally freed from his apprenticeship on reaching his twenty-first year (February 28th, 1873). Leaving the pirate's lair on that day – the day the opera takes place – he stumbles upon a bevy of young maidens and immediately falls in love with the beautiful Mabel (he had never seen a woman before this except for his aged nursemaid Ruth who, being in love with him, had him convinced that she was the most beautiful woman in the world).

In Frederic's solar chart we find the sun conjunct Neptune in Pisces, part of a loose grand trine in water signs, which indicates a soft, vulnerable, idealistic person who is nonetheless a bit woolly-minded and easily imposed upon or deceived. Venus square the Nodes indicates that the deception, and his downfall, is due to women. Mercury square Jupiter also points to confused thinking and misplaced ideals – for when the pirates later realize (and present to Frederic) the ingenious paradox that, by the terms of his apprenticeship, he is bound to them until his twenty-first birthday (not his twenty-first year); and since he was born on leap year day he is actually only a little boy of five (not twenty-one); Frederic's staunch sense of duty impels him to leave his beloved Mabel and return to the detested calling of piracy. Note that Mars retrograde in Cancer (its fall) makes for a wavering, indecisive and fickle temperament; even though Mars conjunct the North Node shows one who is brave and daring, even as a little lad.

Duty is ruled by Saturn, and in the solar chart we find – not surprisingly – Saturn besieged by Uranus and Pluto. This indicates a violent trauma early in the life (c.f. those natives born in 1964-1966), and we can well imagine the effect that being apprenticed to pirates would have upon one of a delicate and sensitive nature. It also shows a readiness to do violence to others, such as his willingness to destroy his former comrades after he'd left them; or to destroy his new patron, Mabel's father, after his return to the pirates – all in the name of duty. The Uranus – Pluto besiegement of Saturn forced Frederic to make an obsession and a fetish of duty in order to control his inner violence and maintain his mental balance. Indeed, transiting Saturn was but five days from an exact square to natal Pluto when the events of the opera took place (2/28/1873), which augurs violence, frustration, obsession, anger. Also transiting Neptune was applying to square of natal Mars, which augurs deception and perfidy. Converse progressed Mercury opposed natal Mars around this time as well, auguring misunderstandings and estrangements.

The close correspondences between Frederic's horoscope on the one hand, and his character and the events in his life on the other, constitute apodictic evidence for the indisputable veracity of astrology.

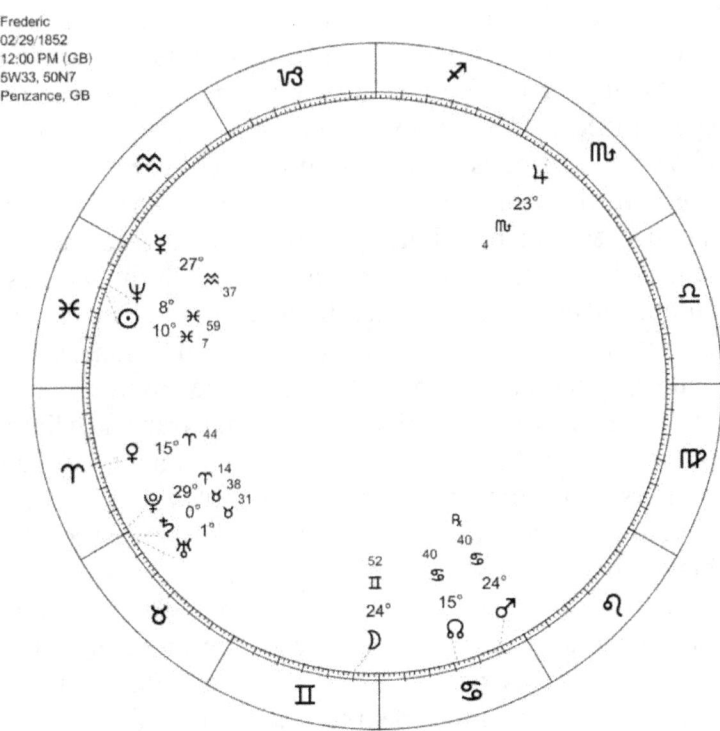

The Politics of Relationship

In every relationship there is a power equation: someone has more control than the other person. The power in a relationship at any given moment resides in the hands of that one of the partners who has the least stake in the continuance of the relationship. Typically, therefore, the power equation in a relationship will teeter-totter back and forth over time (and over different lifetimes) – now this person, now that one, being the one presently calling the shots.

There's no astrological way of determining who's on first in a relationship at any given moment. What horoscopes do reveal, however, is how the individual partners wield the power when it teeters their way; and this is shown primarily by the planet Venus. Where Mercury is the planet of mind, Venus is the planet of desire. Desire is always couched in terms of power – the balance of power between an individual and his or her environment. To desire is to cede power to whomever or whatever can satisfy that desire.

An individual's satisfaction is reckoned in terms of the value of what he or she possesses. In the first instance this means the body, its physical beauty or usefulness in work. Anything of measurable value is symbolized by Venus – it is the impulse to score points for the self. Where self-consciousness (mind, or Mercury) has no measure, self-worth always has a measure. The coin of meaning in the individual case can be Mommy's love, money, social success, sex, heaven; or it can be merely the sense of worth that comes from all the patient suffering undergone in a lifetime. But there must always be something to show for it all in the end – some little blue ribbon or other, some measure of control over the environment, some sense of personal power and effectiveness that translates into self-worth. Venus symbolizes both the native's manner of adapting himself or herself to the environment, and also the concomitant adaptation of the environment to the native – the measure of his or her satisfaction and success (worth).

In contrast to Mercury (mind), Venus (desire) shows a person's dark or hidden side. People readily communicate what's on their minds, but it takes deeper intimacy before they reveal what they're really after. Too, most people know their own minds; and their minds are made up, or they can change their minds. However, they often don't really know what they want out of life; or how to go about getting it; or why it is that their efforts haven't been rewarded. Where mind is expressed as an attitude, desire is expressed as a yearning. It is more symbolic in nature than mind, and it reveals itself to awareness not so much in conscious thoughts as in the imagery of fantasies and dreams. For example, in our fantasy conversations, mind is the logical train of our argument, and desire is the longing for whatever response we hope to elicit from the imaginary interlocutor with whom we are conversing or interacting.

Thus, where mind is concerned with superficial order – rationalizing, filing, and sorting – desire is concerned with power – weighing, maneuvering, and manipulating. Where Mercury presents himself, Venus offers herself, but with the clear intent of subduing that which cannot be seduced. With Venus we're talking about people's strategies of control, manipulation, and avoidance of intimacy (loss of control).

When Venus is oriental – that is to say, a morning star, when she rises before the sun in the east – the desire nature is said to be *possessive*; and when Venus is occidental – when she is an evening star, setting after the sun in the west – the desire nature is said to be *dispassionate*. Just as eager mind (oriental) exhibits the Gemini side of Mercury and certain mind (occidental) exhibits the Virgo side of Mercury, so too does possessive desire exhibit the Taurus side of Venus and dispassionate desire exhibit the Libra side of Venus (see my book *Thought Forms* for a complete discussion of the Mercury cycle in the natal and progressed horoscopes). As is the case also with the eager/certain distinction at Mercury's conjunctions with the sun, there is no hard cusp effect between possessiveness and dispassion at Venus's conjunctions with the sun. On the contrary, the conjunctions exhibit an exaggerated form of the preceding quality: Venus superior conjunction sun can be super-possessive and smothery; Venus inferior conjunction sun (indeed, Venus retrograde, period) can be super-dispassionate and don't-touch-me. But this is another story for another day.

Possessive desire seeks a sense of owning and being owned, and is primarily concerned with alliances and matters of community belonging. Dispassionate desire seeks a sense of personal privilege and prerogative, and is primarily concerned with preserving individual liberty against encroachment.

The tenor of the times for the past several centuries has been a gradual shift away from possessiveness and towards dispassion – at least in the human economy. For example, the gradual shift from feudalism to democracy in political, social, religious, and cultural institutions throughout the world is a shift from a possessive to a dispassionate perspective on power relationships. The institution of marriage, which in its broad outlines has been fundamentally possessive in nature, has been undergoing severe dislocations of redefinition in the past century, and has not yet stabilized itself in a recognizable pattern, except that it is evidently becoming more dispassionate. This has entailed, for example, some diminution of emphasis in the popular mind on marriage for romantic love or pecuniary advantage (which are possessive ideals) and has given more emphasis to the idea of marriage as therapy or a creative collaboration between individuals (dispassionate ideals). This is not to reject or endorse either possessiveness or dispassion: the former is manipulative but warm and gay; the latter is just but cool and somber. However, that half of the population which is dispassionate (those born with Venus placed later in the zodiac than the sun) are more in tune with the times, because the times seem to favor dispassion.

The differences between the possessive and dispassionate Venus types show up most clearly in each one's expectations of marriage. Possessive types are interested in commitment to relationship as an end in itself, to which all else is subordinate; hence, they are less interested in the question of whether or not there is a sharing of philosophies, hobbies, interests, etc. Possessive types bring to marriage expectations of mutual self-sacrifice (especially by the other person), fidelity, and the belief that marriage is above all else a task, which should entail a common purpose, as opposed to mere common interests. The wedding ring is a possessive invention: a pledge of undying constancy; a sign of ownership more humane than a brand.

However, the "loyalty" on which these types pride themselves is not so much to the people themselves as to their images of them; and when the image runs out, they can turn on people with a cry of betrayal. Their warmth can turn in a trice to cold severity. Other people can sense this, which is why they tend to distrust the motives of possessive types in spite of how self-sacrificing they believe themselves to be. Where the dispassionate natives are afraid of consciously acknowledging hurt, the possessive types use their hurt as a fuel to fire resentment. Their security lies in their pride, in their fidelity to their own images; thus, they anchor their emotional stability to the bedrock of their fantasies – to whether this or that image is being actualized in reality. They unabashedly relate to other people in terms of the service they might render or the use to which they might be put; although they are quite willing to serve others in turn. When all is said and done, they are at least willing to trust other people to some extent.

Dispassionate types, on the other hand, bring to marriage expectations of mutual self-sufficiency, little diminution of individual choice for the sake of the relationship – i.e., the belief that marriage is, above all else, a friendship and should entail nothing more than benevolent interest and good faith. Marriage is viewed as a pooling of common interests insofar as such interests can be shared, with only a generalized feeling of goodwill and well-wishing beyond this point. To these natives, there is a relationship only to the extent that there is a commonality of interests.

The dispassionate types are friendly and democratic; they draw no distinctions between people, but are equally open, or closed, to strangers and spouse alike. When they are interested in someone, they can be genuinely solicitous and sympathetic listeners; but when they are not especially interested in someone they can be brusque to the point of rudeness. When they give their attention, they do so wholeheartedly: they stop everything they're doing to help. But most of the time they are too busy for people (unless other horoscope factors intervene – e.g., Aquarius emphasis, or a Mutable Natural Disposition). Their reactions to people are more a function of the mood they're in at the moment than what they expect to get from the people. They always maintain a reserve and privacy that they allow no one to breach. They prefer relationships with a minimum of clinging, self-adjustment, or inconvenience. Where people happen to meet, they meet; and where they don't, they go their separate ways. As Fritz Perls put it, "I do my thing and you do your thing. I am not in this world to live up to your expectations, and you are not in this world to live up to mine. You are you, and I am I, and if by chance we find each other, it's beautiful. If not, it can't be helped." Within a relationship they feel a strong need for psychological elbow room, some way of distancing themselves through individual activity. They must have a life of their own. They will never permit any relationship to become the centerpiece of their existence, nor permit themselves to critically depend upon anyone if they can help it. The wedding ring is a dispassionate invention – something the woman can sell after the divorce.

Dispassionate natives will not commit themselves emotionally to any situation or relationship over which they do not exercise decisive control, so they find it difficult to fully appreciate just how emotionally dependent on other people they actually are. They are impersonal and impassive, quite simply unwilling to allow themselves to be hurt. And when they are hurt, they make a conscious decision to slough it off, to ignore it, and then to turn their attention to their other affairs. Their security lies in maintaining an unobstructed exit, thus emulating the ostrich in strategy and effectiveness. They try to gloss over conflicts and to accentuate the positive. As a result they never really know what their true feelings are, since they refuse to acknowledge their emotional dependencies. They go out of their way to please, to placate, as long as no real sacrifice is required of them. They are quite capable of maintaining a pleasant front while nursing a deep resentment. But at least they are free of the vengeful "I told you so" mentality of the possessive types; they let bygones be bygones, and try to maintain a hopeful, positive, constructive attitude.

Oriental Venus wants to possess and be possessed – to merge individual identities and surrender individual initiative in order to create something greater; whereas Occidental Venus prefers a free, easy, laissez faire relationship that serves merely as a springboard or a base of support from which to operate.

To dispassionate types, the idea of commitment to a relationship as an end in itself seems quite foreign and bizarre, and these natives tend to view possessive types as clingy, overbearing, and a bring-down. Possessive natives, on the other hand, regard the idea of a community of interests as quite superficial, and these natives see dispassionate types as cold, aloof, and selfish.

One might suppose, therefore, that marriage would be more likely to succeed between natives of the same type: both possessive or both dispassionate. In a "mixed" marriage the individual partners soon discover that they're not going to get what they want from each other, nor is the other person going to be satisfied with what they have to offer. The respective partners have contradictory expectations of marriage. In the politics of relationship, the fact that the power in a relationship resides in the hands of the party who has the least stake usually gives the dispassionate party an edge in the normal course of things; but possessive types have a way of upsetting the apple cart when they feel they've been dispossessed. In yin-yang fashion, at the bottom of the dispassionate psyche there lurks an unrecognized possessiveness, a dependency usually unacknowledged until the relationship terminates (or threatens to terminate). And at the bottom of the possessive psyche there lies an unrecognized dispassion – a cold, brusque, utilitarian independence to which the native resorts when he or she is blocked.

Marriage between two Venus oriental natives or between two Venus occidental natives is in some ways easier than a "mixed" marriage, because then the partners possess a like spirit of cooperation and can take the same assumptions about marriage for granted: they at least share the same basic map of marriage. However this is no guarantee of success because even in this case one usually finds the other partner reading the map upside down. Even though their basic expectations of marriage may be in accord, this does not mean that the common interests that bring two dispassionate natives together at the beginning will be enough to sustain them through the years; nor does it mean that the total union, which the two possessive natives seek will be harmonious in all its specific implications.

The universal struggle of marriage is the slow and excruciating acceptance of the fact that this person who stands before you doesn't fit the image that you had of them; nor will they satisfy the needs you hoped they would. A marriage between two natives of the same phase is as likely to underscore respective insecurities as it is to address respective needs. On the other hand, mixed marriages have greater potential for growth – if the initial divisiveness can be overcome – because each partner is challenged to defer to the other, to give up something of his or her self (which when all is said and done limits one's scope), to find happiness in a situation that he or she cannot fundamentally control. In other words, mixed marriages require and teach greater trust.

If we are going to manipulate other people and exploit them for our own ends – and everyone is doing this all the time with everyone else (this is what the action of the planet Venus is all about) – there is no point in being shameless and pretending that we aren't doing this. Rather we should try to be skillful in our machinations. This means appreciating other people and what they do for us (also the action of Venus), being able to see things from their point of view and not taking them for granted. We should be gentle and kind to them, instead of just grabbing what we want from them and then tossing them aside.

Both possessiveness and dispassion can be strategies for avoidance of intimacy: possessiveness a strategy of control and dispassion a strategy of escape. Both can become strategies of self-protection, refusal to take responsibility for there being a relationship, and thus both can be wrong. The right strategy is to be willing to make a total commitment (as the possessive types do), while also maintaining one's own individuality (as the dispassionate types do).

Control is avoidance of intimacy. The dispassionate types aim for control in a day-to-day sense, whereas the possessive types seek long-term control; thus dispassion and possessiveness can be viewed as natural divisions of labor in the economy of marriage. It's up to the dispassionate types to keep things on an even keel – to keep things light and in perspective; and it's up to the possessive types to keep things grounded and take a long-term view. Then the types can work in collaboration instead of competition.

Assessing Partnership Compatibility

People have been having problems with their relationships for as long as they have been having relationships. Even Adam and Eve, under the most ideal conditions imaginable, failed to make a decent go of it. It's not surprising, therefore, that synastry–the astrology of relationships – has always been one of the most popular branches of the stellar art. In the second century A.D. Claudius Ptolemy wrote in his *Centiloquy* (XXXII): "Concord between two persons is produced by an harmonious figuration of the stars, indicative of the matter whereby good will is constituted, in the nativity of either person. Love and hatred are discernible, as well from the concord and discord of the luminaries, as from the ascendants of both nativities."

Ptolemy's method was to compare the suns, moons, and Ascendants in the two horoscopes because these are the points where the natives are in closest touch with the world outside of themselves. All of the other planets, cusps, parts, etc., are derivative from these three, both in terms of their mathematical motion, and in the psychological sense of being more conditioned or subject to karma. It is in the three vital centers that one looks for the natives' free will – the ability to recognize and discard choices that have outlived their usefulness, and go on to make new ones. This is why a comparison of the harmonies and disharmonies between the vital centers in two horoscopes is so revealing of the internal adjustments two people have to make when they join together in a relationship.

Note that this technique doesn't provide the entire story by any means – the cross-aspects between planets in the two horoscopes describe the situation in greater detail (see the following essays). However comparison of the vital centers is a good place to begin. In what follows, marriage will be given primary attention, but the same technique can be used to evaluate any relationship between two people.

Two centers are harmonious if they are either both in masculine signs, or if they are both in feminine signs. If one is in a masculine sign and the other is in a feminine sign, then they are disharmonious. A single sign is harmonious with itself, so two centers that lie in the same sign are in harmony with each other. For example, Leo is harmonious with Gemini, since both are masculine; and Capricorn is harmonious with Cancer, since both are feminine.

But Leo is disharmonious with Capricorn, since the former is masculine and the latter is feminine. The procedure is to compare separately the two sun signs, then the two moon signs, and then the two rising signs, to ascertain which of these pairs of vital centers are harmonious or disharmonious.

All of the signs of the same gender are taken to be harmonious with one another because in this context "harmony" means similarity, or likeness. When a pair of vital centers lies in harmonious signs, then those centers operate in much the same way. The two parties to the relationship can always rely upon one another in that respect, or take that facet of the relationship completely for granted. If the two sun signs are harmonious, then each person respects the other's views on life and living, and they can help one another to follow out the dictates of their individual consciences and destinies. If the two moons lie in harmonious signs, then there is a feeling of good will that underpins the relationship; both parties have a genuine liking for each other, and truly wish one another the best. If the two rising signs are harmonious, then there is a commonality of everyday interests and habits that bind the two people together; they fulfill each other's images of what they are seeking in a partner.

When a pair of vital centers lies in disharmonious signs, then there is a point of conscious difference in the relationship that can become a matter of concern or even conflict. Contrasts always impose themselves upon the awareness more forcefully than similarities do, so the attention tends to go to them. When the two sun signs are in disharmonious signs, there is a clash of wills. The two parties often find it difficult to unite their goals and aims in life. When the two moon signs are disharmonious, there is a polarity in the feelings which often shows up as a lack of emotional warmth or sympathy. When the two rising signs are disharmonious, there is a conflict in the way in which the two people express themselves, and a tendency for communications between them to break down.

Ptolemy's technique illustrates an important principle of astrological interpretation which Dr. Marc Edmund Jones (in *The Essentials of Astrological Analysis*) termed "Negative Indication": *if all but one criteria in a well-defined set are present in a natal horoscope* (e.g. planets in earth-air-water but not fire; planets in succedent and cadent houses but not angular; etc.), *then the emphasis goes to the absent criteria, but with a twist of the symbolism – like a parody of what it should mean – as if in overcompensation for a felt psychological lack or need.* In the present case, if only one pair of the vital centers is disharmonious, then the attention in the relationship tends to dwell upon the disharmony, like an itch that can't quite be reached and scratched, often at the expense of the enjoyment of other areas in which there is a natural accord. Instead of focusing on where there is agreement – which is what happens when only one pair of vital centers is harmonious – the focus tends to dwell upon areas of disagreement. That is to say, relationships in which only one pair of vital centers is in harmonious signs tend to be smoother, less fractious than relationships in which two (and only two) pairs of vital centers are in harmonious signs. The examples which follow are taken from biographies and memoirs.

From the foregoing it might appear that the ideal relationship occurs **when the two sun signs, moon signs, and rising signs are all harmonious**, but this is not necessarily the case. If that were true then President Bill Clinton and his erstwhile mistress Monica Lewinsky would be the ideal couple, since they have all three pairs of vital centers in identical signs (Leo suns, Taurus moons, and Libra Ascendants). Too much harmony in a relationship can produce a static or stagnant situation. Have you ever met someone and recognized in him or her some quality or trait remarkably similar to one of your own? You immediately understand that part of the person, but at the same time you are left with an unsettled feeling, or an unresolved question, like a gear that encounters another cog where it should have meshed with a space. Similarities tend to reinforce themselves on one level, rather than move to new levels. Relationships mature through a continual giving way or relinquishing of individual desires in order to maintain a greater unity. Few of us are strong enough to give up our desires by ourselves; we need other people whose desires conflict with ours to give us a reason to change and mature. Relationships, like pearls, seem to require a certain amount of irritation in order to grow. But when all three pairs of vital centers are in harmonious signs, this irritation – and with it something very vital – is largely missing. The relationship may seem somewhat nebulous or insubstantial since there aren't any solid differences to grab onto or push against. Instead of being a challenge, the relationship may become a competition, or a game of one-upmanship.

For example, in the words of one of the Fitzgeralds' biographers, "Both Scott and Zelda had entered a new period in their lives: both drinking heavily, and seemingly to dare each other to ever more reckless and outrageous acts. ... They both dived into the Mediterranean from a great height, and drove their car too fast along winding roads. Once, after a fight with Scott, Zelda threw herself under the wheels of their car and dared him to run over her – and he even started to move the car." When all three vital centers are harmonious, each party tends to confirm him or herself all the more in their own individual resolve, rather than join with the other to move to some new level of realization. The focus of attention, therefore, has to be kept outside of the relationship itself if it is to lead anywhere. Some outside objective or goal to which both parties are dedicated should always be kept in view. These people have many common interests: the more they can concentrate on the final result rather than on who is going to have the privilege of accomplishing it, the more will the harmony between them pay off in a smooth efficiency and ability to avoid getting side-tracked.

The converse situation, **when all three pairs of vital centers are in disharmonious signs**, makes for rather intriguing relationships, on the principle that opposites attract. People who are quite unlike us can provide us with a fascinating complement by helping us to recognize exactly where our strengths and limitations lie. They embolden us to exhibit different facets of ourselves, to try out different roles, to experiment. We can learn a great deal from these people, not only because they present us with an alternative point of view and way of doing things, but also because in the mirror of their reactions to us we see ourselves and our aspirations standing out in bold relief. There is a sense of newness and freshness that grows out of the continual awareness of differences – you never know what to expect next! As an example, consider the first meeting of Isadora Duncan and Gordon Craig: "Here stood before me brilliant youth, beauty, genius; and, all inflamed with sudden love, I flew into his arms with all the magnetic willingness of a temperament which had for two years lain dormant, but waiting to spring forth. Here I found an answering temperament, worthy of my metal (sic). In him I had met the flesh of my flesh, the blood of my blood." This type of relationship, however, is generally better for romance than for marriage, since the fact that none of the pairs of vital centers is harmonious means that the paths in life diverge sharply, and so a frustrating gap between the two people can come into being. At every turn there are differences of approach that must be reconciled; one or the other must always give way. Hence an exceptional amount of inner adjustment is incumbent on both parties in order to make the relationship work. Each must learn to recognize when the other is more in tune with the situation at hand, and forgo their own inclinations and impulses at such times. By the same token, each must learn to sort out their own ideas and feelings to determine where they must "draw the line" and let their own desires prevail. These relationships both bestow and require a peculiar fluidity and ability to adapt.

When the two sun signs are harmonious, while the two moon and rising signs are disharmonious, then there is a basic similarity of outlook on life, or a sense that the two lives are heading in the same direction. These people can come back together again after years of separation and pick right up where they left off, because the essential thing is the long view: life in its more ultimate or long-range aspects. Friendship, therefore, seems to be the most pronounced feature of the relationship. However, there are numerous areas of more superficial division: the two personalities are quite distinct, and opinions are apt to differ on how things are to be done in actual practice. Nonetheless each is willing to free the other to go their own way and do what they feel they must do to fulfill themselves. Whether they cherish or obey is moot, but they certainly honor one another. As an example consider John F. and Jacqueline Kennedy: "The marriage had become, by now, little more than a matter of mutual convenience – a union of two mercurial, strong-willed, stubborn people who, like so many children of the rich, were rather used to getting their own way, and were not happy when they didn't. Any romantic love that might have once existed between them had long since evaporated. ... And so a perfectly sensible business deal was struck during those first White House months. She would supply the elegance, the charm, the class that he wanted. And he, in turn would let her do pretty much whatever else she chose."

When only the two sun signs are disharmonious (with harmony between the two moon and rising signs), then there is likely to be disagreement with regard to life philosophies, and ultimate aims and goals. Often the backgrounds and upbringings contrast; in any case the two parties have very different views of the world and their places in it, and they shape their lives toward different ends. There may be some possessiveness, or a tendency for each to try to force the relationship to fit their own image of how it ought to be. The resulting conflict of wills can make mutual commitment over the long haul a matter of concern, especially in the initial stages of the relationship. In the case of Elvis and Priscilla Presley, "Elvis would 'lock' his women in. It was rough for her because Elvis was a pretty jealous man, too, and with a woman as beautiful and fine as Cilla, you could see why. ... Hence the double standard that developed in Elvis's treatment of his wife. (Elvis's producer) wanted to cast Priscilla in movies. She also had numerous other opportunities. Nobody knows exactly what happened to these opportunities, but it is assumed that she disregarded them at Elvis's command." In counterbalance to this separative tendency on the ideological level, there is a strong emotional bond and usually a shared set of everyday interests and tastes. Both like to do the same sorts of things, and they like to do them together. When only the sun signs are harmonious, it is every-day functioning that becomes a problem; when only the sun signs are disharmonious, it is the overview, the question of where the relationship is heading in terms of each party's individual aspirations, that is at issue. Each must learn to let the other make their own way in life, and respect the other person's choices.

When two people have their moons in harmonious signs (while the two sun and rising signs are disharmonious), then their personalities and temperaments are in accord. Their reactions to things and feelings about life are similar, so they can be perfectly candid and reveal their deepest feelings to one another. There is a strong empathy and tenderness between them; rarely do they need to explain themselves or justify their actions to one other. Each intuitively understands the other's motivations and accepts them for what they are, rather like a mother accepts her children for what they are, unquestioningly. And like a mother who knows her children will leave her when they grow up, these people are aware that their life paths diverge, and that each will want to make their own place in the world. There is a recognition that there are limits to what they will able to accomplish working together, that they can help each other best by providing moral support, and cheering the other on in their struggle with life's vicissitudes. They know they always have someone who is receptive and kindly disposed towards them to whom they can return to unburden themselves and rest their spirits. Even if the relationship breaks up, the breakup is usually amicable and by mutual consent. For example, after Jane Fonda's separation from Ted Turner after eight years of marriage, she commented: "Ted is a soulmate. I care about him. He means the world to me. He taught me to be happy." They separated, she said, "because we changed. I changed. ... Are we happier by ourselves than we were together? It's not clear."

When only the two moon signs are disharmonious (with both sun and rising signs harmonious), then the feelings tend to be at odds, or at least not meeting. Individual likes and dislikes are apt to differ. Frequently the parties have separate outside friendships rather than share the same friends in common, since each needs people outside the relationship with whom they can hope and dream. Within the relationship there is often a distance or detachment where a sympathy and understanding would normally be. Each party may feel at pains to fulfill real or imagined expectations of the other, and so find it difficult to relax comfortably in the relationship and just be themselves. There may be an air of formality and impersonality, with the two parties hurting one another either inadvertently or quite consciously as they struggle to express their needs to each other. Breakups are especially acrimonious and spiteful; Prince Charles and Princess Diana are a good example, as are Woody Allen and Mia Farrow who had a huge, explosive break-up when Farrow found pornographic pictures of her adopted daughter Soon-Yi with Allen in Allen's apartment. Their split was replete with bitter accusations and legal volleys. On the other hand, in these relationships there is a sense of common direction in life and a mutual moral commitment, as well as the ability to see past the momentary emotional obstacles that occasionally keep them apart. Each party has to keep their own preferences and inclinations on a leash, and learn to take satisfaction in the happiness of the other, neither judging nor rejecting that which the other person holds sacred.

When the two rising signs are harmonious (while the two sun and moon signs are disharmonious), then there is a similarity in the roles that the two people play in life. Each is willing to accept the other pretty much on his or her own terms, in hail-fellow-well-met fashion. Their fondest images of themselves are mutually reinforcing: they do things like walk in the rain and watch sunsets together. They can really sit down and talk to one another; even without talking they understand each other very well because their relationship is based on an instantaneous communication. This is one reason why it is helpful for an astrologer to have his or her rising sign harmonious with that of a client. Nevertheless, the parties in such a relationship recognize that there are wide differences between them on deeper levels, which incline them to maintain their distances and not place undue reliance upon one another to come through in a pinch. Even though they have the best of intentions towards each other, they are not always able to give the kind of emotional support that the other needs. These people help each other most, in bad times as well as good, by supplying an abundance of friendly interest and help in not taking things too seriously. For example, after going public and receiving approbation for her outspoken opinions on such matters as women's rights and abortion, Betty Ford felt "it bothered me that while I was getting so much praise Jerry was getting criticism. He was a good sport. He was proud of me and even in cases where he didn't agree with my views, he was all for my spouting them. ... You know, if you bring up a subject long enough with a man, why finally he gets so tired of it he agrees to anything. There might be a woman on the Supreme Court now if I'd just brought it up more often."

When only the two rising signs are disharmonious (with both sun and moon signs harmonious), then there is some source of misunderstanding or non-communication that often bogs down an otherwise smooth relationship. Each party wants to talk while the other is interrupting. They are able to see through one another quite clearly, and so they may become impatient with each other's posturing on the one hand, and overly thin-skinned or sensitive to criticism on the other. They may try to outguess or keep one jump ahead of each other, or keep bringing up the same old divisive issues as if for the sport of contention. They allow the present moment to escape them in a welter of verbiage. They may try to force one another to live up to an impossible image. For example, after a trip to India to visit the birthplace of his idol Gandhi, Martin Luther King, Jr. (in the words of his wife) "felt, as in India, that much of the corruption in our society stems from the desire to acquire material things – houses and land and cars. Martin would have preferred to have none of these things. He finally said to me, 'You know, a man who dedicates himself to a cause doesn't need a family.' I was not hurt by this statement. I realized that it did not mean he loved me and the children less, but that he was giving his life to the Movement and felt he therefore could not do as much for his family as he might in other circumstances. He saw a conflict between duty and love ... But I knew that, being the kind of man he was, Martin needed us." The inability to communicate can be very frustrating, since there is usually a profound emotional tie that binds them: a good deal of what each has to accomplish in life as an individual, the two of them can accomplish as well together. Each must learn to put aside their own train of thought and really listen to the other, permitting them their whims and peculiarities, and taking care not to tread upon their aplomb.

The foregoing descriptions of the various combinations of harmony and disharmony may appear somewhat extreme. The individual case will be more or less so, depending upon the type of relationship involved (since we tolerate different things in our intimate relations than in our casual acquaintances), and also upon the maturity of the two people. Learning how to turn obstacles into advantages is what growth is all about. In synastry, as in every department of astrology, free will is the overriding factor.

Sexual Significators in Synastry

I find it amusing when people state that they "don't believe in astrology." If people only knew how much information they were giving out when they reveal their birth time, date, and place, they would be much more circumspect. In particular, sexual signatures are an infallible guide to when there is an innate sexual attraction between two people. This doesn't always lead to out-and-out sex; but it can be useful in getting one's way with people. A few years ago my girlfriend introduced me to her boss (for business reasons). The boss, she warned me, was bitchy, critical, and impossible to please. But when I saw that the boss's horoscope and my own shared both major sexual significators, I knew that she and I would get along just fine; and so it proved (and my girlfriend's relationship with her boss improved as a result of our interaction).

Sexual turn-on is strongest when the man's sun, Mars or Jupiter conjoins or opposes the woman's moon or Venus. We will allow 6° orbs of inexactitude in measurement, but this is just a rule of thumb. Even 10° orbs "work", but the effect is lessened. This might be a good place for a statistical study (perhaps using a polygraph or MRI to measure sexual turn-on). For example, if a man's sun, Mars, or Jupiter is in 12° Leo; and a woman's moon or Venus is between 6° and 18° Leo (conjunction) or Aquarius (opposition); then there is a powerful sexual attraction between the two people. However, the sexual attraction is obviously stronger the closer the conjunction or opposition is to exact. In this context oppositions are not considered malefic; on the contrary, oppositions between horoscopes are better in sexual relationship. Opposites attract. However some of the effect is vitiated if the conjunction or opposition occurs over the line of the sign (e.g. from, say 29° Aries to 1° Taurus or Scorpio). Note that the reverse case (e.g. man's moon or Venus conjunct or opposed to woman's sun or Mars) is not a sexual signature – it merely indicates that the woman wears the pants in the relationship.

Of these cross-aspects between horoscopes, the sun-moon and Mars-Venus combinations in particular are the most Pavlovian sexual bell-ringers. Oftentimes I've met a woman who had her moon on or opposite my sun; or her Venus on or opposite my Mars; and I made a mental note of the fact at that time. But nothing happened, and I certainly didn't provoke anything. However inevitably, at some future time, perhaps years down the line, without any conscious purpose on either side, there unexpectedly came a moment when we happened to look into one another's eyes and suddenly *FLASH!*

If you go back over all the people you've ever had such a flash with in your life and compare their horoscopes to your own, you'll see exactly what I'm getting at.

The Mars-Venus connection (when the man's Mars lies on or opposite the woman's Venus) is pure sexual attraction – fun, light, flirty, and ready to boogie. On the other hand the sun-moon cross-aspect (when the man's sun falls on or opposite the woman's moon) indicates a more profound connection; it's unquestionably sexual, but goes much deeper than the Mars-Venus combination. When you are with someone who shares this signature with you, you feel like you are home, with the person you are meant to be with, with the person who fulfills your deepest needs. There's a profound understanding between you two with no need for words; a tender sympathy and sense of belonging.

In other words, the existence of any of these sexual signatures between two people's horoscopes assures a strong sexual attraction, even if this is going on beneath the surface, unconsciously. In our sexually-repressed society, most people do not consciously acknowledge their true sexual feelings; they pretend they are not feeling them. Nevertheless these feelings are shown in the horoscopes. When once you become aware of these signatures you can see it in the other person's eyes; behind their eyes, really. There are a lot more sexual agendas going on between people than they acknowledge consciously.

When parents have signatures of sexual attraction with their children, it can mean that in a previous lifetime the parent and child were lovers, and the sexual attraction between them remains in this lifetime, albeit unconsciously on both sides. Of course, they will try to pretend they are not feeling this attraction; but it is often quite visible to an outside observer. Indeed, when parents find themselves fighting with a child of the opposite sex, particularly as the child reaches sexual maturity, it is often because the parent is sexually turned on and is trying to deny the attraction by substituting its negation.

The absence of any sexual signature between two people's horoscopes doesn't necessarily deny sexual attraction. People with Scorpio prominent (sun, Venus or Mars in Scorpio) tend to confuse the issue because they sexually attract and are sexually attracted by everybody. However, I am convinced this is a Scorpio "ploy" which they use – consciously or unconsciously – to manipulate people (rather than being true sexual attraction). When there is no sexual signature between the horoscopes of people in a relationship, then there could be a problem due to one or the other person becoming bored with the sexual side of the relationship.

For gay men sexual attraction is shown when one man's sun, Mars or Jupiter conjoins or opposes the other's sun, Mars, or Jupiter. Here the sun-Mars combination is the strongest.

For lesbian women sexual attraction is shown when one woman's moon or Venus conjoins or opposes the other woman's moon or Venus. The moon-Venus combination is stronger than two moons or two Venus's.

Having stated the foregoing rules for sexual attraction between horoscopes it behooves me to state the First Law of Stalking, or Keeping Your Neck Out Of Other People's Nooses: all sexual attraction and infatuation are phony. When sexual electrons are going back and forth is when you should immediately put your guard up and be very careful of what you are doing, rather than blunder ahead into commitments that you could very easily regret. Sexual attraction can be, and often is, a cover for extremely difficult karma which will have to be dealt with if action is taken without forethought. Be warned, be smart, save yourself a lot of grief. Take a look at the other cross-aspects between the horoscopes.

How to Compare Two People's Horoscopes

It's often difficult for us to know how we truly *feel* about the people around us. The roles we try to make them play for us too easily get in the way of relating to them as just plain folks. If our parents, spouse, or children (for example) don't fulfill our expectations and needs, we tend to condemn them for disappointing us – even though underneath it all we may very well like them and regard them as good eggs when all is said and done, even though they may have let us down. On the other hand, it can also happen that we have superficially cordial and affable relationships with people with whom we are nonetheless faintly distrustful, or even slightly disgusted.

Astrologically speaking, your true feelings about people are shown by the cross-aspects which you have with them. For present purposes we will take into account only conjunctions and oppositions in longitude, and we will allow an orb of 5 degrees from exactness in measuring these.

For example, Princess Diana's Mercury in 4° Cancer lies within 5° of Prince Charles' Uranus in 30° Gemini, and within 5° of opposition to his Jupiter in 30° Sagittarius. Therefore he is a Mercury person to her, and she is both a Jupiter and a Uranus person to him. Note that a cross-conjunction between the same outer planet in two charts is not considered in the case of natives who were born close enough together in time so that the planet hadn't yet moved very far.

We will not distinguish here between the conjunction and opposition: the particular combination of planets involved in the contact has more to do with its basic felicity or infelicity than whether it is a conjunction or opposition (however Dr. Marc Edmund Jones believed that oppositions in cross-aspects were more powerful than conjunctions). When the contact is by conjunction, the relationship tends to be more personal and intimate. When the contact is by opposition, the relationship is more impersonal, noncommittal, with a sense of holding each other at arm's length. It must be noted, however, that certain planets are just naturally ornery and contentious (particularly Mercury, Mars, Saturn, Uranus, and Pluto), and when two of these are joined by opposition aspect, the resulting relationship can exhibit superficial conflict and trivial bickering as a matter of sport, even though the combination may be nominally favorable.

Also, there are certain cross-aspects which are powerful sexual bell-ringers (such as a man's sun, Mars, or Jupiter contacting a woman's moon or Venus). And there are other contacts – such as Jupiter-Saturn – which favor relationships such as employer-employee, advisor-client, or doctor-patient (in this case it really doesn't matter which is Jupiter and which is Saturn; the point is that Jupiter and Saturn trust one another).

What we are interpreting here is how you *feel* about the people you know, not whether you *like* them or not. For example, you may dislike your boss because she's impatient, cranky, brusque, and unappreciative. Yet at the same time you may respect her dedication, industriousness, self-discipline, etc. Thus although you don't *like* her, you nonetheless may have good *feelings* about her. You may have cast her in the role of your oppressor in this lifetime; however she still positively reinforces your own assiduous, hard-working side.

What is shown by the analysis of cross-aspects is your *feelings* about the people you know (which actually transcend a particular lifetime) rather than the transient roles – such as parent, spouse, employer, stranger, lover, tormentor, acquaintance, friend – which they are playing for you in this lifetime. If what you want is information on how happy or successful your marriage, for example, will be, then you must look to your natal Venus for testimony as to intimacy and happiness generally, to your natal 7th house and its ruler for specific information on marital prospects, and so forth, to determine how the role-playing features of the relationship will tend to work out. Analysis of cross-aspects will indicate how you feel about people, but not necessarily how well they are fulfilling your roles and expectations for you.

You cannot deduce from the analysis of cross-aspects whether a relationship will be of major or minor significance in your life. All you can deduce is what part of your own personality you are mirroring in it. If this part of your personality is problematical (if the relevant planet is afflicted in your natal chart), then the relationships which are symbolized by that planet will have a similarly problematical character.

All that other people can ever do or be for us is mirror our own selves. Our Mars people, for example, will mirror how we are using our Mars energy. If Mars is well-aspected and strong by sign and house in the natal chart, then our Mars energy will flow freely, we will be bold and audacious, and we will tend to click with our Mars people who egg us on; thus the positive interpretation will apply. Conversely, if natal Mars is afflicted or weak, then our Mars energy will be timid and inhibited, and we will tend to find our Mars people threatening or inhibiting, so that the negative interpretation will be more obvious. Since what we're talking about here is feelings, the interpretation must be a matter of feeling as well.

If you want to get more specific than this in the analysis, you must take into account the type of relationship and the astrological correlates involved. For example, your mother is usually signified by the moon and the 10th house; and your spouse is signified by Venus (for a man) or Mars (for a woman) and the 7th house. So even though planets in the charts of both your mother and spouse contact your natal Saturn (let us say), the characters of the two relationships may be quite different depending upon the conditions of the respective significators. If the moon and the 10th are natally afflicted, then your relationship with your mother will tend to emphasize negative aspects of her planets which contact your Saturn. Whereas if the moon and 10th are natally strong, then your mother will be more of a positive Saturn person for you. But if your Saturn is natally afflicted, then even your positive Saturn people will bring up certain problem areas in your personality. And so on.

However, it is true that certain types of relationships are intrinsically more or less harmonious than others. These are symbolized by the favorable and unfavorable combinations of planets. The table indicates which planetary pairs tend to combine favorably (+) and which tend to combine unfavorably (−). En passant, note that the following table can also be applied to transiting planets, e.g. Transiting Uranus conjunct natal Mars is intrinsically favorable, whereas transiting Uranus conjunct natal Venus is intrinsically unfavorable. This factor influences the extended interpretations given at the end of this chapter.

The difference between the favorable and unfavorable combinations is that the former are easier, more intimate, more validating; whereas the latter are more reserved, cramped, and non-validating. Every planetary combination (like every relationship) has both its positive and its negative characteristics. However we tend to be more aware of the positive features when the planetary combination is intrinsically favorable; and we tend to emphasize the negative features when it is intrinsically unfavorable.

Table of Favorable and Unfavorable Planetary Combinations

	SU	MO	ME	VE	MA	JU	SA	UR	NE
MO	+								
ME	−	+							
VE	−	+	−						
MA	+	−	+	+					
JU	+	+	−	+	+				
SA	−	−	+	−	−	+			
UR	+	−	+	−	+	+	+		
NE	−	+	−	+	−	+	−	+	
PL	+	−	+	−	+	−	−	−	−

People whose **planets conjunct your Ascendant** manifest a self-sufficient insouciance – they make no excuses or apologies for being who they are. These people impress you with their sheer gumption, with their pride in their own fitness of place in the scheme of things. You tend to be fond of these people even though there may be little warmth in the relationship, and you willingly open up to them. You accept each other, and thus your Ascendant people inspire you to accept yourself.

Perhaps the most important cross-aspects, hence the first ones to look at, are those between natal planets in one chart and lunar Nodes in the other. Right off the top this information indicates whether the relationship is fundamentally progressive or detrimental: ultimately helpful, or ultimately debilitating. The Nodes, more than the planets, reveal karma from past lives which impinges upon this one. The difference between North and South Nodes in relationships – both natally and in synastry – is that South Node is where you put your expectations of others (for better or worse – these people either really turn you on or really turn you off, but in either case they mirror a self-indulgent side of yourself); whereas North Node people are blessings pure and simple – even if the relationship is infelicitous, they give you what you really need.

People with planets conjunct your South Node are not intrinsically bad people; they just tend to bring out the worst in you. For example, the Tar Baby unquestionably had his Mars or Pluto conjunct Br'er Rabbit's South Node. There was nothing bad about the Tar Baby – quite the contrary; everything that happened there was Br'er Rabbit's projection. This is why you must be very, very wary of people who turn you on sexually and who have planets on your South Node.

People whose planets conjoin your North Node touch you with their altruism and unselfish concern. They are role models who manifest admirable qualities which you recognize are latent in yourself as well. You receive a great deal of positive interest and encouragement from these people – they wish you to succeed. They appeal to your nobler sensibilities and selfless impulses. By putting their faith in you, your North Node people inspire you to put faith in yourself.

North Node: People who have planets in their natal charts conjunct your North Node will appear to you as if they had those planets conjunct the North Node in their own charts. They will be people who encourage you, accept you for who you are, and respect your feelings and space. They are the people you instinctively trust and open up to; they are a true blessing to you. Therefore, you must pay especial attention to everything these people have to say, since often their pronouncements are messages from your Higher Self. These people are candid, open, and accepting of your feelings. They respect you and what you are trying to accomplish in life. Their presence is like a breath of fresh air. No matter what else may be going on in the relationship, they have a genuine liking and esteem for you, and they help you to tune into your most prepossessing and gracious impulses in turn – your charitable, benefit-of-the-doubt side.

South Node: People who have natal planets conjunct your South Node will appear to you as if they had those planets conjunct the South Node in their own charts – they touch your more selfish side with their own. They will tend to be manipulative, exploitative, distant, and unsympathetic. These relationships are marred by self-serving ulterior motives, by struggles for power and control, and by emotional undercurrents which are being capitalized on but which are not being openly addressed (such as strong sexual agendas).

These people either attract you in a somewhat sleazy fashion; or else they rub you the wrong way; they are jarring rather than soothing. You can't really connect with these people because there's too much suspicion, defensiveness, or one-upsmanship going on. They tend to use you or to be used by you. You must take care with these people, be on your guard, since they arouse in you dubious impulses. Where your North Node people are a blessing, your South Node people bring out the worst in you – their machinations quicken your most self-indulgent impulses – there's no way they'll ever be able to help you or fulfill your expectations. Whether you are strongly attracted to your South Node people or whether you are thoroughly repelled by them, you'll find they indulge their self-pity in much the same way that you do.

For example, in Prince Charles' natal horoscope, his North Node conjoins the moon and his South Node conjoins Mercury, so (judging just from his own chart) he is natural, relaxed, comfortable with himself and with other people; and yet at the same time he is a bit of a know-it-all: astute, yet curt and autocratic.

In Princess Diana's natal horoscope her North Node conjoins Mars and Uranus, and her South Node conjoins the moon, so (judging just from her own chart) she was bold, decisive and determined; also mentally clear and capable of penetrating insight. However, at the same time, she was huffy, pouty, and easily offended.

So much for the natal situation. From the point of view of synastry (horoscope comparison), Prince Charles' South Node falls on Princess Diana's Neptune, so to him she seemed secretive, suspicious, unrealistic, irresponsible, and disinclined to talk openly about what she was really feeling. At the same time, her North Node widely (7°) conjoins his Saturn, so to her he seemed staunch, composed, collected, and responsible. He was better for her than she was for him.

By paying close attention to the points where our Nodes contact the charts of other people we can get beneath surface images and expectations, and understand the true karmic lessons we seek to learn from the people we know. Once the fundamental karmic situation is understood by considering the Nodes, then the other planets are examined.

Sun people are those with planets conjunct or opposed to your sun; thus they are living out or reflecting your own solar impulses for you: they mirror your self-assurance and manifest an admirable staunchness and resoluteness. You tend to see their stately, dignified, self-possessed side. You esteem these people for their sense of self-worth, their independence of spirit, and for what they are trying to achieve in life. That is, you tend to see these people in terms of their own sense of purpose. You respect them for their uncompromising courage, boldness, and willingness to follow out their own destinies. In turn they stimulate these solar impulses within you. These people strike a familiar chord of anguish or pathos that is the human condition. In one fashion or another they symbolize your highest self, your willingness to follow your own aspirations no matter where they may lead, without need of validation from others.

Because they demand to be met as equals on their own ground, they command your respect. Hence the central feature of your relationships with them is challenge. Because your sun people are uncompromising, inflexible, and impervious (especially in the case of the oppositions) they stimulate your own sense of resolve and determination: you have to hold your own with them, validate your own self-worth under their scrutiny. On the negative side your sun people can also mirror your lack of true self-assurance: here you see them as vain and prissy, stiffly pretentious and haughty. Even if you are put off by their overweening noblesse oblige, however, something in you nonetheless applauds their bravado and sense of flair. Their all-sufficient dignity calls forth your own.

Favorable (moon, Mars, Jupiter, Uranus, and Pluto): These are the people on whom your own self-assurance "works". They are suitably impressed or deferential, granting you your due respect and treating you as an equal.

Sun conjunct or opposition sun is a true meeting of minds. There is mutual respect, friendship, and admiration.

Moon gives you considerable sympathy and leeway. She accepts you pretty much on your own terms, makes you feel relaxed and "at home".

Mars is rooting for you all the way. He appeals to your daring, impudent, devil-may-care side.

Jupiter is lofty and detached, but truly admires you and wishes you well. He is interested in you as a person whether he agrees with you or not.

Unfavorable (Mercury, Venus, Saturn, and Neptune): These people are patronizing or touchy. They show up flaws in your own self-assurance, or mirror your own self-doubts. You can't project or sustain your ease of manner and sense of fitness with them.

Mercury always has a better idea. He thinks a lot like you do, but it's hard to connect with him on a heart level.

Venus genuinely likes you and accepts you, yet you don't have all that much in common or much to communicate or share on deeper levels.

Saturn withholds approval – he may be critical or competitive, or he may feel superior to you. In any case he keeps his distance.

Moon people (who have planets conjunct or opposite your moon) mirror your sense of connection to the world around you. They appear simple, natural, and straightforward; manifesting sensitivity, tenderness, and pathos. They are conscientious and quite aware of the consequences of their behavior. You see them as being introspective, diligent, sensitive to their environment, and highly attuned to nuances of feeling. You have a heartfelt appreciation of their trials and travails. They quicken your sympathies; you identify with their anguish as your own. They touch your life with a profound seriousness, a humility born of awe. They treat you and your feelings with consideration and delicacy; hence they tend to bring out your own humane and protective instincts. They touch you on a deep level of tenderness and compassion.

On the other hand, when they mirror your lack of true connectedness, you see them as being self-absorbed, sulky, and unctuously petulant. Their pouting and insistent dwelling upon themselves tends to arouse your own feelings of morbidity, of being used, or of needing to salve yourself. Your moon people stimulate your sense of longing: you can never reach out to them and touch them as you might like, not so much from reserve as from a delicacy of feeling, a vague sense of eternal separation. They make you aware of your aloneness in the world, that each person is distinct in his or her suffering and hope.

Favorable (Sun, Mercury, Venus, Jupiter, and Neptune): It's easy to connect with these people – they encourage you with their hopefulness and good cheer.

Sun is an inspiration to you. You admire his independent and pioneering spirit and his joie de vivre even in travail.

Moon heightens your susceptibility and sensitiveness. You have a deep sympathy and spiritual kinship with her.

Mercury charms and delights you with his freshness and disarming plainspokenness.

Venus is sweet and appealing. She appreciates you and has true affection for you.

Jupiter has a philosophy or outlook on life which is consonant with your own. Your basic points of view harmonize.

Unfavorable (Mars, Saturn, Uranus, and Pluto): There is empathy here but it's hard to get past the emotional barriers and walls these people have up against you.

Mars and you have such divergent interests and goals that intimacy is difficult in spite of a genuine attraction and fondness.

Saturn is quite capable of turning cold on you and standing on his dignity, which makes it hard for you to fully trust him.

Mercury people mirror your own basic attitude towards life. When you are tolerant and laid-back, you'll find people with planets contacting your Mercury to be practical and down-to-earth, showing good common sense and little pretense. They manifest excitement, enthusiasm, and joie de vivre. You appreciate their ideas, their intellectual integrity and vigor, and their fidelity to their own impulses – you find good fellowship in their company. You applaud their reasonableness, right-mindedness, and earnestness. You usually find yourself convinced by them or in broad agreement with them because they validate your own viewpoint: you both make a lot of the same assumptions about life. The focus in your relationships with these people is on good communications – you encourage each other to spin out your fondest plans and schemes. It is not so much that these people agree with your thinking as that they accept it, as you accept theirs, in good will, even when there is considerable ground for disagreement (which is often the case with the opposition). Your Mercury people stimulate your eager, alert side with a shared spirit of oneness.

On the negative side they can take too much for granted, presume too much, and rub you the wrong way with their smug self-congratulations. You can see their blind spots (and they can see yours) very clearly, and this may lead to a critical or judgmental tendency on the part of both of you. You can get huffy or become sticklers with one another, each one blocked by whatever the other is overlooking.

Favorable (moon, Mars, Saturn, Uranus, and Pluto): These people go along with your self-images. They validate and encourage you – they tend to see you as you see yourself.

Moon is very open to your ideas and tolerant of your quirks. She is sympathetic and really enjoys listening to you.

Mercury shares many of your opinions and suppositions, and also many of your biases and prejudices. This can be stimulating and delightful, but can also (especially when the Mercury's are in opposition) produce competition and one-upsmanship.

Mars is charming and vivacious. He dazzles you with his wit, dexterity, and impetuosity.

Saturn is dignified, forceful, and direct. You like the way he looks you squarely in the eye and talks to the point.

Unfavorable (Sun, Venus, Jupiter, and Neptune): These people stubbornly cling to their own opinions. Although they clearly understand your point of view, they refuse to validate it for you.

Sun is cool and standoffish. Even though you respect him, he is too wrapped up in himself to give you much attention.

Venus is a bit too chintzy or overly delicate for your taste. Even though you do basically like her, your relationship can be too formal or restrained for you to relax into.

Jupiter is fun and cheerful, but he can also be brusque and perfunctory, riding roughshod over your sensibilities and limits.

Venus people reflect your own mood and moodiness; you respond to their candidness, their artlessness, and their naïveté. People with planets contacting your Venus have an inviting, childlike manner and manifest warmth, simplicity, and good cheer. They have a twinkle in their eye for you and a jaunty irreverence. These people possess an impish sense of irony, and they have a conspiratorial mischievousness which appeals to your own playful side. Their sauciness and sense of style makes you feel light and happy when you are around them: it's fun being in their company, even if nothing in particular is going on or being said. They appeal to your sense of delight and call forth your own spontaneous, childlike impulses, and appeal to your benevolent side. You feel protective towards them, and truly wish them well.

On the other hand, they shy away from complex, emotionally sticky matters. They don't care to discuss deeper feelings, and they staunchly resist being emotionally committed or pinned down. Thus you are inevitably confronted with a dark, brooding side of them which they refuse to admit exists. Your relationships with them – albeit joyous on one level – often have a lot of strong emotion churning beneath the surface which isn't being dealt with consciously. You mirror each other's narcissism (vanity, glory-seeking) in a way which is embarrassing to admit openly, so you agree to be gay and carefree and sweep the rest under the rug.

Favorable (moon, Mars, Jupiter, and Neptune): These people are friendly and companionable. They usually aim to please and be pleasing.

Moon gives you considerable sympathy. She shows you her soft, vulnerable side and calls up a corresponding tenderness from you.

Venus strongly attracts you (naturally – that's what narcissism is all about). You delight in each other's company – she lives out many of your own fancies and fantasies.

Mars is a good role model for you of steadiness and cheerfulness in adversity. You admire his stiff upper lip and his no-nonsense force of personality.

Jupiter sends genuinely benevolent and generous impulses your way, and you in turn esteem him and wish him the very best.

Unfavorable (Sun, Mercury, Saturn, Uranus, and Pluto): These people are quite likable, but have questionable or grasping impulses that give you pause.

Sun attracts you but comes on very strong – you've got to keep on the qui vivre so as not to be bowled over by him.

Mercury connects with your blithe, humorous side, but tends to keep your relationship rather superficial and chatty.

Saturn likes you but maintains his reserve. There's often a manipulation or lack of trust here.

Mars people mirror your own vigor and dynamism: you relish their spunk and naïve ardor – their pride in their own fitness and their readiness to tackle anything. They call forth your own boldness and élan, and live out your own brassy, sassy side with their irrepressible determination to just be themselves and let it all hang out. They have an unabashed self-certainty which makes no excuses for itself but just plows on ahead regardless of the opinions of others. They can manifest a coolness, distance, or undue sensitivity to imposition or trespass. There is a degree of standoffishness or aloofness about these people that calls up a similar reserve on your part. The focus in your relationships with them tends to be on some sort of competitiveness, a having to feel one-up on each other. There's a measuring and being measured going on, a vague suspiciousness or implied criticism (especially with the opposition) which precludes real intimacy. Therefore, you tend to conflict with your Mars people: your interactions with them confirm each of you in their own sense of superiority or rectitude.

On the negative side you have to contend with their impatience with everything (including you); their know-it-all cockiness; and their disinclination to listen to reason. You can find them self-willed and contentious, always pulling in some other direction, and this in turn lessens your own willingness to be flexible and cooperative with them.

Favorable (Sun, Mercury, Venus, Jupiter, Uranus, and Pluto): You find these people obliging and ready to go along with your ideas; and you in turn are enthused by theirs.

Sun encourages you by his own enterprising spirit to try your wings and fly. He is a paradigm and role model for your own aspirations.

Mercury can understand you and your point of view even when he basically disagrees with you, and you in turn tend to go along with his thinking and general outlook on life.

Venus and you are strongly attracted to one another – she wins you over with her easy, familiar manner.

Mars is a model of gutsy independence and dedicated effort; he mirrors your own bold, staunch, pioneering spirit.

Jupiter admires your spiritedness and encourages you to express yourself openly and confidently.

Unfavorable (moon, Saturn, and Neptune): Albeit attracted to these people, you almost immediately clash with them on minor issues. They can be abrasive or make you lose patience.

Moon wins your heart – you respond to her zest and joy – but you find her easily bruised and hurt, overly sensitive, so you have to handle her with unnatural restraint and delicacy.

Saturn forces you to contend with his brazen superiority, his overweening pride, and his stiff dignity.

Jupiter people reflect your own generous, disinterested impulses: they manifest breadth of vision and scope. You feel personal regard for these people because of their sincerity and their absence of pretense. You value their frankness and perspicacity. They hold you in high regard, so you feel you can relax and take your ease in their presence. Even when their personalities and life interests are quite different from your own, they maintain a disinterested concern for you that appeals to your own benevolent side. You trust these people and they in turn animate the side of you which seeks to be worthy of trust. They accept you for yourself, withholding judgments and criticism. As a result you find it natural to overlook their little foibles and frailties; to offer them the same broad-minded consideration and avuncular bonhomie they give to you. Your Jupiter people stimulate your integrity, your sense of the validity of your own life and personal history.

On the other hand, you are inclined to over-indulge them, to play up to their little idiosyncrasies and vanities, to curry them. Relationships can become a bit too cozy and superficial. To disagree with them is to lose their interest – to run up against their stuffy, huffy side. There's not much tolerance in these relationships for divergence or conflict: where you harmonize you can meet, and where you don't the relationship stops right there.

Favorable (sun, moon, Venus, Mars, Saturn, Uranus, and Neptune): You share genuinely benevolent feelings of good will with these people: they help you expand yourself and your horizons.

Sun radiates self-confidence and calm pride. You esteem his uncompromising integrity and out front common sense.

Moon elicits your warm, gentle feelings. She soothes you with her calm presence and makes you feel at home.

Venus strongly attracts you; she awakens your most refined impulses. You are charmed by her graciousness and delicacy of feeling.

Mars is boisterous and rough around the edges, but you are captivated by his drive, his gutsiness, and his cocky faith in himself.

Jupiter is very simpatico. He is most generous with you and he arouses your most charitable and compassionate instincts.

Saturn feels personal concern for you: he is protective and takes a parental interest in you. He is a sober, steadying influence.

Unfavorable (Mercury and Pluto): The good feeling is present in these relationships but not the good communications. There is a sense of running on different tracks.

Mercury is mental, stiff, inhibited. Albeit quick and perceptive, he seems trapped in his own rationalizations, too sure of himself to appreciate your viewpoint.

Saturn people mirror your sense of discretion and discreteness – your need for private space and solitude. You respect their determination and grit; their self-sacrifice; and their ability to steel themselves against adversity and to bear up under life's burdens. Yet relationships with your Saturn people are rarely warm: they are characterized by a certain formality or propriety. These people are brisk and aloof; they take things (including you) in their stride. They manifest discrimination, detachment, remoteness, so that you must contend with their finickiness and their sense of individual space and personal privacy. Although they are genuinely interested in you, you can't expect them to go out of their way for you. They offer you understanding and a model of forbearance rather than enthusiasm or intimacy. There is a perfunctoriness about these people that makes you feel as though you were being categorized rather than related to directly, and this in turn calls up your own sense of personal prerogative and self-protective instincts. By calling your attention to their lines which are not to be crossed, your Saturn people reveal to you where you in turn place yours.

In some sense they reflect your need for protection and distance. They openly enact certain features of your own personality which you tend to repress or inhibit. In other words, you see in them some immovable, intransigent, pig-headed quality which forces you to erect your own stout boundary lines which are not to be crossed. You must be careful that you don't overstep yourself with them, and you must watch that they don't presume too much of you.

Favorable (Mercury, Jupiter, and Uranus): These people have a friendly interest in you, of a "ships that pass in the night" sort. There is a feeling of impersonal good will and comradeship.

Mercury buttresses your own thinking and helps you to put your feelings into words.

Jupiter gives you a poignant, heartfelt compassion. You touch him and he touches you on a deep, unspoken level.

Saturn gets down to brass tacks with little wasted emotion or effort. You admire his sharp, no-nonsense, businesslike approach to life.

Unfavorable (sun, moon, Venus, Mars, Neptune, and Pluto): These people make you put on your brakes. Somehow you have to restrain yourself with them, or draw back into yourself.

Sun preempts your own demand for special consideration. You respect him, but find him overly magisterial or dominating.

Moon is likable but circumstances are such that it's hard to really get together with her – there are too many obstacles to connecting.

Venus is sweet but overly vulnerable. You tend to hurt her without meaning to; or else you find her touchy and easily offended.

Mars is too brash and demonstrative for your taste. He mirrors a wilder side of yourself that you may be repressing.

Uranus people are your role models of rugged individualism and emotional independence. You admire their self-possession and authoritativeness, their unflinching determination, their scorn for assistance or succor, and their willingness to stand proudly on their own feet to uphold their principles. They have a quixotic charm and happy-go-lucky naïveté which calls to your own freedom of spirit and heightens your confidence in your own personal power and prowess. You appreciate the originality of their point of view and their self-sacrificing dedication to their own ideals, even though these usually differ from your own. Often the scope of your relationships with these people is restricted to one or several specific areas of interest held in common, and there is no particular communication on any other level. The language being spoken is that of competence. You must meet your Uranus people in a spirit of professionalism and with a confidence in your own adequacy.

On the other hand, you can also find your Uranus people to be thorny, supercilious, and irascible. They are petulant and given to tiffs. They can have an abrasive emotional reclusiveness which rejects even common politeness and social niceties, which in turn arouses your own cool detachment and brusqueness.

Favorable (Sun, Mercury, Mars, Jupiter, Saturn, and Neptune): You enjoy these people's vivaciousness and gameness – their willingness to fly with their impulses.

Sun encourages you to try new activities and to strike out in new directions. He is a ready enthusiast or mentor.

Mercury has bright ideas and a cheerful, optimistic outlook. He woos you with his pixiesque charm.

Mars is a model for you of resolution and alacrity – willing to stand his ground and take responsibility for his decisions.

Jupiter takes a benevolent (if detached) view of you and your projects. He gives you intellectual and moral encouragement.

Saturn is a toughie who challenges you to keep alert and on your toes. You enjoy his masterful sense of authority.

Unfavorable (moon, Venus, and Pluto): These people are admirably staunch but also maddeningly independent. You may suspect one another's motives.

Moon is rather emotional, private, and overly sensitive. Although you genuinely like her, you are puzzled by her, and she finds you too brusque or forward.

Venus appeals with her effervescence and freedom of spirit, but you find her overly delicate; she holds you at arm's length. You can never get down to brass tacks with her, or get her to commit herself.

Neptune people mirror your own vulnerability and defenselessness. You regard these people as being naïve and unsophisticated, trying to live up to high ideals. They manifest an ethereality or sense of not being altogether rooted in this world. Although the roles they play in life can deviate from your own personal standards and norms, these people touch you with their guilelessness and good faith. They may be a bit eccentric or spaced-out, but they charm you with their spontaneity and derring-do. You see in even their quixotic side the irrepressibility of the human spirit. They are very solicitous of you, and so you in turn try to make every allowance for them. They approach you with a ready openness which calls forth a corresponding openness on your own part. Your Neptune people call forth your more tender impulses and your trust in the underlying goodness of the world. These are the people whom you want to believe you can trust, since they seem to be laying all their cards out on the table. You tend to see in them what you want to see in them.

Actually, these are often the very people whom you are asking to deceive or disappoint you, since they tend to be the ones you idealize or upon whom you pin unrealistic hopes and expectations. The precise extent to which you lack faith in your own motives (distrust yourself) is the extent to which you'd better keep a close watch on your Neptune people.

Favorable (moon, Venus, Jupiter, and Uranus): These people inspire you. You have an intuitive trust in them and they put you in touch with your open, innocent side.

Moon and **Venus** offer you a strong sense of emotional bond and kinship – an understanding which transcends words and disarms your customary reserve.

Jupiter and you share a basic philosophy or outlook on life. He calls forth your better instincts and benevolence.

Unfavorable (Sun, Mercury, Mars, Saturn, and Pluto): You tend to overlook your own manipulativeness in your dealings with these people, hence you can't quite trust their motives either.

Sun can be annoyingly distant due to his dominating personality and presumption.

Mercury has a lot of spirit and élan, but you find him flighty, equivocal, and hard to pin down.

Mars has admirable firmness and courage, but you tend to run into his cold and aloof side.

Saturn has a lot of inner strength and self-certainty, but you find him too controlled and inhibited to really be able to relax with him.

Pluto people reflect your own clear-minded self-sufficiency. They are shrewd and headstrong, possessing a piercing intelligence and a commanding, dominating presence. They have themselves under tight control, and thus come across as being both intent and intense. They manifest a degree of severity and cold detachment. You feel restrained with these people: there is usually some question of imposition on one side or the other; of using or being used. Even when these relationships are superficially amicable there is often some sort of power equation being worked out. I.e., these relationships have an occult side – a chess game aspect – that quickens your own vigilance and guardedness. Because your Pluto people require deft handling, they call forth your own tact, adroitness, and self-control. They animate your own spirit of jaunty hubris.

On the other hand they are self-willed, gratuitously defiant, and constitutionally incapable of compromise. They are quick to take umbrage and to gear up for the attack. Your frustration with their self-obsessiveness shows the unmoved and unmoving parts of your own personality. You find yourself either in awe of their faith in their own impulses and willingness to blast on ahead; or else thoroughly revolted by their bumptiousness and preening.

Favorable (Sun, Mercury, and Mars): You have a feeling of camaraderie with these people, and a mutual respect as equals. You encourage one another to reach beyond your normal limits.

Sun has admirable courage and independence of spirit. He unabashedly follows his own impulses and encourages you to do the same.

Mercury and you think very much alike. You learn from him how to articulate your thoughts and feelings.

Mars' directness captivates you: he minces no words but gets down to business smoothly and cleanly.

Unfavorable (moon, Venus, Jupiter, and Saturn): These people have an energy level much lower or slower than your own. You feel held back by them.

Moon has a dark, soft, indulgent side which plays up to your own vanity or self-reflectiveness.

Venus is magnanimous but also emotionally remote. You find her overly delicate and fastidious.

Jupiter is broad-minded and genuine, but you dislike his intransigence and stick-in-the-mud complacency.

Saturn affects you on a profound level; yet there are too many unspoken vibrations going on to allow you to relax with one another or to feel at ease in the other's presence.

Willie and Maud – A Spiritual Marriage

William Butler Yeats – poet, playwright, and Nobel laureate; and Maud Gonne – actress, journalist, social activist, and revolutionary; shared a half-century long relationship which both considered a "spiritual marriage." Although they never actually lived together, they were both members of the Order of the Golden Dawn. Together they carried out experiments in thought transference over distances, visited one another in dreams, and conducted spiritual investigations (into claims of stigmata, etc.). Willie also wrote plays for her (not to mention reams of poetry), and (in the beginning at least) shared her revolutionary designs. As is usually the case with two people who have all three of their vital centers in harmonious signs, they shared many common interests, although there was also a tendency to one-upsmanship – a struggle for control. Willie conceived of his spiritual marriage to Maud as two "lives devoted to mystic truth." And, spiritual though it may have been, the spiritual marriage contained its share of possessiveness, jealousy, duplicity, and quarreling.

The couple first met on January 30th, 1889. "I was twenty-three years old when the troubling of my life began. I had heard from time to time in letters from Miss O'Leary, John O'Leary's old sister, of a beautiful girl who had left the society of the Viceregal Court for Dublin nationalism. In after years I persuaded myself that I felt premonitory excitement at the first reading of her name. Presently she drove up to our house in Bedford Park with an introduction from John O'Leary to my father. I had never thought to see in a living woman so great beauty. It belonged to famous pictures, to poetry, to some legendary past ... I was in love but had not spoken of love and never meant to speak, and as the months passed I grew master of myself again: 'what wife could she make,' I thought, 'what share could she have in the life of a student?'"{40-43}

At the time of this first meeting Willie was having his Jupiter return, which occurs in a horoscope roughly every twelve years. The month of one's Jupiter return brings joyous and serendipitous events – new projects, hobbies, and relationships – which often have great importance in the future. The principle attractive cross-aspects between Willie's chart and Maud's are his Jupiter conjunct her sun and opposed to her moon; and his sun and Uranus opposed to her sun and conjunct her moon (in the analysis of cross-aspects between horoscopes we only employ conjunctions and oppositions, and we use 6° orbs in defining these. Maud's moon at 28° GE 37' lies 5° 46' from Willie's natal sun at 22° GE 51'.

Unquestionably, the strongest indicators of sexual attraction between a man and a woman are his sun, Mars, or Jupiter conjunct or opposed to her moon or Venus (the sun-moon and Venus-Mars combinations, in particular, are especially intense); and here we find both Willie's sun and Jupiter contacting Maud's natal moon (and her natal Venus too, if you extend the allowable orbs a bit). In other words, there was a tremendous sexual tension in this relationship for both parties, and it was heightened at the time of Jupiter's transit over all these cross-aspects in January and February of 1889.

What Willie didn't realize at this first meeting was that Maud was already the mistress of another man, Millevoye, in France, and would soon become pregnant by him: her son Georges was born in January 1890. In the summer of 1891, she sent Willie a letter "telling of a dream of some past life. She and I had been brother and sister somewhere on the edge of the Arabian desert, and sold together into slavery ... I returned to Dublin at once, and that evening, but a few minutes after we had met, asked her to marry me. I remember a curious thing. I had come into the room with that purpose in my mind, and hardly looked at her or thought of her beauty. I sat there holding her hand and speaking vehemently. She did not take away her hand for a while: I ceased to speak, and presently as I sat in silence I felt her nearness to me and her beauty. At once I knew that my confidence had gone, and an instant later she drew her hand away. No, she could not marry – there were reasons – she would never marry; but in words that had no conventional ring she asked for my friendship."{46}

She returned to France suddenly, telling Willie that she had been summoned by a secret society to which she belonged. In truth, her lover had written her that her son Georges was sick; he died of meningitis shortly after. Maud wrote Willie "a letter of wild sorrow. She had adopted a little child, she told me, some three years ago, and now this child had died."{47} Maud returned to Ireland on the same boat that, coincidentally, brought the corpse of an Irish political leader: "She was dressed in extravagantly deep mourning, for Parnell, people thought, thinking her very theatrical. We spoke of the child's death ... She was plainly very ill ... We were continually together; my spiritual philosophy was evidently a great comfort to her. We spoke often of the state of death, and it was plain that she was thinking of the soul of her 'Georgette.'"[48] Note that Maud was not only lying to Willie about the baby being her biological child, but also about its sex.

Continuing, he writes: "She had come to have need of me, as it seemed, and I had no doubt that need would become love, that it was already becoming so. I had even as I watched her a sense of cruelty, as though I were a hunter taking captive some beautiful wild creature. We went to London and were initiated in the Hermetic Students, and I began to form plans of our lives devoted to mystic truth."[49] Thus the "spiritual marriage" with the apparently unattainable beauty had begun.

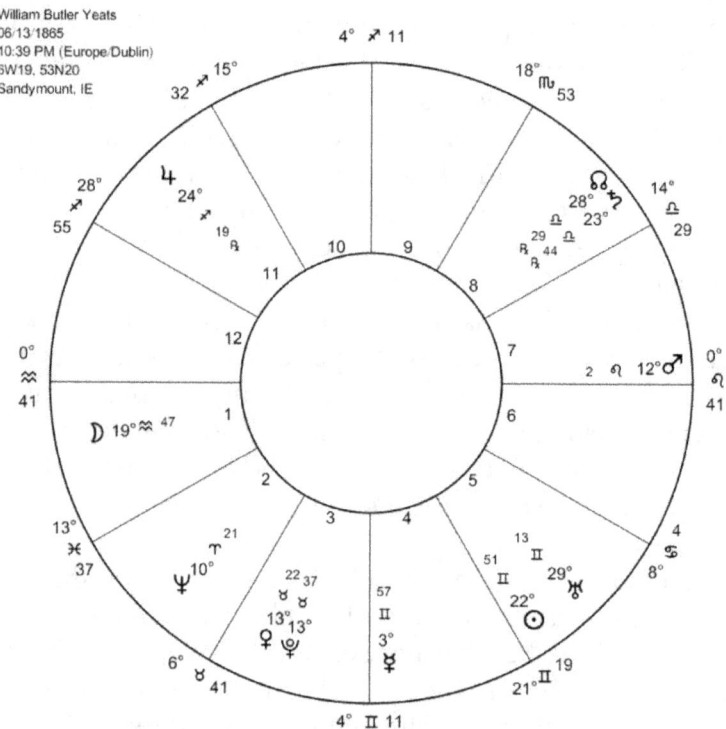

"Sometimes, when I had gone to sleep with the endeavour to send my soul to that of Maud Gonne, using some symbol, which I forget, I would wake dreaming of a shower of precious stones.

Sometimes she would have some corresponding experience in Paris and upon the same night, but always with more detail. I thought we became one in a world of emotion eternalized by its own intensity and purity, and this world had for its symbol precious stones. No physical, sexual sensation ever accompanied these dreams and I noticed that once the excitement of the genital ceased, a visionary form, that of Aedain, approached."{128}

When analyzing relationships, it is first necessary to analyze the conditions of the respective natal horoscopes – particularly those of Venus in the two charts. Although Willie's natal Venus is posited in Taurus, its own ruling sign; and it is two days past Greatest Brilliancy (which are signs of his creative genius and popularity); nonetheless it closely conjoins Pluto. In my book *Planetary Combination* I say of Venus conjunct Pluto, "In intimate relationships there can be a self-centeredness which is impatient and exacting, requiring unstinting allegiance and subservience (which you also offer in return). At times it may seem as though you are more in love with an image that you have – a Beatrice or Dulcinea– rather than a real, live person, since your attentions can become unduly smothering or devouring; or else you lose your own center and willingly become a submissive slave to the object of your affection. You grab on hard; and it's hard for you to let go. In any case your relationships tend to become struggles for supremacy rather than relaxed and easy-going give-and-takes – with you it tends to be either all give, or all take.

The natal conjunction of any planet with Pluto indicates fierce obsessiveness and tenacity, and also sudden shocks in the areas ruled by the conjoined planet, as the system seeks balance against the distortions induced by Pluto's intense clinging by violently snapping back to equilibrium. Any planet conjunct Pluto means violent reversals in the area of life ruled by that planet – either sudden, 180° about-faces; or complete wipe-outs in which everything is lost and the native must rebuild again from scratch. Venus conjunct Pluto shows a tendency towards romantic obsessiveness, which brings recurring periods in the native's life in which he is completely wiped out emotionally and forced to let go of his clinging. Here the Venus-Pluto conjunction forms the short leg of a T-Cross between Mars in the seventh house (of partnership) and the moon in the Ascendant. A T-Cross generally carries much of the same meaning as a conjunction with Pluto: concentration and intentness upon the path beneath one's feet; super self-seriousness, obduracy; lack of objectivity and perspective. T-Crosses give a tendency to go through empty motions, to fan the breeze with vague discontent, to run around in little circles. Here the T-Cross specifically refers to issues of partnership (seventh house) versus self (first); and conflicts (Mars) with women (moon – Willie's mother was mentally ill and died young); all focused through obsessive love relationships (Venus-Pluto).

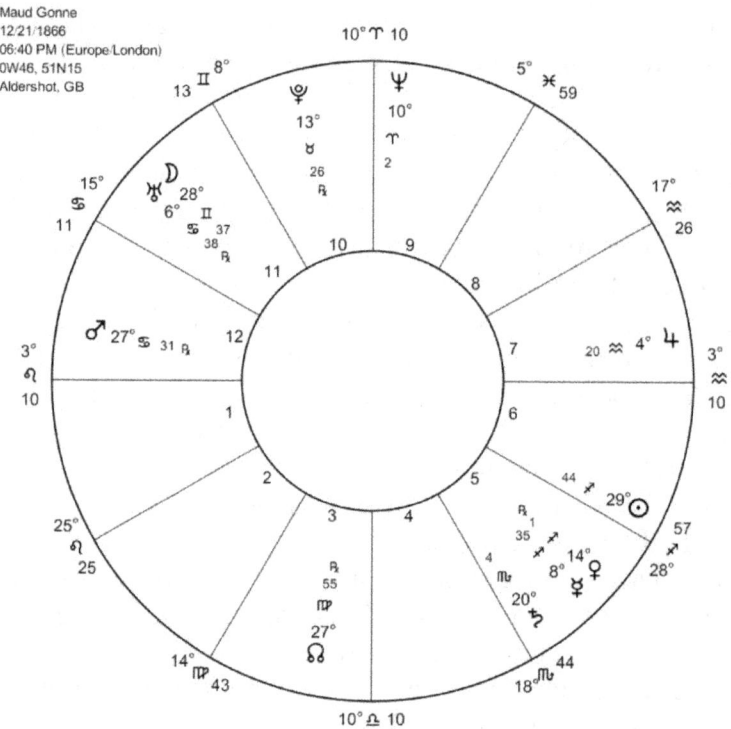

"I heard much scandal about her, but dismissed the grosser scandal at once, and one persistent story I put away with the thought, 'She would have told me if it were true.' It had come to seem as if the intimacy of our minds could not be greater, and I explained the fact that marriage seemed to have slipped further away by my own immaturity and lack of achievement ... She was complete; I was not."[63] This is another feature of possessive Venus: the tendency to idealize the object of one's affections (dispassionate Venus does nothing of the kind, but views her significant other critically and with detachment).

In the autumn of 1893, Maud again became pregnant by Millevoye. Willie made his first trip to Paris to visit her there in February 1894: "[O]ur relations, which were friendly enough, had not our old intimacy."{73} He certainly didn't realize that she was pregnant. Her daughter Iseult was born in August of 1894.

Maud's natal Venus conjoins Mercury (a disharmonious combination), which gives a tendency to subsume emotional and romantic desires under some mental image – to regard relationship as a means to some idealized end: "You are light and breezy; and on the negative side can be overly detached, non-committal, and trifling. Intimates may complain that you are vague and unreachable, just shrugging off anything which you find distasteful or simply don't want to have to face." Furthermore Venus is retrograde, which has a similar meaning as the conjunction with Mercury: the native feels isolated from the world around her; avoids mundane entanglements; senses that she has been set aside for a special destiny, and that any relationships or emotional commitments she makes must serve that destiny. Venus is also widely opposition Uranus, which also gives a dislike of being tied down emotionally (in spite of her possessive Venus). In *Planetary Combination* I say of Venus opposition Uranus: "you are a free-wheeling maverick with considerable perspicuity and panache. However, your usual state of mind is disgruntlement with the status quo, and you possess a snide or disparaging view of your fellow bipeds. You expect the worst from people and situations, and focus on their deficiencies and shortcomings rather than take a detached or sympathetic view. Your congenital impatience and hypercritical intolerance for any sort of stricture tend to bog you down and make you a target, so that your life becomes an unending struggle against limitation rather than a quest for transcendence: 'I am a rock; I am an island.'"

In Maud's case, she was a political revolutionary and mesmerizing platform speaker, wholly committed to the cause of Irish freedom, and rather perfunctory in her commitment to love relationships. "Her power over crowds was at its height, and some portion of the power came because she could still, even when pushing an abstract principle to what seemed to me an absurdity, keep her own mind free, and so when men and women did her bidding, they did it not only because she was beautiful, but because that beauty suggested joy and freedom."[274]   Venus retrograde natives are not so much loners – on the contrary, they are usually quite outgoing and sociable – as they are uncompromisingly free-spirited. They just don't need intimacy in the same way that most other people do. And this of course was a problem for Willie: "I came to hate her politics, my one visible rival ... We had a quarrel, and even after she had gone to France and returned again, there was a slight estrangement."{63} "Upon my side, my emotions were exasperated by jealousy, for everyone that came near Maud Gonne made me jealous, and by the strain upon my nerves of that perplexed wooing."{65}

One morning in December 1898, Willie "woke in my hotel somewhere near Rutland Square with the fading vision of her face bending over mine and the knowledge that she had just kissed me. I joined her after breakfast ... She said, 'Had you a strange dream last night?' I said, 'I dreamed this morning for the first time in my life that you kissed me.' She made no answer, but late that night when dinner was over and I was about to return home she said, 'I will tell you now what happened. When I fell asleep last night I saw standing at my bedside a great spirit. He took me to a great throng of spirits, and you were among them. My hand was put into yours and I was told that we were married. After that I remember nothing.' Then and there for the first time with the bodily mouth, she kissed me.

"The next day I found her sitting very gloomily over the fire. 'I should not have spoken to you in that way,' she said, 'for I can never be your wife in reality.' I said, 'Do you love anyone else?' and she said 'No,' but added that there was somebody else, and that she had to be a moral nature for two. Then bit by bit came out the story of her life, things I had heard all twisted awry by scandal, and disbelieved."{131-2} Willie was completely shocked by her tale of a pact made with the devil; her affair with Millevoye; the birth and death of her son Georges; the birth of her daughter Iseult. But in true-blue Venus conjunct Pluto fashion, Willie kept the faith and proposed to her once more. "She was now always very emotional, and would kiss me very tenderly, but when I spoke of marriage on the eve of her leaving said, 'No, it seems to me impossible.' And then, with clenched hands, 'I have a horror and terror of physical love.'"{124}   At the time of these revelations, transiting Neptune (illusions/delusions) was retrograding over Willie's natal sun; and Uranus (sudden shocks) was crossing his Midheaven and opposing his natal Mercury (images). On her side, transiting Saturn was crossing Maud's natal Venus (stonewalling / blocking romance).

Although a physical marriage thus seemed impossible, Willie and Maud continued their spiritual marriage: "My own seership was, I thought, inadequate; it was to be Maud Gonne's work and mine. Perhaps that was why we had been thrown together. Were there not strange harmonies amid discord? My outer nature was passive – but for her I should never perhaps have left my desk – but I knew my spiritual nature was passionate, even violent. In her, all this was reversed, for it was her spirit that was gentle and passive and full of charming fantasy, as though it touched the world only with the point of its finger."{124}

Thus it was with great consternation that Willie received word from Maud in late January 1903 that she intended to marry Irish revolutionary John MacBride; "I am getting old and oh so tired and I have found a man who has a stronger will than myself and who at the same time is thoroughly honorable and who I trust. .... As for Willie Yeats, I love him dearly as a friend but I could not for one minute imagine marrying him."^154^ This illustrates another point about Venus retrograde – and Venus opposition Uranus – natives: they tend to be rather quirky (rather than practical or commonsensical) in bestowing their affections.

Willie's spiritual marriage with Maud was not only one of his fondest ideals, but also the subject of many of his poems and indeed an integral part of his occult philosophy: "It was our work to teach a few strong aristocratic spirits that to believe the soul was immortal & that one prospered hereafter if one laid upon oneself an heroic discipline in living & send them to uplift the nation. You & I were chosen to begin this work & just when you and I come to understand it fully, you go from me & seek to thrust the people down further into weakness ... now I appeal, I whose hands were placed in yours by eternal hands, to come back to yourself. To take up again the proud solitary haughty life which made you seem like one of the Gods."^165^

At the time Maud dropped this bomb-shell, transiting Saturn was crossing Willie's Ascendant (which always causes a big shakeup in one's self-image, forcing a major reexamination of who one is and what one is doing in life); and transiting Uranus conjoined his Jupiter (sudden shocks requiring considerable generosity of mind). At the time of Maud's marriage in late February 1903, transiting Saturn had reached her natal Jupiter.

Willie not only felt betrayed personally, but also that his ideal spiritual marriage had become a mockery: "As the husband is, the wife is; thou art mated with a clown. And the grossness of his nature will have weight to drag thee down."[31]

Willie's prediction proved correct: in January 1904, Maud gave birth to a son, Sean, but her marriage to John MacBride was short-lived: he was a drunkard, he beat her, and made sexual advances to her daughter Iseult; so in little more than a year Maud filed for divorce. Meanwhile, Willie engaged in several love affairs to console himself, but his and Maud's correspondence continued.

By 1907, she was indicating an interest in returning to a spiritual marriage with him; and in December 1908, on a trip to Paris to visit her, she *finally* had sex with him (his progressed sun was trine his Midheaven at the time), although she immediately abjured what they had done: "Dearest [the first time she had thus addressed him]: It was hard leaving you yesterday, but I knew it would be just as hard today if I had waited. Life is so good when we are together & we are together so little! ... You asked me yesterday if I am not a little sad that things are as they are between us – I am sorry & I am glad ... I am glad & proud beyond measure of your love, & that it is strong enough & high enough to accept the spiritual love & union I offer ... I have prayed so hard to have all earthly desire taken from my love for you & dearest, loving you as I do, I have prayed & I am praying still that the bodily desire for me may be taken from you too ... The struggle is over & I have found peace. I think today I could let you marry another without losing it – for I know the spiritual union between us will outlive this life, even if we never see each other in this world again."[258] Needless to say, this episode inflamed once again all of Willie's desire for her.

In spite of the strong sexual linkage between his sun and Jupiter and her moon (and Venus), Maud's natal Saturn widely opposed Willie's Venus-Pluto conjunction. This is a stonewall: the Saturn person will always block and frustrate the Venus-Pluto person's amorous designs, and the Venus-Pluto person will intrude in the Saturn person's space in his attempt to manipulate her to his own ends (Pluto is very manipulative). Moreover, Willie's and Maud's natal Mercury's are in opposition, which indicates a contradiction between their respective images: to Maud, it was just a friendship – a true spiritual marriage; to Willie, it was a very powerful sexual attraction: the spiritual marriage was the best he could do to bind her to him, and so he tried to make the best of it.

Maud's divorced husband, John MacBride, was killed during the Irish uprising on Easter 1916, and Maud sent her twenty-one year old daughter Iseult to London, where Willie took her under his wing, introduced her around, and in June 1916 traveled with her to France. He commented that "[s]he is quite a commanding person now, no longer a fanciful child."[378]

On July 1st, Willie once again proposed to Maud with the usual result, but then he surprised her by asking her if she would object to his marrying Iseult. This rather fanciful proposal was probably due to Neptune's final transit of Willie's Descendant, which was exact two weeks prior. Maud gave her permission for the match, but added that she didn't believe Iseult would accept the proposal (which she didn't).

By summer 1917, at age fifty-two, with transiting Saturn crossing his Descendant, while transiting Uranus conjoined his moon, Willie seemed to be desperate to marry someone, anyone. Saturn crossing into the seventh house tends to focus attention on partnership issues – new partnerships are begun, or old partnerships require profound adjustments. Uranus on the moon brings sudden changes or upsets in relations with women. Willie returned to France in August to woo Iseult: "Iseult and I take long walks, and are as we were last year affectionate and intimate and she shows many little signs of affection."[391] In the end, Willie gave her an ultimatum: if she did not marry him now, then he would marry someone else. "Poor Iseult was very depressed on the journey and at Havre went off by herself and cried. Because she was so ashamed 'at being so selfish' 'in not wanting to marry me and so break her friendship with me.' I need hardly say she had said nothing to me of 'not wanting.' Meanwhile, she has not faltered in her refusal of me, but as you can imagine life is a good deal at white heat."[391]

"Now that your tongue cannot persuade the child till she mistake
    Her childish gratitude for love and match your fifty years?

O let her choose a young man now and all for his wild sake."^41^

Disconsolate though Willie may have been, he was determined to marry, so on his return to England – when transiting Saturn passed over his seventh house Mars – he proposed to the twenty-five year old Georgie Hyde, and on October 20th, 1917, he married her. This was ten days before transiting Uranus turned direct on his natal moon (sudden, precipitate changes involving intimate relationships); also Willie's converse progressed Mercury turned retrograde now. This usually occurs at a time when the native feels a need for more direction and organization in life; some situation pops up which engages all one's attention and interest, and releases one's pent-up energy. It gives a real sense of purpose in life that was lacking before, and a deeper understanding of who one really is and what one really desires from life. A new enthusiasm and zest replace the frustration one felt before.

In Willie's case, his immediate reaction to what he had done was horror – he felt he had made a big mistake in marrying Georgie rather than Iseult:

"But O! my Heart could bear no more when the upland caught the wind; I ran, I ran, from my love's side because my Heart went mad."^41^

However, Willie was in for a big surprise: "On the afternoon of October 24th 1917, four days after my marriage, my wife surprised me by attempting automatic writing. What came in disjointed sentences, in almost illegible writing, was so exciting, sometimes so profound, that I persuaded her to give an hour or two day after day to the unknown writer, and after some half-dozen such hours offered to spend what remained of life explaining and piecing together those scattered sentences."#8#

These automatic writings formed the basis for his astrological/cabalistic magnum opus *A Vision*. Thus converse progressed Mercury's change of station brought Willie not only a wife, but also a new, overarching philosophical orientation and system of thought.

One of the central principles of this philosophy is the concept of being *in-phase* or *out-of-phase*. When a person is acting in accord with his or her true purpose in this life – their reason for incarnating

– then they are said to be in-phase; and when they are just acting on a level of social conditioning in mindless, knee-jerk reactivity, they are said to be out-of-phase.

Yeats' life is a good example of what it means to be both out-of-phase and in-phase. For most of his adult life Yeats dabbled in mysticism and oddball occult groups, always seeking something of profound significance, but never finding it. And for most of this same period he was hopelessly in love with a selfish, deceitful woman who completely trashed him emotionally. After thirty years of this frustrated romanticism something deep inside Yeats decided to stop chasing the fantasy woman and marry someone truly worthy. And four days later his new wife began channeling *A Vision*. In other words it was Willie's decision to act on a deeper level than his illusions and daydreams that turned him from out-of-phase to in-phase – that fulfilled his true purpose in incarnating in this lifetime.

But the saga of Maud and Willie didn't end with his marriage. They continued to be good friends and correspondents, and Willie's wife Georgie got on quite well with both Maud and Iseult. As time went on, however, Willie and Maud drifted apart politically (the opposing natal Mercury's): during the Irish civil war she was on the radical side, and he became a senator in the conservative government. In early January 1923, Maud was arrested, and Willie tried to get some blankets to her in her cell: "The day before her arrest she wrote to say that if I did not denounce the Government she renounced my society for ever. I am afraid my help in the matter of the blankets, instead of her release (where I could do nothing) will not make her less resentful."[429] Transiting Jupiter was exactly opposed to Willie's natal Venus-Pluto conjunction at this time.

The letters continued off and on for the next fifteen years, until Willie's death in January 1939. Maud died in 1953, Iseult in 1954. Six years after Willie's death, Maud wrote: "Politics had separated us for quite a long while, we got on each other's nerves over them & neither wanted to see the other, but at the last we had come together & the last time I saw him at Riversdale he was planning things we would do together when he returned – but he seemed to me so ill, I felt unhappy for I didn't think we would meet again in this life – not that one should feel unhappy about death for the pattern will be clearer to us I think after."[453]

Willie's retrospective on the spiritual marriage is summed up in his *Autobiographies* thusly: "I was involved in a miserable love affair, that had but for one brief interruption absorbed my thoughts for years past, and would for some years yet. My devotion might as well have been offered to an image in a milliner's window, or to a statue in a museum, but romantic doctrine had reached its extreme development."[298] But what is the point of being a poet if you're not going to be romantic?

Interpretation of Transits

I have long been an admirer of the heuristic method employed in Ronald Davison's *Astrology* – perhaps the best beginner's book on natal astrology ever written. The basis of this system is a set of keywords and a concise but elegant set of key phrases and ideas. Davison succeeded magnificently in reducing natal astrology's complexities to a bare-bones armature, over which the neophyte astrologer could drape his or her own ideas and intuitive insights. I have often wondered whether the same sort of systemization might not be applied to the theory of transits (R.C. Davison's book *The Technique of Prediction*, while also excellent, is aimed at advanced students of astrology rather than beginners. Also, it is concerned more with secondary progressions than with transits).

The basic system for interpretation of transits given here is meant to be suggestive, not definitive. You could call it a rough sketch. Only transiting conjunctions and oppositions are taken into account here; not because other aspects cannot be effective – they often are (particularly transiting squares). But by only taking transiting conjunctions and oppositions into account are we obeying Dr. Marc Edmund Jones' injunction to keep things as simple as possible (which Dr. Jones invoked as the principle of "Occam's Razor"; and which contemporary computer theory embodies in the principle of KISS – Keep It Simple, Stupid.) This system of interpretation is based upon the fundamental idea that when a transiting planet conjoins or opposes a significant point (planet, angle, etc.) in your natal chart, then:

1) the nature of the expected event is described by the symbolism of the transiting planet;

2) the nature of your emotional response – or the area of your life affected – is described by the symbolism of the natal point contacted.

Following this assumption, the following table of Keywords results:

Table of Keywords for the Transiting and Natal Planets:

Transiting Planet (nature of external event)		Natal Point (nature of your response)
DECISIVE	SUN	DETERMINATION
HEARTFELT	MOON	ASSURANCE
ENCOURAGING	MERCURY	UNDERSTANDING
SOCIABLE	VENUS	INTIMACY
FORCEFUL	MARS	ADVANCEMENT
CHEERING	JUPITER	FULFILLMENT
CHALLENGING	SATURN	DISCIPLINE
SURPRISING	URANUS	LIBERATION
UNUSUAL	NEPTUNE	ATTUNEMENT
REVEALING	PLUTO	CLARITY
	NORTH NODE	GUIDANCE
	SOUTH NODE	GRATIFICATION
	PART OF FORTUNE	NOVELTY
	ASCENDANT	REORIENTATION
	MIDHEAVEN	HOPE
	DESCENDANT	COOPERATION
	LOWER MERIDIAN	RESOLUTION

See Appendix I below for more detailed interpretations for the transiting and natal planets.

Before giving some examples of how to apply these keywords to actual cases using Theodore Roosevelt's life and horoscope as the model, let us consider some basic issues in transit theory. What follows below is meant to be a mere suggestion – a set of pointers – based upon one practitioner's own experience. This is not to imply that there aren't other approaches which can be equally or more effective in a given horoscope or for a given practitioner. Astrology – like healing – is a science; but it is even more so an art. There's no right way or wrong way of doing it: all approaches made in good faith, in a true spirit of searching for truth, are valid.

Overall Expectation: The technique of transits – like that of zodiacal primary directions – tends to produce concrete physical events in one's outward life (whereas secondary progressions tend to produce emotional or psychological states – karmic lessons – rather than actual events per se. Although they can and do). Transits – unlike zodiacal primary directions – fail frequently. Also, major events in the life can and do occur without any relevant transit, progression, or direction which can be held to account for that event. That's life. Astrology is not a tocsin which unfailingly sounds the alarm at the precise moment it's supposed to. This doesn't mean that we have to use every astrological point imaginable – e.g. the transit of the moon's Node to the quincunx of the Chiron – Lillith midpoint – to "prove" anything. Nor does it mean – as the rationalistic materialist critics of astrology would have it – that astrology is a false doctrine. On the contrary, astrology models life perfectly, because life is imperfect.

Note: the given interpretations do not take into account whether the transiting planet and the natal planet contacted are intrinsically harmonious or disharmonious in nature, which modifies the interpretations. For example, a transit to natal Mars by a planet intrinsically disharmonious with it would tend to impede or block ADVANCEMENT rather than facilitate it. See the *Table of Favorable and Unfavorable Planetary Combinations* on page 88.

The Natal Chart: It is often said that transits cannot bring events which are not promised in the natal chart; but I haven't found this guideline especially useful in interpretation. House positions and rulerships do not seem to be as important in determining how a transit will operate as do the essential meanings of the transiting planets and natal points involved. Do, however, pay attention to any aspect in the natal chart between the planet which is transiting and the planet or point being transited, since e.g. a natal sextile or trine will tend to bring fortunate events even if the transiting aspect is an opposition or square (though usually these necessitate expending effort or overcoming conflict in order to benefit the native); and a natal square or opposition will tend to bring conflicts or disappointments of inflated hopes even to nominally benefic transits.

Transiting Planets: In a general way, the transiting conjunctions and oppositions of Uranus and Saturn, respectively, are the most effective. Transiting Jupiter and Mars can be quite effective, especially when transiting their own positions in the natal chart. The effects of Neptune and Pluto tend to be more vague; but not necessarily (the point is, don't count too much on them). The other, swifter, planets tend to be less effective, except in combination. That is to say, when transiting swift planets conjoin or oppose each other within a degree or two of a significant position in the natal chart, then this mutual transit is likely to produce a noticeable event. For example, the Superior Conjunction of Mercury or Venus (the transiting Superior Conjunction of these planets with the sun) in conjunction or opposition to a significant point in the natal horoscope, usually produces a noticeable event within orb of a day or two.

Orbs: Outer planets which transit the same natal position three times (direct, retrograde, direct) or five times (direct, retrograde, direct, retrograde, direct) may produce an event anywhere within the time frame between the first and last direct transits; but the overall tendency is for the event to occur at – or shortly after – the first direct transit (and in the case of the slower planets, the following year or two is spent in clean-up or reorganizing in response to the effect of the first direct transit). But this is not always the case: Jupiter's return to its natal place often produces CHEERING events which bring FULFILLMENT at the end of the three transits; and an informal study of the Demi-Uranus Return (Uranus' transit to opposition its natal place – see the essay "The Chance of a Lifetime" – which occurs in early 40-something natives) shows that the expected SURPRISING event which brings LIBERATION can occur anywhere between the first and last direct transits.

Transiting Uranus tends to produce events sharply-defined both in nature and in timing. Transiting Saturn produces events which – albeit sometimes associated with a particular moment in time – even then spread their effects out over a period from a few months before, to a year or two after, the exact date of the first direct transit. Transiting Neptune is vaguer (of course); transiting Pluto can produce definitive, transformative events (like 180-degree changes – deaths and rebirths), whose repercussions go on over a year or two of time. Jupiter's return to its natal place – and sometimes its transits of the other planets and angles – produce joyous, serendipitous events within a month of the exact transit date. The swifter planets in combination refer to events that should be timable within a day or two of the exact time of the transit.

Your emotional response – or the area of your life affected– here we follow traditional astrological symbolism, e.g. that the **Sun** symbolizes honor, reputation in the world, career, life work, life purpose; the father, the husband, boss or authorities. The **Moon** symbolizes feelings, mood, past life influences, the mother, the wife, the home, the public, employees; and lacunae in one's quotidian life (travel, sickness, psychic experiences – any break with wonted routines). **Mercury** symbolizes mind – the particular set of self-justifications and images with which you present yourself to the world for approval (or rejection); as well as routine issues and relationships: siblings, neighbors, coworkers, children. **Venus** is love in the sense of infatuation, embellishment, art, creativity, sociability, the girlfriend or female lover, art for art's sake. **Mars** is aggressive energy – courage, valor, athletics, self-sacrifice for a cause; male friends and lovers, dynamism. **Jupiter** is enthusiasm, benevolent impulse with no thought of reward; money, religious / philosophical interests; aunts and uncles, as well as detached advisors and friends who wish the best. **Saturn** is discipline, limitation, karma. We all have dues to pay – which are accessible in our past life regressions – and Saturn symbolizes where (by house position) and how (by sign position) we have to slow down and wake up to the lessons which our life is teaching us. It symbolizes frustration, obstruction, older people, difficult people. **Uranus** introduces an element of disruption and surprise into our lives, without which we could never understand the meaning of freedom. **Neptune** is psychic, intuitive, otherworldly knowledge (or its opposite – spaced-out irresponsibility). **Pluto** is cunning and obsession; as well as complete transformation – ability to begin anew after total wipeout.

Examples of Interpretation of Transits

In these examples the cookbook interpretations – cobbled together from the keywords in the Table and the Detailed Interpretations from Appendix I – are given first; and these are followed by a description of what actually happened in Theodore Roosevelt's life at that time. Examples for the slower planets (which often spread their effects out for a year or more) will be listed first; followed by examples for the swifter planets (which are usually effective only for a day or two).

Jupiter: Transiting Jupiter's return to its natal place every twelve years usually brings a month of serendipitous events – new spiritual or business connections, new ideas, new relationships – which become of great importance in the future. In TR's case Jupiter's return in June 1906 brought a CHEERING event: an opportunity to lighten up, join together with others, and take a detached, generous, and conciliatory overview; and this event brought him FULFILLMENT– he found that things fell right into place with no effort on his part. He got to do something he'd wanted to do for a long time.

This month saw the triumphal passage of most of TR's progressive legislation: a bill allowing him to proclaim national monuments on federal land (in particular protection for Niagara Falls from hydroelectric despoilment), worker protection legislation, immunity for witnesses in antitrust cases, Oklahoma statehood, "and the three major laws Roosevelt most wanted": the Railroad Rate Regulation Act, the Meat Inspection Act (in response to Upton Sinclair's exposé of the meat packing industry), and the Pure Food and Drug Act. "It had been an historic session, he felt, one that had greatly extended the authority of centralized government."[448]

Saturn: Transiting Saturn's aspects are not necessarily bad; but even the good ones require considerable discipline or sacrifice. Also, what Saturn giveth, Saturn taketh away. In TR's life, transiting Saturn opposed Venus and conjoined Jupiter just before crossing his Ascendant from summer 1884 through summer 1885, which one might expect would bring a CHALLENGING event – having to overcome obstacles directly; not shrinking from difficulties but holding his own ground and securing his position in life. This event emphasized INTIMACY and FULFILLMENT and brought REORIENTATION: he attended to family, social, or relationship matters which impacted on his gregarious, romantic, enthusiastic side; and found that things fell right into place with no effort on his part. He got to do something he'd wanted to do for a long time; and he began a new phase or epoch in his life.

The preceding fall he made his first trip out west and *loved* it. That winter his mother and wife died suddenly (the same day) which completely shattered him emotionally, and to get his mind off it he returned to Dakota in June 1884; made some important new friends;

found a perfect site for a ranch house, and bought it. He returned east in October and spent the winter writing *Hunting Trips of a Ranchman*. In April 1885 he returned to Dakota and finished building his ranch house, bought a herd of cattle, and spent the month of June on a roundup through the Badlands. According to his biographer this experience changed him drastically: "Some extraordinary physical and spiritual transformation occurred during this arduous period. It was as if his adolescent battle for health, and his more recent but equally intense battle against despair, were crowned with sudden victory. The anemic, high-pitched youth who had left New York only five weeks before was now able to return to it 'rugged, bronzed, and in the prime of health.'"<303> Long afterward he said that "If it had not been for my years in North Dakota, I never would have become President of the United States."<374>

Another example: Transiting Saturn conjoined TR's natal moon and opposed his Mars between summer 1886 and late spring 1887, which augured a CHALLENGING event to his ASSURANCE and ADVANCEMENT. Obstacles had to be confronted directly; he couldn't shrink from difficulties but had to hold his ground and secure his position in life. His deep-seated instincts came to the surface and he had to pay attention to what his own inner voice was telling him. Since Saturn is disharmonious with moon and Mars we take a negative interpretation from Appendix I: his forward motion was blocked; his plans and projects shattered; and he was depressed by failure and despair for the future.

TR remarried in December 1886, but the event to which this transit probably refers is the destruction of his western ranching business and dream due to the terrible winter of 1886-87, which killed all of his cattle. He made a trip out west in April 1887 to survey his losses, and returned east thoroughly depressed. "The losses are crippling. For the first time I have been utterly unable to enjoy a visit to my ranch. I shall be glad to get home."<373> Returning broke, with no political prospects, he determined that he would have to write for a living, and so began working on his magnum opus *Winning the West*.

Uranus: Transiting Uranus crossed TR's natal Venus – Jupiter opposition from late 1901 through late 1902. This SURPRISING, unexpected, serendipitous event shook TR out of his ordinary routines and doldrums and brought him INTIMACY and FULFILLMENT: he attended to family, social, and relationship matters which impacted on his gregarious, romantic, enthusiastic side. He found that things fell right into place with no effort on his part, and he got to do something he'd wanted to do for a long time.

This period corresponds to TR's first year in the White House, which he entered the preceding September 1901 upon President McKinley's assassination. It was like releasing a fish into water: that first year he began the first major national anti-trust case (against Northern Securities); he introduced his plan for a Panama Canal; he settled a major, violent strike in the anthracite coal fields; and he squared off with Germany over a crisis in Venezuela. It was a year of triumph and success on all fronts (except for a serious accident suffered on 9/03/1902 when his carriage was hit by a trolley car, which killed his bodyguard; almost killed him; and was the beginning of a life-long leg pain which required many operations over the next few weeks). But by the end of 1902, TR was assured of re-nomination in 1904: "The power of one man thus to cover his party with the mantle of his own strength is unprecedented in the history of American politics."[170]

Neptune and Pluto: Transiting Neptune crossed TR's natal moon – Mars opposition; and transiting Pluto crossed his Ascendant; from late summer 1908 through mid-1910. Transiting Neptune produces UNUSUAL events – odd, out-of-the-ordinary occurrences; strange vibrations and undercurrents; which provoke powerful attractions or repulsions on his part. The event impacted upon his ASSURANCE (his deep-seated instincts came to the surface; he had to pay attention to what his own inner voice was telling him) and also impacted his ADVANCEMENT – impelling him forward to make new plans or projects, motivated by a sense of progress, accomplishment, and hope for the future. At the same time the interpretation for transiting Pluto conjunct Ascendant is a REVEALING (disorienting, transformative) event which forced him to take command, rise to the occasion, get on top of things. This event produced a major REORIENTATION: he began a new phase or epoch in his life.

This period embraced TR's last few months in office and the victory of his hand-picked successor (Taft) whom TR believed would follow his policies. Just before he left office, TR's Great

White Fleet returned from its round-the-world cruise, which one of his biographers called "the apotheosis of Roosevelt."[637] From March 1909 – March 1910 he went on a safari in Africa which was the fulfillment of a long-held dream; and he wrote a series of articles on his adventures. He returned to the U.S. on 6/16/1910 to a triumphal welcome (a parade up Broadway hosted by the mayor of New York). His friends considered that he had become a changed man; in the words of one of them: "He was just the same in manner, in appearance, in expression, yet there was something different. We, all of us who had been closely associated with him in the past, felt it. I spoke of it. Senator Lodge spoke of it. Secretary Meyer ... spoke of it; and so did Nick [Longworth]. Loeb and I, for we rode together in the procession, talked almost entirely of him and each of us felt that there was a change in him. Mr. Meyer thought he had grown older, but it wasn't that. Loeb, Senator Lodge, and I figured it out to be simply an enlarged personality. To me he had ceased to be an American, but had become a world citizen. His horizon seemed to be greater, his mental scope more encompassing."[670]

The swifter transiting planets produce transient events – perhaps within a day or two of the precise date they are due. They fail often. Transiting changes of station (from direct to retrograde or retrograde to direct) usually work quite well; mutual transits (the conjunction or opposition of two transiting planets falling on or opposite a significant point in the natal horoscope) are usually more effective than single-body transits. For copious examples of mutual transits in TR's horoscope, see the essay on "Mutual Transits"

Mars: Transiting Mars conjoined its natal place on 3/2/1879, bringing a FORCEFUL event: intense involvements with other people (though not necessarily conflictive) in which he had to take a position, stand up for himself, be willing to fully commit himself; the upshot of which brought him ADVANCEMENT: impelling him forward, motivating him with a sense of progress, accomplishment, and hope for the future. What happened was that the previous day TR embarked on a fabulous two-week hunting trip to Maine, where he made some fast friends for life: "The emerging politician got great satisfaction out of his ability to converse, on equal terms, with backwoodsmen as well as Boston Brahmins. So, too, did the hunter exult in chasing a caribou for thirty-six hours through the snowy forest, with neither tent nor blankets to protect him. The naturalist collected specimens, while the sometime invalid worked up 'enough health to last me till next summer.'"[111]

Venus: Transiting Venus opposed its natal place on 4/22/84, indicating a SOCIABLE event – encounters, gatherings, or events which play upon his affections and may symbolize a poignant moment in a personal relationship; and accentuated INTIMACY – social or relationship matters which impact on his gregarious, romantic, enthusiastic side. On this day Assemblyman TR went to the state Republican convention which was split between two presidential candidates with himself "in his favorite position – at the balance of power."[252] He manipulated and "allowed his personality to penetrate every corner of the auditorium. From that moment on, there was no doubt as to who was controlling the convention"[254] and the following day he overwhelmingly won the delegate-at-large status he had sought. On an emotional level "He knew now that it was time to unrope himself from [his old political friends] whose horizons extended no further than New York State, and eagerly search out new altitudes, wider vistas."[255]

Mercury: Transiting Mercury turned Stationary Direct conjunct natal Venus on 12/26/1872, signifying an ENCOURAGING event which heightens INTIMACY – an event which changed his attitude, viewpoint, or self-image. He saw himself in a new light, in a new role vis à vis other people, and needed tact, aplomb, and confidence in his own abilities. He attended to family, social, or relationship matters which impacted on his gregarious, romantic, enthusiastic side. What happened was that 14 year-old TR had been traveling with his family on a houseboat down the Nile River, and on Christmas day he received a shotgun of his own "and the boy's delight knew no bounds. 'He is a most enthusiastic sportsman,' wrote Theodore Senior, 'and has infused some of his spirit into me. Yesterday I walked the bogs with him at the risk of sinking hopelessly and helplessly, for hours ... but I felt that I must keep up with Teedie.'"[66]

Appendix I: Detailed Interpretations

I: Detailed Interpretations for Transiting Planets
(nature of event)

Sun: DECISIVE – Calls for an exercise of will in which you have to follow your heart and stay your course; do what you feel is right.

Moon: HEARTFELT – Something out of the ordinary which affects you on a deep level. May bring messages or guidance from the spirit world.

Mercury: ENCOURAGING – An event which changes your attitude, viewpoint, or self-image. You see yourself in a new light, in a new role vis à vis other people, and need tact, aplomb, and confidence in your own abilities.

Venus: SOCIABLE – Encounters, gatherings, or events which play upon your affections. They may symbolize a poignant moment in a personal relationship, or creative, artistic expression.

Mars: FORCEFUL – Intense involvements with other people (though not necessarily conflictive). You have to take a position, stand up for yourself, be willing to fully commit yourself.

Jupiter: CHEERING – An opportunity to lighten up, join together with others, and take a detached, generous, and conciliatory overview.

Saturn: CHALLENGING – Obstacles which have to be confronted directly. You cannot shrink from difficulties but must hold your ground and secure your position in life.

Uranus: SURPRISING – Unexpected (serendipitous or calamitous) events which shake you out of your ordinary routines and doldrums.

Neptune: UNUSUAL – Odd, out-of-the-ordinary occurrences; strange vibrations and undercurrents. May provoke powerful attractions or repulsions on your part.

Pluto: REVEALING – Events of a disorienting, transformative nature. You have to take command, rise to the occasion, get on top of things.

II. Detailed Interpretations for Natal Planets
(nature of your response)

Sun: DETERMINATION – You have to stand up for yourself, let your own views be known, make your own will prevail. You must disencumber yourself and take a step forward.

Moon: ASSURANCE – Your deep-seated instincts come to the surface. You must pay attention to what your own inner voice is telling you.

Mercury: UNDERSTANDING – You must meet or communicate with others of like mind (opposition inclines to conflicts). You may begin new projects or relationships.

Venus: INTIMACY – You attend to family, social, or relationship matters which impact on your gregarious, romantic, enthusiastic side.

Mars: ADVANCEMENT – You are impelled forward, make new plans or projects, and are moved by a sense of progress, accomplishment, and hope for the future.

Jupiter: FULFILLMENT – You find that things just fall right into place with no effort on your part. You may get to do something you've wanted to do for a long time.

Saturn: DISCIPLINE – You must work hard, dedicate yourself, exercise self-control. You have to adjust yourself to limits imposed from outside.

Uranus: LIBERATION – An expansion of your personal space and horizons. New doors open for you, and you have to release old assumptions.

Neptune: ATTUNEMENT – You need to overcome doubt, confusion and uncertainty and trust in your ability to just go with the flow and be open to inspiration.

Pluto: CLARITY – You must be calm and steady, and use sober, objective analysis. You have to put the situation into proper perspective.

North Node: GUIDANCE – You need to reconsider your position, to be fluid and receptive to change.

South Node: GRATIFICATION – Your ego gets a boost; you collect some debt from the past.

Part of Fortune: NOVELTY – You find you are able to take things in stride, to relax and enjoy yourself in a unique situation.

Ascendant: REORIENTATION – You begin a new phase or epoch in your life.

Midheaven: HOPE – You are given something to set your sights on or to shoot for.

Descendant: COOPERATION – You change the tone or direction of a close relationship.

Lower Meridian: RESOLUTION – You are required to stand your ground and consolidate your position.

Mutual Transits

The present essay is meant to be a tutorial on how to use the mutual transits of planets. It is assumed that the reader has a basic working knowledge of the symbols of astrology: what the different planets mean, and what aspects are and how to measure them. The best book (and one of the least expensive) for complete beginners is Ronald Davison's *Astrology*.

We will arbitrarily take 2° orbs in longitude and 2-day orbs in time so as to keep our focus narrow. We hearken to Dr. Marc Edmund Jones' injunction not to multiply unnecessarily the factors we are taking into account – the principle of Occam's Razor. It's not that difficult to find astrological correspondences for pretty much anything in retrospect, by taking enough midpoints, Arabian parts, asteroids, minor aspects, etc. etc. into account. Looking backwards, astrology works like a dream. What we're trying to do here, however is to predict the *future*, not make excuses for the past. Therefore we will concentrate on major factors: conjunctions and oppositions of the ten planets and angles; and we'll throw the moon's Nodes and the Part of Fortune into the mix since they usually are effective also. In other words, we'll keep our focus of attention on those factors which jolly well had better work if there's anything to astrology at all. In fact, these transits do indeed produce events much of the time. For detailed information on how to use these transits to cast spells, see my book *Planetary Hours*.

Interpretations of Transiting Conjunctions and Oppositions to Natal Planets

Sun Conjunct Mars = You may have to take decisive, committal action, but you have the confidence and élan to bring it off. Try to avoid conflicts with men now. Good time to take risks, and to ask favors of men (sun hours if father/boss/authorities; Mars hours if brother, husband, lover, male friend). Also good for rituals to attract a male lover (use a red candle in person's image and a Mars hour).

Sun opposition Mars = Avoid conflict, especially with men. You cannot enforce your own will now, so try to be patient in the face of obstruction and frustration. If you must confront others, use a sun hour. It is, however, a good day to do a Scat ritual to get rid of any man in your life who is bringing you down (use a Mars hour for this).

Sun Conjunct Jupiter = An excellent day to approach men for favors or ask for a raise (sun hours); and to borrow/lend/invest money (Jupiter hours) and launch new projects generally. Also to make prayers or cast spells for money: choose a Jupiter hour for this (and, if possible, a time when sun-Jupiter cross an angle at your locality).

Sun Opposition Jupiter = Some plan or purpose may not live up to expectation, but you'll find that you get what you need in the end. Not good for money matters. It's best to approach superiors / authorities / men from whom you wish a favor during a sun hour; other people during a Jupiter hour; but don't expect a whole lot.

Sun Conjunct Saturn = May bring disappointment or onus. You may come eyeball-to-eyeball with someone or have to take the bull by the horns in a difficult situation. You must be decisive and unflinching without being oppressive yourself. Act during sun hours if possible; or during Saturn hours if dealing with difficult, intractable people.

Sun Opposition Saturn = This brings conflict, opposition, frustration; however it is a good time to call something quits, or make prayers or cast spells to banish negative people or situations. This should be done during a Saturn hour.

Sun Conjunct Uranus = Surprising news, or a breakthrough or critical moment in which you have great clarity and decisiveness. Good time to make a complete break or radical change in your situation or relationships to free yourself of encumbrances (use a sun hour).

Sun Opposition Uranus = This may bring tension, conflict, and stress, especially vis à vis father, boss, authorities, men generally. Keep your cool. If you find that you must confront, do this during a sun hour.

Sun Conjunct Neptune = You may receive inspiration or intuitive understanding. An excellent time to initiate spiritual practices; to meet with spiritual teachers and counselors, to invoke spirits, and to cast spells asking for spiritual enlightenment and understanding. Use a white candle during a sun hour.

Sun Opposition Neptune = There may be some underhandedness going on, especially vis à vis men, superiors, authorities.

Be careful not to deceive yourself, or be too trusting. It's easy to fall for delusions now; you have to face up to reality, not pursue fantasies or will-o'-the-wisps.

Sun Conjunct Pluto = Deep insight into others' motivations may bring the solution to a problem (tackle it during a sun hour). You are detached, objective, and confident of your abilities now, and are in a decisive mood.

Sun Opposition Pluto = There may be a conflict of wills or bad faith going on. Be alert to duplicity. Your viewpoint is not going to be accepted or appreciated so you had better just hold your tongue now (let go of obsessions). If it is unavoidable, arrange to approach others (especially men / boss) during a sun hour.

Mercury Conjunct Venus = Get things straight with a loved one or friend, particularly women (Venus hour), clear up misunderstandings (Mercury hour). Don't let communications problems bog you down; plan to enjoy yourself. A good day for dating, travel, recitals, art exhibits, parties, children.

Mercury Conjunct Mars = A good time to get things straight with other people, especially men (Mercury hours) or confront them forcefully (Mars hours). Hastiness may occasion mistakes – there is a need to take a detached overview. Best to ignore provocation now.

Mercury Opposition Mars = Disagreement, anger, conflict. Sharp tongues may bring about confrontations which will be regretted later on. You're not going to convince anyone or get your own way now, so best defer or go quietly.

Mercury Conjunct Jupiter = You're bright-eyed, bushy-tailed, and in good spirits and humor. New ideas and inspiration now; also helps in reaching agreement and accord. You can take a positive, bright, optimistic view and thereby win the support and encouragement of other people. This is a good time to travel or visit / join with others, sign contracts, invest money, particularly during Mercury and Jupiter hours.

Mercury Opposition Jupiter = Inflated expectations may lead to a let-down. Your enthusiasms aren't appreciated. Avoid signing papers or investing money. Communications are misunderstood or unappreciated; but if unavoidable approach other people during Jupiter hours.

Mercury Conjunct Saturn = There is a call for sobriety and serious-mindedness. You may need patience in dealing with others, but you can understand their viewpoints objectively and are called upon to facilitate or teach. Good for long-term commitments and undertakings.

Mercury Opposition Saturn = Things come to a head today; you are misunderstood and blocked. Don't count on others for support or believe everything you're told; be prepared to cut loose and go it alone.

Mercury Conjunct Uranus = A sudden flash of understanding and illumination – like a bolt from the blue. Good day to pray / cast spells for creativity and guidance. You must keep your wits about you and be alert to opportunities.

Mercury Opposition Uranus = Unexpected upsets. There may be some tension or conflict based on misunderstandings or differing interpretations. There seems to be pigheadedness on all sides. Best just to cool it now.

Mercury Conjunct Neptune = A great time to begin spiritual projects or studies, invoke spirits, or learn how to channel. Also good for travel and romance, since you are highly intuitive and full of creative ideas and projects.

Mercury Opposition Neptune = There are apt to be misunderstandings or misleading promises (betrayal of trust). You shouldn't believe everything you hear now, especially not rumors; nor should you act until you have all the facts.

Mercury Conjunct Pluto = You can see very clearly what is really going on beneath the surface. You are objective and disinterested and can facilitate accord (use a Mercury hour to approach others)

Mercury Opposition Pluto = There may be misunderstandings and conflict due to stubbornness on all sides. Not a good time to approach others or start projects since your own thinking is obsessive rather than objective.

Venus Conjunct Mars = There may be a romantic attraction or attachment, or an enjoyable time with one's present significant other, or just a member of the opposite sex. Good to ask someone out for a date. Also good time to cast a love spell: use a Venus hour (straight women or gay men can use a Mars hour instead – particularly if sex is more important than companionship).

Venus Opposition Mars = Disappointment or conflict in an intimate or social relationship. Not a good day to meet with others or try to reach agreement. It is a good day, however, to break things off (or do a Scat ritual to get someone out of your life).

Venus Conjunct Jupiter = A joyous, harmonious time in which social and financial matters take a turn for the better. Excellent time for launching new projects; indeed, one of the most favorable aspects of the entire year, so you should do something enjoyable today (use Venus or Jupiter hours), or cast a spell for love, money, artistic creativity, or social success. Choose a Venus (for love) or Jupiter (for money) hour for this.

Venus Opposition Jupiter = Inflated hopes or expectations may bring disappointments. There may be estrangements or misunderstandings with friends or family members. This is not a good time to borrow / lend / invest money, but if you must approach others use a Jupiter or Venus hour.

Venus Conjunct Saturn = Expectations are disappointed. Tact and discretion are needed in addressing the feelings of a friend or family member, or else feelings may be hurt on both sides. On the other hand, this is a good day to break things off (use a Saturn hour).

Venus Opposition Saturn = Conflict, disappointment, separation, or betrayal in an intimate relationship. Avoid being too trusting, or bringing up problems now on your own account – you can't win. Good day to do a Scat ritual to get rid of someone undesired.

Venus Conjunct Uranus = You may feel unexpected attractions or receive sudden creative inspiration and new ideas. It's a good time to make prayers or to cast spells to bring romance (choose a Venus hour for this).

Venus Opposition Uranus = This may bring sudden estrangements or disruptive actions by a friend or family member. It may be best to leave the other person in peace and go your own way; unavoidable contacts should be made during Venus hours.

Venus Conjunct Neptune = Good for romance and for creative and artistic activities in general; though there may be a tendency to see through rose-tinted glasses and idealize other people. A good day for musicians, artists, writers, etc. to ask for creative inspiration and spiritual help (use a blue candle and a Venus hour).

Venus Opposition Neptune = Expectations of others are likely to be disappointed now. Try to be aloof and unconcerned (rather than to indulge your worry and fear) since things aren't as bad as you might think.

Venus Conjunct Pluto = There may be hidden feelings or unspoken agendas that must be addressed consciously to avoid hurt. Objectivity (rather than obsessiveness) is called for – seeing the other person's motivations clearly, and not being clingy.

Venus Opposition Pluto = Intimate or family matters may come to some kind of a head. There may be some intense, obsessive feelings in the air which need to be brought out into the open and addressed consciously. Use a Venus hour to confront others.

Mars Conjunct Jupiter = Good for bold, daring action, risk-taking, speculation (Mars hours). Launch new ventures now (Jupiter hours), or cast spells for money, courage, success in athletic competition or protection (for yourself or another) in war.

Mars Opposition Jupiter = Be careful of over-optimism or overreaching these few days; avoid investing/lending/borrowing money or launching new projects. There is a difference between daring and mania. Be suspicious rather than trusting; watch your temper.

Mars Conjunct Saturn = Conflicts, obstacles, delays, frustration are rife now. If you must be confrontational, arrange to do it during a Mars planetary hour if possible (not a Saturn hour), but best dig in your heels and bear it. It is a good day, however, to break things off, especially with older or intractable people; or do a Scat ritual to get rid of an undesired someone from your life.

Mars Opposition Saturn = Conflicts, obstacles, frustration, betrayal, anger. Avoid conflict if at all possible, and if not try to arrange it for a Mars hour (not a Saturn hour); but best avoid making forward moves or contacts now. On the other hand, this is a good day to do a Scat ritual to rid yourself of a person or situation which is oppressing you (use a Mars hour).

Mars Conjunct Uranus = Sudden, surprising events – either a breakthrough or (more likely) stress and turmoil – force a major change of plans or thinking. You are bold, decisive, even reckless; and while this is a good day to make a stand or take risks, you should avoid provoking conflicts and feeding anger.

Mars Opposition Uranus = Tends to bring accidents, tension, anger, open conflict which surfaces in a sudden, unexpected blast. This is definitely not a good time to make changes or depend on other people. If you must confront, do it doing a Mars hour for determination and strength.

Mars Conjunct Neptune = May bring worries, paranoia, deception, betrayal. Don't be too trusting of other people; nor of your own fears and impulses (for better or worse, things probably won't work out the way they seem to be going). Definitely avoid conflicts now.

Mars Opposition Neptune = This may bring deception, duplicity, or general worry and paranoia. Avoid drugs and alcohol. Don't be too trusting or too credulous; don't believe everything you hear. If you must confront others, try to do it during a Mars hour.

Mars Conjunct Pluto = You can see very clearly into other people's hidden motivations, but must use this objectivity wisely (not obsessively cling to your own agendas). A little patience and detachment are more useful now than bull-headed aggressiveness.

Mars Opposition Pluto = Things come to a head or boil over. Anger, impatience, conflict tend to flare up. You must cool it rather than react obsessively; try to avoid confrontation altogether now (certainly don't provoke it yourself).

Jupiter conjunct Saturn = A profound realization which brings you up short and impels you to assume greater responsibility for the course of your life; but at the same time broadens your scope and deepens your understanding.

Jupiter opposition Saturn = There may be disappointments, estrangement, opposition: some sort of occurrence which requires you to consider the meaning of your life and the seriousness of your purpose. You have to cop to something unpleasant. It's not so much a question of inadequacy or failure as of recognition, admission, and willingness to try again.

Jupiter conjunct Uranus = A good time to do some devil-may-care thing that you've always wanted to do. Be prepared for the unexpected, and be ready to throw out your preconceived ideas and plans and just fly with the flow.

Jupiter opposition Uranus = You are forced by circumstances to release previously held expectations or taken-for-granted assumptions, and take a broader and less encumbered perspective.

Jupiter conjunct Neptune = Inspiration, benevolent impulses, divine guidance. You may have an opportunity to share wisdom or reach out to other people in a spiritual way; or you may receive a spiritual gift from others. Good day to trip, or to cast spells for enlightenment. Also an excellent day to start channeling your spirit guides

Jupiter opposition Neptune = Disappointment or results falling short of expectation. Not a good time to begin projects, invest money, or trust other people since your judgment may be clouded.

Jupiter conjunct Pluto = Some sort of realization or coming to grips with underlying motivations; you are shrewd and decisive, and can take a detached, overall view of things to make your own will prevail.

Jupiter opposition Pluto = You are not believed or appreciated, nor are your views taken into account (perhaps because you are overly sanguine and too focused upon your own ends).

Saturn conjunct Uranus = Someone pushing your buttons, or a sense of frustration and helplessness. Stress, turmoil, intense feelings which must be dealt with tactfully and patiently (qualities which you may lack now).

Saturn opposition Uranus = There may be sudden, unexpected setbacks or bolts from the blue. Intransigence or unavoidable obstacles cause a great deal of frustration and tension now. Anger may flair and bad feelings are rife. Definitely control your temper or things may spin out of control – don't try to butt your way through, but wait as patiently as you can before taking action.

Saturn conjunct Neptune = There may be betrayal or deep disappointment and a tendency to brood or feel paranoiac. This is a time of contraction: best to pull your wagons into a circle and assume a defensive stance.

Saturn Opposition Neptune = Things may get a bit depressing or frustrating, there may be vague worries or dashed hopes, especially regarding goals or relationships in which you have a major emotional investment. It's best to withdraw now rather than to trust or depend too much on others.

Examples from the Life of Theodore Roosevelt

Some of the events listed below fit the planetary symbolism better than others do. It's possible that the listed event isn't really what the planetary symbolism meant in Theodore Roosevelt's life at all, but some other event which is not recorded in his biographies. For the most part we don't really know what was happening in TR's personal life; we only know what was happening in his public life. Also these transits often refer not so much to events as to emotional responses; new ideas and plans and dreams; things that a biographer wouldn't know about.

It's also necessary to consider the background – the progressions, directions, and transits to a person's individual horoscope. The approach to analysis suggested in this tutorial does not take into account the unique features of each individual horoscope which groove prediction in the individual case.

For example, Neptune intrinsically symbolizes otherworldliness: on the positive side it rules true inspiration and contact with the spiritual realm; on the negative side it rules woolly-mindedness, irresponsibility, drugs and alcohol, illusions and delusions. Thus Neptune is not usually thought of as a planet associated with worldly matters or worldly success (which are usually considered to be the realm of the sun and Jupiter).

However in the specific case of Theodore Roosevelt's horoscope, Neptune is in the 10th house of career / life's work / reputation / fame; and Neptune is very strong. It's the most elevated planet in this chart; it's in a zodiacal sign, Pisces, which favors Neptune; it's the short leg of a T-Cross based on the mutable opposition of setting Venus and rising Jupiter. Neptune is also the mediating planet of the wedge based on the cardinal opposition of Mars and the moon: Neptune receives a sextile from the powerful Mars (in Capricorn, where he is exalted) and a trine from the powerful moon (in Cancer, which she rules). All of these indications increase Neptune's strength and importance in this particular horoscope. Additionally Neptune lies on the fixed star Markab, which according to Vivian Robson "gives honour, riches, fortune, danger from fevers, cuts, blows, stabs and fire, and a violent death." (TR's death was not violent, but he came close to it numerous times; the rest is correct). Therefore, beyond Neptune's intrinsic symbolism of otherworldliness, in TR's individual case Neptune relates specifically to his public career and great success in life. Indeed, transiting Neptune was exactly trine TR's Midheaven when he became president. As a perusal of the following example transits will show, it is often the case that Neptune's transits coincided with major career openings and opportunities: moments of advancement and triumph; but this is not at all what Neptune symbolizes in most people's horoscopes.

The following list of examples does not include the conjunctions of sun-Mercury and sun-Venus. These are discussed separately in the essay on the "Transiting Synodic Cycles of Mercury and Venus". A *Table of Keywords for the Transiting and Natal Planets* contacted appears on page 118.

The list is ordered by transiting planets, then by natal planet contacted, rather than chronologically. This is done to stress similarities in tone between different transits by the same planet at different times in TR's life.

Format:

(Transiting Planets) conjunction or opposition Natal Planet(s) = date
TRANSITING PLANETS KEYWORDS – NATAL PLANET(s) KEYWORDS
= event (allow a time orb of ±2 days from exact date of transit to event)

Using the Keywords:

The keywords can be used to cobble together cookbook interpretations, as is done below. However they are intended more to provide an intellectual point of departure, or as a springboard for intuition. Interpretation cannot be carried out mechanically; the keywords are only meant to be suggestive. What we are trying to do here is provide examples from one person's horoscope and a barebones technique to illustrate how interpretation is actually carried out in practice – i.e., a very simplified explanation of what the symbols basically mean and how they interact. As one's intuitive grasp of what the different planets symbolize deepens, interpretation is done by feel rather than thought. For example:

Mars conjunct Neptune on February 7th, 1878 occurred at 4°55' of the sign Taurus, which opposes Theodore Roosevelt's natal sun at 4°20' Scorpio. TR received a telegram at Harvard in the late afternoon of February 9th, 1878 that his father was critical; and he immediately left for New York. His father died that night before TR arrived. <see page 94 of *The Rise of Theodore Roosevelt* by Edmund Morris>. This information is abbreviated as:

(MA conj NE) opp SU = 2/7/78
FORCEFUL-UNUSUAL event which accentuates
DETERMINATION
= news that TR's father was dying, and his father's death. His diary entry for 2/9/78: "'My dear father. Born Sept. 23, 1831.' Here his pen wavered and stopped."[94]

An experienced astrologer would be aware that the sun symbolizes the father (also boss, superiors, authorities; also career / honor) and that a Mars-Neptune event would produce unhappy, conflicting emotions – perhaps something like paranoia or a betrayal of trust. The astrologer might not hit the nail exactly on the head, but would perhaps predict something like "Turbulent feelings unleashed with regard to a person of power and authority; or a besmirched reputation." The interpretation given earlier in this essay reads: "Mars conjunct Neptune = May bring worries, paranoia, deception, betrayal. Don't be too trusting of other people; nor of your own fears and impulses (for better or worse, things probably won't work out the way they seem to be going). Definitely avoid conflicts now."

Moreover the astrologer would be aware of other influences in the person's chart at the same point in time – in this case, TR's Saturn conjunct Lower Meridian (IC) by zodiacal primary direction, which was the "real cause" of his father's death at this time in TR's life. The (Mars conjunct Neptune) opposition sun transit was merely the trigger for the primary direction.

Another example: (SU conj MA) conj SU-ME = 10/25/80, which occurred at the time of TR's first marriage, was merely the trigger for the underlying primary direction of Uranus conjunct Ascendant. The point is that true astrological prediction involves an analysis of the most important influences – namely the primary directions to angles, secondary progressions, and transits of the outer planets to natal planetary positions. These mutual transits are then added on as a fillip or extra detail added to the analysis; and they are useful in making elections (planning your daily life to take advantage of prevailing karmic currents).

Mutual Transits in the Life of Theodore Roosevelt:

(SU conj MA) conj SU-ME = 10/25/80
DECISIVE-FORCEFUL event which accentuates
DETERMINATION-UNDERSTANDING
= 1st marriage: "Our intense happiness is too sacred to be written about."[133]

(SU opp JU) opp SU conj PL = 4/25/99 (+ 3 days)
DECISIVE-CHEERING event which accentuates
DETERMINATION-CLARITY
= final day of NY legislative session; Governor TR, by a bold and risky stroke, forced a vote which discredited his political enemies and was a great personal triumph: "Looking back over the session in the first flush of his victory, Roosevelt felt some relief and no little pride in what he had accomplished as Governor."[99]

(SU conj JU) opp NE = 9/13/97
DECISIVE-CHEERING event which accentuates ATTUNEMENT
= excellent meeting with President McKinley, who was very agreeable and flattered his Naval undersecretary. At this meeting TR requested the president to give him a military appointment in case war should break out with Spain (which later came true).[585-6]

(SU opp UR) opp SU = 4/25/92
DECISIVE-SURPRISING event which accentuates
DETERMINATION
= TR had provoked a House investigation to discredit a political enemy who now retaliated and "launched into a speech which must have made Roosevelt boggle when it appeared in the evening paper" because it was, from TR's point of view, full of calumny and lies.[448]

(SU conj UR) conj IC = 8/22/78
DECISIVE-SURPRISING event which accentuates RESOLUTION
= huge fight with his girlfriend which "seems to have kindled some sort of rage in Theodore" and led directly to their breakup (which paved the way for his getting together with the woman he eventually married).[98]

(SU-VE conj UR) opp NE = 9/17/83
DECISIVE-SOCIABLE-SURPRISING event which accentuates

ATTUNEMENT
= TR made the deal to buy cattle for his new ranch (i.e. the beginning of his ranching business); two days later on a hunt he killed his first buffalo: "Roosevelt now abandoned himself to complete hysteria. He danced around the great carcass like an Indian war-chief, whooping and shrieking, while his guide watched in stolid amazement."[221, 224]

(SU opp UR) conj ASC 3° and (VE conj MA) conj JU = 6/19/04
DECISIVE-SURPRISING event which accentuates REORIENTATION
SOCIABLE-FORCEFUL event which accentuates FULFILLMENT
= Republican convention opened in Chicago. As incumbent TR was a shoo-in for the nomination and orchestrated every detail.[328, 331]

(SU opp NE) conj SU-ME = 10/26/76
DECISIVE-UNUSUAL event which accentuates DETERMINATION-UNDERSTANDING
= insulted at Harvard political rally; one witness recounted "Every student there was profoundly indignant. I noticed one little man, small but firmly knit. He had slammed his torch to the street. His fists quivered like steel springs and swished through the air as if plunging a hole through a mattress. I had never seen a man so angry before. 'It's Roosevelt from New York.' someone said.'" This was TR's 1st political involvement, "the first sign of any political interest in young Theodore."[82]

(SU conj NE) conj JU = 6/13/98
DECISIVE-UNUSUAL event which accentuates FULFILLMENT
= After many delays and logistical screw-ups TR's Rough Riders *finally* sailed for war in Cuba.[631]

(SU conj NE) conj ASC = 6/18/00
DECISIVE-UNUSUAL event which accentuates REORIENTATION
= nominated V.P. "McKinley and Roosevelt were nominated by votes of 926 and 925 respectively – the Governor casting the convention's only vote against himself. After that final gesture to his lost independence, he proclaimed himself a loyal member of the team, and offered his services to Hanna for the duration of the campaign."[729]

(SU opp PL) conj VE opp JU = 12/12/03
DECISIVE–REVEALING event which accentuates INTIMACY-FULFILLMENT
= TR's 1904 candidacy had been opposed by the Robber Barons. But now he received the endorsement of the Republican National Committee.<304>

(SU conj PL) conj JU opp VE = 6/11/03
DECISIVE–REVEALING event which accentuates INTIMACY-FULFILLMENT
= dinner with Sec'y of State and French ambassador, in which TR "launched beaming into an account of his adventures. ... As he talked on and on, Roosevelt began to free-associate earlier western memories; of sharing a bed with the judge who jailed Calamity Jane, of Hell-Roaring Bill Jones chasing a lunatic across the prairie ... Roosevelt's extraordinary frankness, his high-pitched mirth (punctuated with table thumps and chortles of 'Hoo! Hoo!'), were such that the ambassador could conclude only that France was being vouchsafed some sort of privileged audience."<241>

(SU conj PL) conj JU and (VE opp MA) opp PL = 6/12/05
DECISIVE–REVEALING event which accentuates FULFILLMENT
SOCIABLE-FORCEFUL event which accentuates CLARITY
= two days after his successful negotiation of Russo-Japanese treaty TR spent his first weekend at new forest dacha / retreat with his wife: "It really is a perfectly delightful little place."<392>

(SU conj PL) conj ASC and (ME conj MA opp UR) conj MO opp MA = 6/15/08
DECISIVE–REVEALING event which accentuates
REORIENTATION
ENCOURAGING-FORCEFUL-SURPRISING event which
accentuates ASSURANCE-ADVANCEMENT
= Republican convention opened with Taft (TR's candidate) a shoo-in to be nominated as TR's successor.<525>

(SU conj PL) conj ASC = 6/18/10
DECISIVE–REVEALING event which accentuates
REORIENTATION
= return to US from one-year African safari "Roosevelt descended

the gangway to more cheers, then entered a carriage for a parade up Broadway. ... For five slow miles north, the hero rode a wave of adulation through a sea of sound."[669-70]

(SU opp PL) conj DESC = 12/16/08
DECISIVE–REVEALING
event which accentuates COOPERATION
= dinner with his outgoing Cabinet: "I don't feel any resentment at all (at Taft's pursuing an independent course). Only I hope he will take care of the men who served me here."[544]

(SU opp PL) conj DESC = 12/16/07
DECISIVE–REVEALING
event which accentuates COOPERATION
= his great fleet launched on around the world cruise to his great pride: "By George! ... Did you ever see such a fleet and such a day?"[502]

(ME opp MA) opp ME = 5/15/73
ENCOURAGING-FORCEFUL event which accentuates UNDERSTANDING
= age 14, during a boring family trip to Europe he now left for Germany to stay with a family for the summer to learn the language and to be independent from his family.[70]

(ME conj MA) opp SA = 2/3/00
ENCOURAGING-FORCEFUL event which accentuates DISCIPLINE
= V.P. nomination machinations (his political enemies in New York state trying to kick him upstairs): "I am going to declare decisively that I want to be Governor and do not want to be Vice President."[717]

(ME conj JU-SA) conj PL, opp SU-ME = 5/6/81
ENCOURAGING-CHEERING-CHALLENGING event which accentuates DETERMINATION-UNDERSTANDING-CLARITY
= defeated by Republican regulars: "His very first political maneuver was in the direction of rebellion and reform ... the party machine was opposed to the measure; and on May 5, after 'rather a free fight' Theodore found himself 'with only some half-dozen votes out of three or four hundred.'"[145]

(ME conj JU) conj DESC = 12/31/00
ENCOURAGING-CHEERING event which accentuates
COOPERATION
= last day as governor of NY: "I think I have been the best governor of my time."[732]

(ME conj SA) opp VE = 6/25/84
ENCOURAGING-CHALLENGING event which accentuates
INTIMACY
= in the Dakota Badlands he met Marquis De Mores, who later became his friend and then enemy; also he found and purchased the perfect place to build his ranch house: "No place could be more remote from the world, yet more insulated from the wilderness. Roosevelt knew he had found his 'hold' in Dakota."[277]

(ME conj SA) opp UR = 11/18/97
ENCOURAGING-CHALLENGING event which accentuates
LIBERATION
= birth of 6th child (and favorite) Quentin ... also drafted bellicose letter advocating war with Spain.[589]

(ME conj VE conj SA) conj NO = 2/22/06
ENCOURAGING-SOCIABLE-CHALLENGING event which accentuates GUIDANCE
= TR's pure food bill passed overwhelmingly: "The tone of the Republican Senators is not so defiant as it was a few weeks ago, and one hears on all sides predictions that Mr. Roosevelt will carry all the various measures upon which he was to have been overthrown."[438]

(ME opp SA) conj MC = 7/28/05
ENCOURAGING-CHALLENGING event which accentuates HOPE
= W.H. Taft, representing TR on secret mission, got desired peace objectives from the Japanese government: "Taft wanted a statesman's assurance that Hawaii and the Philippines would not be menaced in future years. Katsura (the Japanese minister) wanted Korea."[399]

(ME conj UR) opp MO = 1/2/09
ENCOURAGING-SURPRISING event which accentuates
ASSURANCE
= New Year's message to a very hostile Congress: "Seven years of

cumulative frustration exploded in jeers and catcalls. ... After seven hours of mounting rancor, the House handed him a rebuke unprecedented since the days of Andrew Jackson .. but to his great personal glee the House's very action made it seem as if it was indeed afraid of (his investigations). Effectively if not legislatively he came out looking like a political winner."[546-7]

(ME conj UR) conj DESC = 12/8/03
ENCOURAGING-SURPRISING event which accentuates COOPERATION
= TR's rejection of Robber Barons' support: "President Roosevelt has refused to make peace with the trust and railway corporation leaders of New York. They approached the President with an offer to withdraw their opposition to him if he would give them certain assurances as to his future course. The President declined point-blank."[303-4]

(ME opp UR) conj IC = 4/6/91
ENCOURAGING-SURPRISING event which accentuates RESOLUTION
= President Harrison warned him to squash report on electoral corruption: "Aware that he had an ax hanging over him ... Roosevelt drafted his report with extreme caution."[435]

(ME conj NE) conj JU = 6/29/97
ENCOURAGING-UNUSUAL event which accentuates FULFILLMENT
= met Commodore George Dewey and Captain Leonard Wood, both of whom would soon play major roles in his life; and as acting Naval Secretary he received the plans for war against Spain which was exactly what he wanted.[576-7]

(ME conj NE) conj JU = 6/22/98
ENCOURAGING-UNUSUAL event which accentuates FULFILLMENT
= invasion of Cuba: "Roosevelt was left standing on the sand with nothing but a yellow mackintosh and a toothbrush. Fortunately his most essential items of baggage were inside his Rough Rider hat: several extra pairs of spectacles, sewn into the lining. If he was to meet his fate in Cuba, he wished to see it in clear focus."[635]

(ME conj PL) conj JU = 6/26/04
ENCOURAGING-REVEALING event which accentuates FULFILLMENT
= TR's unanimous nomination for a 2nd term; also the satisfactory ending of Moroccan kidnapping crisis (which increased TR's prestige in foreign affairs).<337>

(ME opp PL) opp JU = 11/28/04
ENCOURAGING-REVEALING event which accentuates FULFILLMENT
= visit to World's Fair: "We really had great fun, although we only spent one day at the Fair. ... a perfect whirl." "He was impressed by the beauty of the illuminations, but only one exhibit spoke to him personally. It was his own Maltese Cross ranch cabin from 1884, reverently presented by the State of North Dakota."<367>

(ME opp PL) opp UR = 11/4/86
ENCOURAGING-REVEALING event which accentuates LIBERATION
= came in 3rd in NY mayoralty, extremely disappointed: "This third political defeat in just over two years became one of those memories which he ever afterward found too painful to dwell on." He immediately sailed for England.<357-8>

(VE opp MA) conj NO = 4/10/86
SOCIABLE-FORCEFUL event which accentuates GUIDANCE
= the finale of a 12-day pursuit of thieves through the wilderness, during which TR and his companions ran out of provisions: "There is very little amusement in combining the functions of a sheriff with those of an Arctic explorer. ... after thirty-six hours of sleeplessness, I was most heartily glad when we at last jolted into the long, straggling main street of Dickinson, and I was able to give my unwilling companions into the hands of the sheriff."<329>

(VE opp JU) opp SU-ME = 3/27/87
SOCIABLE-CHEERING event which accentuates DETERMINATION-UNDERSTANDING
= return to NYC from European honeymoon (2nd marriage): "A certain bearish heaviness was noticeable in his physique (he had put on considerable weight in European restaurants), and several friends were seen to wince as he exuberantly hugged them tight."<368>

(VE opp JU) opp ME = 5/23/99
SOCIABLE-CHEERING event which accentuates UNDERSTANDING
= NY Governor TR triumphantly forced through bill to tax corporations, "the most important law passed in recent times by any State legislature," over much enemy opposition.[702]

(VE opp JU) opp SA = 1/5/08
SOCIABLE-CHEERING event which accentuates DISCIPLINE
= "All that was needed to precipitate a final, all-out battle (with the capitalists) was a direct challenge. It came on 6 January, and from an unexpected quarter: the Supreme Court" which struck down one of TR's proudest legislative achievements.[505]

(VE conj JU) conj PL = 5/13/81
SOCIABLE-CHEERING event which accentuates CLARITY
= 1st marriage honeymoon: "Hurrah! For a summer abroad with the darling little wife."[145]

(VE opp UR) opp VE = 7/15/02
SOCIABLE-SURPRISING event which accentuates INTIMACY
= 1st inspection of the presidential yacht: "Sailors were swabbing the *Mayflower*'s decks, and its officers were dressing below, when a rowboat began to splash across the bay. Pulling the oars was a stocky man in a sleeveless swimsuit. The sailors paid no attention until there was a creaking of the gangway ladder, and the President appeared beaming in their midst. 'Bully! Bully!' Roosevelt exclaimed, as he rushed around admiring fixtures and fittings."[128]

(VE conj UR) opp PL = 12/5/92
SOCIABLE-SURPRISING event which accentuates CLARITY
= brother's wife died: "Anna Roosevelt, her frail health broken by two years of humiliation, succumbed to diphtheria at the age of twenty-nine. ... One wonders if this gave any momentary pang to Theodore, who more than anyone else was responsible for their separation."[456]

(VE opp UR) conj NO = 3/24/80
SOCIABLE-SURPRISING event which accentuates GUIDANCE
= medical exam revealed weak heart: "Doctor, I'm going to do all the things you tell me not to do. If I've got to live the sort of life you

have described, I don't care how short it is."[129]

(VE opp UR) conj ASC = 5/9/03
SOCIABLE-SURPRISING event which accentuates REORIENTATION
= 1st visit to California; L.A. flower parade: "Amid all the color and luxuriance, nubile girls in white waved prettily, to the President's obvious pleasure. For four hours, the child California loomed like a rose before him."[226]

(VE opp UR) conj ASC 3° = 6/23/04
SOCIABLE-SURPRISING event which accentuates REORIENTATION
= TR re-nominated by acclamation: "An elemental din built and built, and for twenty-one minutes the convention rocked in pandemonium. Three sergeants at arms carried in Roosevelt's portrait ... They swung the President from side to side, while he gazed with waxy eyes at the party he could at last call his own."[336]

(VE opp PL) conj VE 3° = 11/21/99
SOCIABLE-REVEALING event which accentuates INTIMACY
= the incumbent Vice President died, which removed the last obstacle to TR's nomination as McKinley's next V.P.[709]

(VE conj PL) conj JU = 5/19/06
SOCIABLE-REVEALING event which accentuates FULFILLMENT
= very important railroad regulation bill finally passed Senate: "it's sheer accumulation of legislative weight, from a motion few supported to a majority measure only extreme conservatives opposed, was evidence that the President had started something very big."[447]

(VE conj PL) conj UR = 7/2/86
SOCIABLE-REVEALING event which accentuates LIBERATION
= orator at Dakota Independence day festival. Later that day he spoke with an editor who told him: "'You will become President of the United States.' Roosevelt did not seem in the least surprised by this remark. ... 'If your prophecy comes true,' he said at last, 'I will do my part to make a good one.'"[336]

(VE conj PL) conj UR and (MA opp JU) opp ME = 4/20/87
SOCIABLE-REVEALING event which accentuates LIBERATION
FORCEFUL-CHEERING event which accentuates
UNDERSTANDING
= left Dakota for east devastated and broke since his cattle herd had been wiped out: "The losses are crippling. For the first time I have been utterly unable to enjoy a visit to my ranch. I shall be glad to get home."<373-4>

(MA opp JU) opp SA = 11/2/07
FORCEFUL-CHEERING event which accentuates DISCIPLINE
= against his principles he approved trust to assuage Wall Street crash: "Relief flooded the market, and within hours prices began to rally."<499>

(MA conj SA) opp NE = 10/12/91
FORCEFUL-CHALLENGING event which accentuates
ATTUNEMENT
= fight with administration over TR report: "'As usual, I come back to rumors of my own removal.' ... 'Mr. Harrison could be consoled if Mr. Roosevelt would resign,' *The New York Times* remarked, 'but he will not, and the President will not dare ask him to do so.'"<443>

(MA opp UR) opp UR 3° = 7/18/98
FORCEFUL-SURPRISING event which accentuates LIBERATION
= During the war in Cuba: "On July 20, Roosevelt found himself in command of the whole 2nd brigade. This elevation was due to medical attrition in the higher ranks, rather than his heroism at San Juan, but it was flattering nonetheless. So, too, was the growing flood of letters and telegrams from New York, urging him to consider running for the governorship in the fall."<659>

(MA conj UR) opp NE 3° = 7/19/84
FORCEFUL-SURPRISING event which accentuates
ATTUNEMENT
= against his principles, to maintain his party loyalty, he supported Blaine; he was savagely attacked by his friends and allies for treason to the independent cause: "Most of my friends seem surprised to find that I have not developed hoofs and horns."<280>

(MA conj NE) conj UR = 5/11/89
FORCEFUL-UNUSUAL event which accentuates LIBERATION
= moved from NYC to DC: "When Roosevelt arrived in town on the morning of Monday, May 13, 1889, he was alone, just like thousands of other hopeful newcomers in the early days of the Harrison Administration. Unlike them, however, he had a desk waiting for him, and a commission, signed by the President of the United States, lying upon it."[397]

(MA opp NE) opp UR = 3/5/90
FORCEFUL-UNUSUAL event which accentuates LIBERATION
= anti-TR hearings end with TR exonerated: "The humiliated ex-postmaster sat for three days in his chair, helpless as a trussed turkey, while Roosevelt determinedly pulled out his feathers, one by one. ... Roosevelt seemed determined to show the committee what an angry Civil Service Commissioner looked like in action."[422]

(MA conj NE) conj ASC = 8/24/98
FORCEFUL-UNUSUAL event which accentuates REORIENTATION
= after military triumph in Cuba, invited to run for NY governor by independent party leaders, who said: "I shall never forget the luster that shone about him ... I never before nor since have felt that glorious touch of hero worship."[670]

(MA opp PL) opp JU = 3/16/07
FORCEFUL-REVEALING event which accentuates FULFILLMENT
= stock market crash, "rich man's panic" caused in part by his regulatory reforms: "Sooner or later (the capitalists) will realize that in their opposition to me for the last few years they have been utterly mistaken ... that nothing better for them could be devised than the laws I have striven for."[488]

(MA conj PL) conj JU-ASC 3° = 5/12/08
FORCEFUL-REVEALING event which accentuates FULFILLMENT-REORIENTATION
= hosted nonpartisan conservation conference: "It was the duty of the Governor's Conference, he said, to formulate a national philosophy of conservation based on efficient use of finite resources and scientific management of renewable ones." Also, he now got the

idea of an African safari (which he took for a year starting when he left office as President).[514,519]

(JU opp PL) opp UR = 5/1/88
CHEERING-REVEALING event which accentuates LIBERATION = began writing his magnum opus, *Winning the West*: "I'm a literary feller, not a politician these days."[388]

The Transiting Synodic Cycles of Venus and Mercury
Astronomical Explanation of Venus' and Mercury's Cycles

The synodic cycles of Venus and Mercury are their cycles of orbit around the sun, as seen from the point of view of the earth. These synodic cycles break down naturally into six phases delimited by six marking points: two conjunctions (Superior and Inferior); two stations (Retrograde and Direct); and two points of maximum elongation from the sun (East and West). The astronomical basis of Venus's Synodic Cycle will be explained below; Mercury's cycle is entirely similar. (For an illustration of the Synodic Cycle of Mercury, as well as an explanation of how to apply it in natal and predictive work, see my book *Thought Forms*. Tables of Mercury's synodic cycle for 1900 to 2050 are given in *Thought Forms*, and are also posted online at:

http://www.astro.com/swisseph/ae/mercury1600.pdf).

Because Venus is one of the two inferior planets (those whose orbit around the sun lies within the earth's orbit), from our earth-centered point of view Venus appears to oscillate back and forth around the sun over a period of 584 days. Sometimes she appears to move towards the sun; sometimes she appears to move away from the sun; but she never gets too far from it. Sometimes Venus is visible in the east before sunrise; sometimes she can be seen in the west after sunset.

Venus' synodic cycle begins and ends with the Inferior Conjunction (IC), at which time she is on a direct line between the earth and sun, moving at her maximum retrograde speed (backwards in the zodiac). She falls behind the sun in longitude until her Stationary Direct (SD) point, when she appears to stop moving backwards in the zodiac and resumes forward motion. She then increases speed until she is moving at the same speed as the sun, and is as far from the sun as she will get, at her Greatest Western Elongation (GWE). Note that the terms "GWE" and "GEE," which are the terms used by astronomers, are misnomers since at GWE Venus rises before the sun in the east, and at GEE she sets after the sun in the west.

After GWE Venus catches up with the sun and passes it at Superior Conjunction (SC), at which point she is on a direct line with the earth and sun, on the far side of the sun from the earth. After Superior Conjunction Venus' speed decreases until she is moving at the same speed as the sun, and is as far from the sun as she will get, at her Greatest Eastern Elongation (GEE). Then her speed drops to zero at Stationary Retrograde (SR) and she begins moving backwards in the zodiac, until she once again conjoins the sun at Inferior Conjunction. The entire cycle takes roughly 584 days, so that five Venus cycles correlate very closely with eight earth years (as will be seen by inspecting the Venus tables posted at:

http://www.astro.com/swisseph/ae/venus1600.pdf).

When Venus is oriental – that is to say, a morning star: when she rises before the sun in the east – then the desire nature is said to be *possessive*; and when Venus is occidental – when she is an evening star, setting after the sun in the west – then the desire nature is said to be *dispassionate*. Possessive desire exhibits the Taurus side of Venus and dispassionate desire exhibits the Libra side of Venus (see the essay on "The Politics of Relationship" for details). Venus is at her Greatest Brilliancy when she is a crescent; this occurs between SD and GWE and between GEE and SR about 36 days before and after Inferior Conjunction.

Mercury's synodic Cycle is similar to Venus' Cycle except it has a period of roughly 116 days (rather than 584), so there are three complete Mercury cycles each year. When Mercury is oriental (a morning star) then the mentality is said to be *eager* (or *Promethean*; of the nature of Gemini); and when Mercury is occidental (an evening star) then the mentality is said to be *certain* (or *Epimethean*; of the nature of Virgo – see the essay on "Mental Chemistry" for details).

Interpretation of Venus' and Mercury's Synodic Cycles in the Natal Horoscope

Mercury's synodic cycle shows why people believe that they are *right*; that they are making the correct decisions; that they are on the inside track or are one up on other people. For example, Mercury conjunction sun natives know that they are right because they obediently and unquestioningly carry out the directives that their parents and society have taught them. Mercury elongation natives, by contrast, know that they are right precisely because they haven't believed what they were told, but rather have analyzed everything and figured out all the angles for themselves. For more information on the meaning of the Mercury cycle in the natal, progressed, and transiting horoscopes, see my book *Thought Forms*.

Venus' synodic cycle, on other hand, shows not what people believe they know but rather what they believe they deserve. Venus conjunction sun natives believe that they have to live up to an ideal, to do more or be more than is humanly possible, in order to deserve happiness. This contrasts sharply with the robust egos and emotional resiliency of the Venus elongation types, who believe they deserve (have a right to) whatever they can grab for themselves. When Venus is at her Greatest Brilliancy the natives possess an ease of manner and ability to take things as they come – to adapt to their environments and to get what they want without bending themselves (or other people) out of shape.

Where Mercury is concerned with superficial order – rationalizing, filing and sorting – Venus is concerned with power – weighing, maneuvering, and manipulating to get one's way. With Venus we're talking about people's strategies of control; of intimacy and avoidance of intimacy (loss of control).

The synodic cycles of Mercury and Venus taken together constitute what some psychologists have termed the *Inner Child*. When both Mercury and Venus conjoin the sun the Inner Child – overpowered by the parent – is often very damaged and in a great deal of pain, hence very defensive and quick to attack. When both Mercury and Venus are relatively far from the sun the Inner Child has fully separated from the parent and is able to function calmly and effectively in the world with little pother or wasted motion (see my book *Planetary Combination* for more information).

The Transiting Venus Cycle

The Transiting Venus Synodic Cycle symbolizes the rhythmic cycles of high and low self-esteem in current affairs. These days are points of inflection in life which tend to manifest in terms of ongoing relationships or other self-worth issues – appreciating and being appreciated. Emotional matters are brought to the fore: you may get to do exactly what you want, or that which you fear comes upon you, as the case may be. The positive or negative nature of the event depends in great measure upon the natal planet contacted: transits to natal moon, Jupiter and Neptune tend to produce more felicitous events than sun, Mercury, Mars, Saturn, Uranus or Pluto do. The horoscope of Theodore Roosevelt will be used as an example.

Triple Conjunction of Sun, Mercury, and Venus:
Example: (SU-ME-VE) conj MC = 2/22/1882
DECISIVE-ENCOURAGING-SOCIABLE event which accentuates HOPE
= Theodore Roosevelt was a junior NY state legislator: "On February 21 he again rose to protest a suggested deal with the opposite side, confident 'that enough Independent Republicans would act with me to insure the defeat of the scheme by "bolting" if necessary.' His senior colleagues were aware of this, and the matter was hastily referred to a party caucus that evening. For the next eight hours Roosevelt was besieged by deputations promising him rich rewards if he would withdraw his objections. 'I politely but sweetly declined. ... As no one seemed disposed to take up the cudgels I responded, and pitched into (the Speaker) mercilessly and we had rather a fiery dialogue.' Again the young man was successful: his objections were upheld by a narrow vote. Next morning he woke to find himself, if not famous, at least the hero of some liberal newspapers."[171]

Venus Superior Conjunction: May bring disagreement, conflict, tension. Your credibility or reputation may come under attack, or in some other way your self-image is bruised. However you are able to maintain your élan and poise even though you are in a disadvantageous position.
Example: (VE SC SU) conj MC = 2/18/1890
DECISIVE-SOCIABLE event which accentuates HOPE
= Three weeks earlier Congress had appointed a committee of his enemies to investigate him; on 2/19/90 hearings began: "As always when confronted by a challenge, Roosevelt instantly took the offensive. He intended to so dominate the hearings that he would be entirely vindicated." (which is what happened).[418]

Venus Inferior Conjunction: A surprising event which powerfully engages your feelings. Can be very poignant. It either sweeps you off your feet or knocks you off your pins, but in either case it opens new possibilities and points you in a new emotional direction. You

get to the root of how you are really feeling in a relationship; stand up for yourself, reach out to make your own desires come true.
Example: (VE IC SU) conj MC = 2/21/1878
DECISIVE-SOCIABLE event which accentuates HOPE
= returned to Harvard after father's death two weeks before: "On February 23, 1878, his first night back at Harvard after the funeral, Theodore noted casually: 'I am left about $8000 a year: comfortable though not rich.' His duty was clear. Grief or no grief, he must balance the numerator of his independence with the denominator of work. With remarkable self-discipline, given the hysteria of his private emotions, he at once resumed his studies, and within a week had scored 90 percent in two semiannual examinations."[96]

Venus Stationary Direct: A turning point in an intimate relationship which requires sensitivity and delicacy on your part. You must be sensitive to undercurrents and attentive to other people's feelings. You can get past something that was separating you from other people.
Example: (VE SD) opp ME = 5/22/1889
SOCIABLE event which accentuates UNDERSTANDING
= as Civil Service commissioner, TR took an investigative trip which he realized could be used to make political hay: "As a preliminary attention-getting exercise, Roosevelt went on May 20 to New York, where the press knew him (to investigate corruption in the administration of Civil Service Exams), and issued a fiery report accusing the local examinations board of 'great laxity and negligence,' 'positive fraud.' ... The Eastern press was watching him now; it was time to get Western newspapers to do the same."[402]

Venus Stationary Retrograde: Encounters, gatherings, or events which play upon your affections. There may be a poignant moment in a personal relationship; or creative, artistic expression. You reach a new depth of understanding or appreciation of other people.
Example: (VE SR) conj MC = 1/24/1902
SOCIABLE event which accentuates HOPE
= "On 24 January, Roosevelt attended his first Gridiron Club dinner as President of the United States. Mark Hanna was another guest of honor. Both men laughed heartily as an actor impersonating an

obsequious Frenchman bowed, scraped, and presented the Senator with a gold brick labeled PANAMA."[86]

Venus Greatest Western Elongation: You can reach out and make an important heart connection with someone or some ideal, but this may necessitate modifying your own preconceived conceptions or expectations. You can be practical and see other people's points of view.

Example: In lieu of an example of Venus GWE from Theodore Roosevelt's horoscope we shall examine one of Abraham Lincoln's: (VE GWE) at 25°LE44' opp natal SU at 23°AQ28' and conjunct DESC at 28°LE59'= 10/5/1836
SOCIABLE event which accentuates DETERMINATION and COOPERATION
= his first court case and the beginning of his law partnership: "On October 5 he was in a Springfield court, appearing in a case for John T. Stuart, the beginning of their partnership as a law firm."[Carl Sandburg, *Abraham Lincoln*, Harcourt 1974 p49]

Venus Greatest Eastern Elongation: There is a need for support and encouragement, which may have to be won by standing up for yourself and sticking to your guns. You have to assert yourself by going with your own feelings and instincts rather than by trying to curry favor.

Example: (VE GEE) conj UR= 7/9/1889
SOCIABLE event which accentuates LIBERATION
= President Harrison backed TR against attacker: "This placed Roosevelt in a highly embarrassing position. ... On July 10 a telegram summoned the three Commissioners to the White House. Roosevelt may have wondered if he was about to go the same way as Shidy, but he was pleasantly surprised by Harrison's attitude. 'The old boy is with us ... in his talk with us today did not express the least dissatisfaction with any of our deeds or utterances.'"[406]

Venus Greatest Brilliancy: May bring poignant moment in intimate relationship, for better (conjunction) or worse (opposition). You may get the opportunity to really shine – reach a pinnacle of social acceptance / approbation – able to bring your creativity and personal prowess into manifestation for all to behold. It's best to just let things unfold naturally rather than try to manipulate them your way.

(Note that Venus Greatest Brilliancy can have wider orbs than her other transits – say, a week or so on both sides).
Examples: (VE GB) at 3°TA14' opp SU (4°SC20') and ME (2°SC58') = 6/01/1897
SOCIABLE event which heightens DETERMINATION and UNDERSTANDING
= as leader of "Manifest Destiny" warhawks TR made a stirring speech at the Naval War College on June 2nd – a call to arms which "was printed in full in all major newspapers and caused a nationwide sensation. From Boston to San Francisco, from Chicago to New Orleans, expansionist editors and correspondents praised it, and agreed that a new, defiantly original spirit had entered into the conduct of American affairs."[569-71]

(VE GB) at 0°TA58' opp ME (2°SC58') = 5/31/1905
SOCIABLE event which heightens UNDERSTANDING
= four days after the Russian fleet was annihilated at Tsu Shima, the Japanese government asked TR if he would "directly and entirely of his own motion and initiative ... invite the two belligerents to come together for the purpose of direct negotiation."[389-90] TR solicited the Tsar's concurrence, and a week later Tsar Nicholas II agreed that TR should broker the peace settling the Russo-Japanese War.

The Transiting Mercury Cycle

Mercury's synodic marking points tend to bring news – new information which causes a change of plans, calculations, or attitude. In a general sort of way the transiting (like the progressed) elongations seem to refer more to relationships than the conjunctions or stations. The conjunctions are more "Aha!'s" – sudden bursts of insight when the truth becomes clear – whereas the elongations tend to be shifts in perspective (often because you now must take another person's point of view into account). With the conjunctions, something that was hidden comes into plain view, whereas with the elongations it's more a matter of having to see a larger picture. The stations are more dynamic – "thought in action" – than either conjunctions or oppositions; and the realizations you have at these times tend to move you past a blind spot (a sticking point or hang-up).

Mercury Superior Conjunction: The Superior Conjunction tends to be favorable and often involves a joining together or communicating with others. Sensitivity and receptivity to other people's views are required. This is usually a good day for making moves, for travel, and for making forward-going progress in personal and business relationships.

Example: (ME SC SU) conj ASC = 6/18/1879
DECISIVE-ENCOURAGING event which accentuates REORIENTATION
= proposed marriage, rejected: "He had been tense as a wire the night before. But now his mood was tranquil. Never had he spent such a pleasant day; never had Alice looked 'sweeter or prettier.' Then it was time for Alice to go home. He had much to ponder. Alice had rejected him – but in such a way he could not be wholly despondent. She would, he knew, remember him fondly at least through summer, and he had a tacit invitation to resume his suit in the fall."[115]

Mercury Inferior Conjunction: This tends to be more intense than Superior Conjunction, and also intrinsically somewhat malefic. The realization which one has now involves having to go it alone, make it on one's own, not depend on or rely on other people. Decisive action on your part may be required to be true to yourself and hold your own.

Example: (ME IC SU) conj South Node = 8/29/1905
DECISIVE-ENCOURAGING event which accentuates GRATIFICATION
= Breakthrough in Russo-Japanese war negotiations which TR was conducting: "… the low point of the conference, with Witte and Komura staring at each other in silence. … Rumors spread over the weekend that the Russians were asking for their hotel bills. On Monday Roosevelt concluded that he could do nothing more. … On Tuesday, 29 August, Witte suddenly placed a sheet of paper on the table. … Komura sat impassive. Silence grew in the room. Eventually, Komura said in a tight voice that the Japanese government wanted to restore peace, and bring the current negotiations to an end. The Russo-Japanese War was over." TR's comment: "It's a mighty good thing for Russia, and a mighty good thing for Japan. A mighty good thing for me, too!"[414]

Mercury Stationary Direct: A new departure or new outlook on your current affairs. You may get past something that was hindering you, or launch new projects or relationships which become important later on.
Example: (ME SD) opp JU = 1/1/1899
ENCOURAGING event which accentuates FULFILLMENT
= first day as governor of NY: "On the icy midnight of Sunday, January 1, 1899, the silence brooding over Eagle Street, Albany, was disturbed by the sound of smashing glass. Theodore Roosevelt, Governor, had stayed out late after dinner with the result that forgetful servants had locked him out of the Executive Mansion. Unwilling to disturb his sleeping family, he had no choice but to break into his new home." The next day was his triumphal march to capital and 1st annual message.[690-1]

Mercury Stationary Retrograde: A breakthrough, perhaps quite unexpected, in your current situation or relationships. Your optimism and enthusiasm are fired up and you are able to make progress in the realization of your life goals.
Example: (ME SR) conj JU = 5/26/1883
ENCOURAGING event which accentuates FULFILLMENT
= at a party TR met Single-Tax advocate Henry George,[342] but more importantly "A chance meeting occurred which directly influenced the future course of his life. There was at the party a certain Commander H.H. Gorringe. ... Gorringe had just been West, and was in the process of opening a hunting ranch there himself. When Roosevelt wistfully remarked that he would like to shoot a buffalo 'while there were still buffalo left to shoot,' Gorringe, scenting business, suggested a trip to the Bad Lands of Dakota Territory." This was the very beginning of TR's cowboy life and ranching business in Dakota.[198]

Mercury Greatest Western Elongation: New possibilities and horizons open up; new beginnings are made. There is a need for optimistic self-appraisal, a hopeful attitude, and a willingness to take risks and fly with gut-level impulses. Your own leadership and fresh ideas may prove decisive.
Example: (ME GWE) opp NE = 10/5/1884
ENCOURAGING event which accentuates ATTUNEMENT

= A bully had "stopped by the ranch-site in late September, accompanied by several drunken gunmen. Finding Roosevelt away" they rode off without incident. When TR returned he immediately set off to the bully's house: "'I understand that you have threatened to kill me on sight.' rasped Roosevelt. 'I have come over to see when you want to begin the killing.' Paddock was so taken aback he could only protest that he had been 'misquoted.' Next morning Roosevelt left for New York, confident that from now on his ranch-site would be left in peace."[288]

Mercury Greatest Eastern Elongation: Things are pushed to the limits, to the edge of what is acceptable. There may be a breakdown in communications, or you have to take a detour from your normal mode of action. You may have to put on the brakes, or adapt your own opinion to the necessities of the time. There is a need for patient understanding of other people's viewpoints and of where one's own limits lie.

Example: (ME GEE) conj MC = 2/3/1902
ENCOURAGING event which accentuates HOPE
= Northern Securities case, TR's first declaration of war upon the Robber Barons and Trusts: "It was 5 February 1902. He had been in office nearly five months, listening to advice and experimenting with power, not always successfully. ... Signs of disillusionment were evident in the press, and on Capitol Hill. Any fool could tell what the public expected of him. (He) must reach, and grapple with, the ogre of Combination. Mail poured daily into the White House, urging him to prosecute various trusts. ... This exceptional case looked strong enough to go all the way to the Supreme Court, yet it was fraught with political risk."[89]

Transits to the Angles

In the essay "Interpretation of Transits", I discussed how to use a system of keywords to assist in interpreting the possible effects of transits in general. In this essay we will take a closer look at one aspect of this subject: the interpretation of transits by the slow planets – Jupiter through Pluto – over the angles in a natal horoscope, using the horoscope of William Butler Yeats as the example. We'll start by summarizing briefly what the different angles and the slow planets symbolize.

The Ascendant (ASC) shows *who* the native is, and has particular reference to casual relationships, whereas the Midheaven (MC) shows *what* he or she does in life, and refers to group relationships. The Descendant (DESC) suggests intimate relationships; and the Lower Meridian (Nadir, or IC for *Imum Coeli*) suggests standing alone.

Transits to the Ascendant produce a necessity for REORIENTATION; whereas transits to the Midheaven give the native reason to HOPE. Transits to the Descendant tend to emphasize issues of COOPERATION; and transits to the Lower Meridian test or strengthen the native's RESOLUTION.

Transits to the Ascendant give rise to a sense of REORIENTATION within the native, which means transformative events – often moves, major journeys, work / relationship changes, new beginnings, or illness (in the case of malefic transits) – which necessitate reinventing oneself. The native's self-image – "*who*" the native conceives him or herself to be – is emphasized, whether because it is being applauded (transiting Jupiter), attacked (transiting Saturn), shook-up (transiting Uranus), dissolving (transiting Neptune), or seen from a distance (transiting Pluto). The point is that transits to the Ascendant are *the* most life-transforming (in the same way that progressed and directed planets conjoining the Ascendant signify *very* important life changes spread out over several months after the exact date of the progression or direction). This is why, if you expect to be able to make decent predictions, it is extremely important to have an exact birth time.

Transits to the Midheaven give the native reason to HOPE, which means events which transform what the native does in life, and how he or she does it. This can mean some advance in life's goals or sense of purpose; or some necessity to change course, whether because of new opportunities or blockages. There may be new directions in career / life's work / long-term ambitions – whether these are occasioned by events that are expansive (transiting Jupiter); obstructive (transiting Saturn), disruptive (transiting Uranus); or whatever. Parental issues or other control issues (with superiors / authorities) may come to the fore. The native may join or found new groups, make new social contacts or networks of support. The native's honor or public face may become an issue: there may be recognition and approbation; or disappointed social expectations, depending upon whether the transiting planet is strong or weak, or in good or bad aspect to the MC, in the natal horoscope.

Transits to the Descendant tend to emphasize issues of COOPERATION or lack of same. There can be new social relationships, or new partnerships (or would-be partnerships), whether romantic or business. In existing partnerships, there can be a heightened intensity of feeling (in either a good or bad way depending on the planet); or some particular focus on relationship issues. The native may also experience a new sense or level of social exploration – of finding out who he or she is by making alliances and social connections. Health may be an issue (since the Descendant opposes the Ascendant).

Transits to the Lower Meridian (IC) emphasize the native's RESOLUTION. There is often a change of home or domestic arrangement which puts the native on his or her own. The native may just go off on a tangent – marching to the beat of a distant drum – or he or she may be thoroughly pragmatic and down-to-earth; but in any case, the native has to stand his or her ground. The IC, like the MC, can symbolize one or the other parent (although usually the MC is the mother and the IC the father); so parental or family issues may come to the fore now.

When planets transit angles in the natal horoscope, the events to be expected (and their approximate timing relative to the exact date of the transit), depend on the individual natures of the transiting planets (see the *Table of Keywords for the Transiting and Natal Planets* on page 118). Usually, when a transit is repeated because of retrograde motion so that it occurs three times (direct-retrograde-direct) or five times (direct-retrograde-direct-retrograde-direct), then the expected event can occur anywhere between the first and last direct transits (although it is more likely to occur near the beginning). Another good rule of thumb is that the slower the planet, the longer the effect endures after the exact date of the transit. Thus transiting Jupiter's effects only last for a month or two (but can bring opportunities which favorably affect the future forevermore). Transiting Saturn's onerous effects can be occasioned by a sudden event; but even then the effect is spread out for a year or more following the exact date of the transit. Transiting Uranus usually brings unexpected (sharp and deep) disruptions in the life; and these can occur anywhere within the period between direct-retrograde-direct transit (although they tend to occur near the beginning). Transiting Neptune and Pluto are more indefinite in their effects, which tend to be spread out over the whole retrogradation period or series of periods (while transiting Pluto can produce transformative events focused in time – life-transforming flashes and realizations, or emotional wipe-outs – still the effect of the transit endures for quite some time thereafter).

Here are delineations for the transits of the slow planets:

Transits by Jupiter bring CHEERING events – serendipitous (or jovial when anticipated) events within the month of the exact transit (or within the range of direct transit-retrograde transit-direct transit – although in the case of Jupiter the expected event tends to occur at the last direct transit). These are events which make the native smile. And they occur without much in the way of stress or strain on the native's part – everything seems to fall into place by itself, as if from heaven.

Transits by Saturn bring CHALLENGING events – events that bring the native up short, like the sudden jerk of a tight leash, or just something that impedes or detours. These events seem to block or disappoint, as if mandated by an angry deity or by the laws of karma. Occasionally, if the inner work has been done prior to the Saturn transit – if the inner discipline and self-limitation have been achieved alone – then the predicted event can mean success and recognition for achievement (but even here, much of the time, it involves taking on heavy new burdens of responsibility; or else the proffered opportunity doesn't pan out in the end). Much depends on the condition of Saturn in the natal horoscope. If the natal Saturn is strong by house and sign – or (especially) if it is in good aspect to that angle in the natal horoscope – then Saturn transits can signify favorable events or lightened circumstances (release from burden).

Transits by Uranus bring SURPRISING events – sudden shocks which are unexpected and disruptive. Everything seems to dissolve (although this can mean barriers as well as dependable structures). In contrast to the other slow transiting planets (which don't so much point to particular events, but rather spread their effects out over the period between the first direct transit; the retrograde transit; and the last direct transit), Uranus' transits point to some sudden, transforming event which occurs at a moment in time, which can fall anywhere within the direct-retrograde-direct time frame; but most often near the beginning. If there is only one direct transit, then the predicted event will tend to occur within a few weeks of this date. Uranus' events can be serendipitous breakthroughs; but they can also cause tremendous shocks to the system – they can signify conflict, anger, tension, and impatience occasioned by stressful events. But in the end these events are a shakeup and shakeout which liberates the native's sense of independence and psychological freedom.

The Transits of Neptune and Pluto often occur five times: direct-retrograde-direct-retrograde-direct. When this happens the expected event can occur anywhere between the first and last direct transits, but is more likely to happen near the beginning. The effect, however, is spread out over the entire period.

Transits by Neptune bring UNUSUAL events – which can be of the psychic, powerful dreams, out-of-this-world type; or can perhaps involve the native's spiritual aspirations – what inspires him or her; or it can simply show creative and artistic high points in the native's life. These are times of spiritual awakening and inspiration (even if the native wouldn't call it that, or think about it in those terms); or else of moodiness and depression. On its negative side Neptune rules drugs and alcohol, disillusionment, and also shirked responsibilities.

Transits by Pluto bring REVEALING events: a sharp jolt which forces a complete mental re-evaluation. The event may occasion a complete wipeout emotionally, financially, or spiritually (or all three); or there may be some kind of 180° about-face, occasioned by a very revelatory event. This event or circumstance forces the native to look at things the way they are with considerable mental clarity and certainty. It's as if the native is forced to let go of obsessions and take a more objective view of his or her life; and to follow that new vision.

Now it's time for a practical example. What follows below is a list of transits by the slow planets to the angles in William Butler Yeats' horoscope (shown on page 106). W.B.Y. was born 6/13/1865 @ 10:39 pm LMT at 6°W19', 53°N20'; and since W.B.Y. was an astrologer himself, the birth data are probably correct. His own version of his horoscope has 0° 41' Aquarius rising. In his *Journal* entry for April 15, 1909 W.B.Y. noted: "April 14 and 15 Mars conjunct asc."[216] which would imply an ASC of 2 ½° Aquarius (instead of 0° 41' Aquarius). If true, this doesn't particularly invalidate the event list below except for transiting Pluto conjunct DESC, which would then occur after his death. However, in his *Journal* entry for March 17, 1909 he stated: "Mars conjunct M.c.p."[189] Mars was then transiting 14° Capricorn, which is indeed the progressed MC for the 0° 41' Aquarius rising chart.

The events in W.B.Y.'s life which are signified by transits, progressions, and directions in his horoscope can be broken down into common categories (love, money, health, etc.) which we will summarize here for the benefit of readers who know nothing about his life:

LOVE: For most of his life, from age 23 to age 52, W.B.Y. was hopelessly in love with actress and revolutionary Maud Gonne – a selfish, treacherous, lying woman who teased him, led him on, and trashed him emotionally (many of the transits in this essay refer specifically to events related to this fruitless love affair – Pluto conjunct Venus in a natal chart does signify obsessive, Gatsbyesque love affairs). At age 52 W.B.Y. desperately tried to entice this woman's daughter to marry him; and after the daughter's rejection he turned around and married a 24-year old woman who the next week started channeling (via automatic writing) notes about reincarnation and occult philosophy which became the basis of Yeats' masterpiece *A Vision*. A virgin until age 30, through most of the rest of his life – even after his marriage (and with his wife's knowledge and consent) – W.B.Y. had numerous love affairs.

MONEY: For most of his life W.B.Y. was poor, albeit not indigent. One drain on his finances was the necessity of helping to support his impoverished family (father, insane mother, and sisters). A blip of income came to him when he won the Nobel Prize for literature in 1923, and he invested this money in railroad stocks which crashed during the depression of the 1930's. The last few years of his life he was awarded a stipend by a group of Irish-Americans who wanted to help him out.

HEALTH: Throughout most of his life – from childhood on – W.B.Y. was very sickly and had very poor eyesight.

POLITICS: Although W.B.Y. surrounded himself with fire-eating radicals, he himself was a moderate Irish nationalist who participated in political action groups and became a senator in the new Irish republic after its founding in 1922.

RELIGION: An enemy of the Catholic Church in Ireland, which attacked his plays mercilessly, throughout his life W.B.Y. dabbled in the occult groups of the day (Theosophical Society, Order of the Golden Dawn, etc.), knew their leaders personally, and became a leader himself. He was a disciple of various Indian swamis; studied astrology; and participated in séances. His wife channeled – and he edited – the occult masterpiece *A Vision*.

ART: Although today he is known principally for his poetry, during his life W.B.Y. was involved mostly in theater. He co-founded a theater company in Dublin to produce new Irish drama, and he wrote numerous plays for it on Irish folk and national themes (which are rarely produced today).

The transiting aspects of Jupiter (every 12 years) tend to point to happy events – gifts from the universe – which usually occur within a few weeks of the exact date of the transit; or around the last direct transit when there are three of them.

Jupiter conjunct ASC (CHEERING events which give rise to sense of REORIENTATION): 6/11/1878 = In the spring of 1878 W.B.Y. was doing very badly in school; but that summer his work improved and he won a science prize in competition against 18-year olds (he was then only 13) [25]

Jupiter conjunct ASC (CHEERING events which give rise to sense of REORIENTATION): 2/22/1890 = In early 1890 W.B.Y. was with Annie Besant et.al. experimenting with mesmerism and magic. On 3/7/1890 he joined the Hermetic Order of the Golden

Dawn[104][453] and he brought many friends, his uncle, and Maud Gonne (his life-long beloved) into the organization.

Jupiter conjunct ASC (CHEERING events which give rise to sense of REORIENTATION): 2/6/1902 = On 1/13/1902 W.B.Y. persuaded Maud Gonne to act the lead role in a play he had written for her.[260] The production of *Cathleen ni Houlihan* on 4/2/02 was a huge success: "There is continual applause."[261][332]

Jupiter conjunct ASC (CHEERING events which give rise to sense of REORIENTATION): 1/21/1914 = On 1/18/1914 W.B.Y. left for a three month lecture tour of the United States.[511] The tour was exhausting, almost brought on a breakdown,[517] but he re-established old ties and made amends with his estranged father and some old friends.

Jupiter conjunct ASC (CHEERING events which give rise to sense of REORIENTATION): 1/5/1926 = In February 1926 W.B.Y.'s occult magnum opus *A Vision* was published:[280,309] "(*A Vision*) has not been out of my mind for years. I have grown well as I got it out of my head. I now have a free mind for the first time in years. ... I do not know what my book will be to others – nothing perhaps. To me it means a last act of defense against the chaos of the world."[280] But it was not success, and he soon saw he'd have to rewrite it.[313]

Jupiter conjunct ASC (CHEERING events which give rise to sense of REORIENTATION): 12/18/1937 = In October 1937 the new edition of *A Vision* – on which W.B.Y. had been working assiduously for the previous twelve years – was published: "As I turn the pages I find here & there the best prose I have written & much passion."[602]

Jupiter's transits of the other angles aren't as definite as are those to the Ascendant (dubiety is indicated by ?? below), so they will just be summarized briefly here.

Jupiter conjunct MC (CHEERING events which give reason to HOPE):

10/26/1876 = Autumn 1876 eleven year-old W.B.Y. lived with his father at a country place out in nature. [24]

2/13/1888-4/28/88R-10/07/88 = The year 1888 was actually a bad time for W.B.Y. financially, and he was depressed and exhausted. But in September 1888 his first real book, *Irish Fairy Tales*, was published and was well received.[76-7]

1/17/1900-6/10/00R-9/14/00 = ?? W.B.Y.'s mother died 1/3/1900;[223] also for most of 1900 he was involved in a power struggle in the Order of the Golden Dawn, which led to its dissolution and reconstruction (none of this fits the Jupiter symbolism; but Saturn was conjunct the DESC by primary direction at this time as well).

12/30/1911 = The production of W.B.Y.'s play *Countess Cathleen* took place on 12/14/1911, and was a great success.[456]

12/13/1923 = W.B.Y. received the Nobel Prize for literature on 12/10/1923,[396] which was not only a great honor but a tremendous financial relief for the next ten years.

11/28/1935 = On 11/28/1935 W.B.Y. left for Majorca with his Swami guru.[535]

Jupiter conjunct DESC (CHEERING events which bring COOPERATION):

9/26/1883-1/16/84R-5/21/84 = In May 1884 W.B.Y. entered art school (not Trinity College, as expected of him),[36] [89] through 1886. Here he met George Russell (A.E.), who became his lifelong friend and supporter.[90]

9/04/1895-3/01/96R-4/17/96 = In February 1896 W.B.Y. moved into his own flat[475]; and he finally became lovers with his girlfriend Olivia Shakespear (at long last lost his virginity).[158]

8/18/1907 = ?? W.B.Y. spent that summer writing at Coole, his friend Lady Augusta Gregory's country home.[370]

8/02/1919 = ?? He spent that summer writing at his home Ballylee.[156]

7/17/1931 = ?? In May 1931 in London W.B.Y. received an honorary degree from Oxford, with a dinner in his honor.[418]

Jupiter conjunct IC (CHEERING events which strengthen RESOLUTION):

5/10/1882 = ?? In 1882 W.B.Y. was writing poetry,[34] and it was the year of the awakening of his sex drive.[79]

4/22/1894 = On 4/16/1894 W.B.Y. met Olivia Shakespear and began courting her (eventually he lost his virginity with her).[152-3]{74} In late April 1894 both W.B.Y.'s *Land of Heart's Desire* and George Bernard Shaw's *Arms and the Man* opened on a double bill. *Arms* was a huge success; *Land* a failure. This began an intense Shaw/Yeats rivalry,[141][221-22] in addition to a rivalry for Florence

Farr, the leading lady. W.B.Y. consoled himself thinking he did not want to be popular.

8/18/1905-11/02/05R-4/04/06 = ?? This entire year there was a power struggle within his theatrical company. He was vindicated on 4/16/1906 when his production of *On Baile's Strand* was a big success.[346]

7/21/1917-12/15/17R-3/09/18 = On 10/20/1917 W.B.Y. married Georgie Hyde, who immediately began channeling the text of what later became W.B.Y.'s occult masterpiece, *A Vision*.[101, 103-4] W.B.Y. spent the next twenty years on this project, and in the end produced a masterpiece which contains an all-encompassing system of symbolism which has geometrical, astrological, psychological, metaphysical, and historical components – a model of the entire universe: "all thought, all history and the difference between man and man."

7/01/1929 = ?? Moved from Italy (where his wife was bored and snappish) back to Dublin.[401]

Saturn's transits every 29 or 30 years are more spread out over time than Jupiter's – even if there is only one transit (as opposed to three – direct, retrograde, and direct) the effects of Saturn transits can unfold over a year (usually after the exact date of the transit), and produce far more profound changes in the life than Jupiter's transits. Notice that in the examples below the event associated with the transit usually occurred near in time to the first direct transit; but this is not always the case.

Saturn conjunct ASC (CHALLENGING events which give rise to a sense of REORIENTATION): 3/13/1873-7/14/73R-12/10/73 = reference is to the death of brother Robert on 3/3/1873. W.B.Y.'s mother went into a depression from which she never recovered: she was a cold and rejecting mother, and an emotional burden to her surviving children thereafter.[13,21] "My realization of death came when ... I was in the library when I heard feet running past and heard somebody say in the passage that my younger brother, Robert, had died. He had been ill for some days. ... Next day at breakfast I heard people telling how my mother and the servant had heard the banshee crying the night before he died. It must have been after this that I told my grandmother I did not want to go with her when she went to see old bedridden people because they would soon die."[55]

Saturn conjunct ASC (CHALLENGING events which give rise to a sense of REORIENTATION): 1/19/1903 = On 2/07/1903 W.B.Y. learned that his beloved, unattainable Maud Gonne was engaged to another man; and on 2/21/1903 she married him. W.B.Y. was completely shattered: "Since December 1898 his great powers of rationalization had been directed towards convincing himself that their 'spiritual' relationship was the better part of passion."<284> W.B.Y. wrote her: "I appeal to you in the name of 14 years of friendship to read this letter. It is perhaps the last thing I shall (write) you. … Your hands were put in mine & we were told to do a certain great work together. For all who undertake such tasks there comes a moment of extreme peril. I know now that you have come to your moment of peril."^164^ The destruction of W.B.Y.'s most cherished expectation was a major turning point in his life: thereafter he stopped being so involved in e.g. radical politics since he no longer lived his life to impress her but rather did his own thing. He now also became closer to Lady Augusta Gregory – his great friend, defender, benefactress, and literary collaborator.<288>

Saturn conjunct ASC (CHALLENGING events which give rise to a sense of REORIENTATION): 2/23/1932-8/13/32R-11/18/32 = On 5/23/1932 Lady Augusta Gregory died. "She has been to me mother, friend, sister, and brother. I cannot realize the world without her – she brought to my wavering thoughts steadfast nobility. All day the thought of losing her is like a conflagration in the rafters. Friendship is all the house I have."{160} This represented not only the loss of his best friend and literary and theatrical collaborator, but also the house where he spent his summers and did most of his writing – "the shifting of his life's centre of gravity:"<439> "These last days (Lady Augusta's daughter) was very kind to me, though we had not always been friends, unlocking without being asked the big room upstairs where I have slept & written when a young man, that I might look my last at the woods through its windows."<438> "He already knew, therefore, how cut adrift he himself would feel when his fellow romantic, her work done, vanished like the swan into darkness."<440> And in the years afterwards W.B.Y. sought summer refuge on the Riviera rather than at Lady Augusta's estate at Coole.

Saturn conjunct MC (CHALLENGING events which give the native reason to HOPE): 12/02/1897 = W.B.Y. was carrying forward a theatrical project in collaboration with Lady Augusta Gregory, whom he had met the preceding summer. She now became his patron, lending him money to get through the winter. "She also introduced him to a new level of London society. ... From his side, he provided artistic stimulation."<188> The work they carried out together in 1898 to obtain a venue for Irish national theater productions led to the founding of the Abbey Theatre six years later.

Saturn conjunct MC (CHALLENGING events which give the native reason to HOPE): 1/10/1927-5/28/27R-10/10/27 = In January 1927 W.B.Y. came down with influenza and inflammatory rheumatism and was in bed for a month and was recuperating through the spring.<338> Even though he wrote scarcely any poetry this year,<385> "From now on he knew that time could not be wasted; he was more and more fiercely impatient with any impediments, obstructions, evasions which might come between his work and what he wanted it to say; and he would pursue that lost vigour with a single-minded commitment, determined to demonstrate that he could recapture the force of youth in his life as well as in his work. The aftershock of 'first serious illness' reverberated not only in his subsequent writing, but in the experiments with politics, philosophy and love which would mark the next phase of his life."<356>

Saturn conjunct DESC (CHALLENGING events which emphasize issues of COOPERATION): 8/18/87-3/10/88R-4/20/88 (also see Pluto conjunct IC below) = his family had just moved from Dublin to London, which he disliked, but he began to meet many people with whom he would collaborate later, such as MacGregor Mathers (whose Hermetic Students – later the Order of the Golden Dawn – W.B.Y. joined on 8/9/1887); and George Bernard Shaw with whom he would later found an Irish theater. On a trip to Dublin in the fall of 1887 he stayed with writer Katherine Tynan: "I wrote many letters to Katherine Tynan, a very plain woman, and ... I began to wonder if she was in love with me and if it was my duty to marry her."{32} A flurry of literary activities in early 1888 left him near collapse from nervous exhaustion,<74> but he was now starting to make a reputation and money.

Saturn conjunct DESC (CHALLENGING events which emphasize issues of COOPERATION): 10/17/1916-12/08/16R-

6/24/17 = W.B.Y. had spent the winter of 1916-17 exchanging letters with Maud Gonne's daughter Iseult in the futile hope of marrying her as a vicar for her mother.<90> Otherwise, 1917 was a year in which his life gelled, things came together for him. It was also a period of religiosity for him,<79> and he lived in the hope and prospect of revelation (which did indeed happen a few months later when he married Georgie Hyde, who began channeling his mystical masterpiece, *A Vision*). On 6/30/1917 W.B.Y. purchased Ballylee, a castle which was the fulfillment of a lifelong dream (and also the first home he ever owned).<85>

Saturn conjunct IC (CHALLENGING events which strengthen the native's RESOLUTION): 6/27/83-12/31/83R-3/08/84 = In the autumn of 1883 W.B.Y.'s family moved to cheaper lodgings "crowding and indignity."<30> He left high school – already conceived of himself as a poet;<33> and in the spring of 1884 he wrote his first play, *Love and Death*.[86]

Saturn conjunct IC (CHALLENGING events which strengthen the native's RESOLUTION): 5/03/1913 = In early May 1913 the possibility of university chair of poetry came up; he applied, but politics kept it from him.<484> (N.b.: note that even when Saturn giveth – even when something good seems to be offered under a Saturn transit – Saturn usually taketh away again). Also in late May 1913 his girlfriend became pregnant, which would mean having to marry her.<488> He was "horror struck ... I am living under much strain and anxiety." By the end of June it was revealed that she wasn't pregnant at all (sometimes when Saturn makes bad things happen, they turn out to be not such bugaboos after all).

Uranus transits produce sudden, unexpected shocks which disrupt and disorganize the native's life; but which in the end give the person much greater scope and freedom of action. Because Uranus' transits point to specific upheavals in the life, they are much easier to pinpoint in time than the transits of Saturn, Neptune, and Pluto.

Uranus conjunct MC (SURPRISING events which give the native reason to HOPE): 12/22/98-7/18/99R-9/6/99 = On 12/8/1898 Maud Gonne – W.B.Y.'s fantasy woman – finally admitted everything: that that she had been lying to W.B.Y. all along – that while she was teasing him and leading him on, she was actually the mistress of a Frenchman and had had two children by him. W.B.Y. was thrown into utter confusion: "MG is here & I understand everything now. I feal (sic) like a very battered ship with the masts broken off at the stump."[202] "All I have gained through so many years is staked against all that I have ever hoped for."[204] Meanwhile this year he was mounting a theatrical production which opened to great success on 5/8/1899, and was the beginning of the realization of his dream of an Irish national theater (this came true five years later when transiting Uranus opposed its natal place in W.B.Y.'s horoscope).

Uranus conjunct ASC (SURPRISING events which give rise to a sense of REORIENTATION): 1/30/12-9/5/12R/-11/11/12 = On 4/9/1912 W.B.Y.'s spirit guide, Leo Africanus, made his first appearance at a séance: "It was perfectly dark. We were seated a very few minutes when we were sprinkled with some liquid – I felt it on my head and hands, a few drops. Medium said it was a baptism. Then there came a very loud voice through the trumpet. It had come for 'Mr. Gates.' Or so the medium heard the voice. I said that was me. Then the voice said, 'I have been with you from childhood. We want to use your hand and brain.'"{264} W.B.Y. spent most of the rest of the year attending séances and taking note of what Leo was telling him. This was the beginning of what became his wife's channeling of spirits five years later, which led eventually to W.B.Y.'s magnum opus *A Vision*.

The transits of Neptune and Pluto spread their effects out for years, so it's not always easy to associate them with particular events. They instead indicate trends in the life, subtle changes of direction. When they do indicate specific events, it can take several years to unravel or work through the consequences.

Neptune conjunct IC (UNUSUAL events which strengthen the native's RESOLUTION): 8/03/89-10/11/89R-5/25/90-1/14/91 R-3/14/91 = In spite of his close friendship with founder Madame Blavatsky, W.B.Y. now resigned from the Theosophical Society since his thinking was too independent: "Presently I was called before an official of the Section and asked with great politeness to resign. I was causing disturbance, causing disquiet in some way. I said, 'By teaching an abstract system without experiment or evidence you are making your pupils dogmatic and you are taking them out of life.'"{24} He joined the more experimentative Hermetic Order of the Golden Dawn, "Now too I learned a practice, a form of meditation that has perhaps been the intellectual chief influence on my life up to perhaps my fortieth year."{27} During this period he was also trying to woo Maud Gonne and he became politically radicalized in order to impress her. He also now began dreaming of creating an Irish national literature, which culminated thirteen years later with the Abbey Theatre: "I knew that the romance of Irish public life had gone, and that the young, perhaps for many years to come, would seek some unpolitical form for national feeling."[115] This was also the time when W.B.Y. began to be successful: by late 1890 – early 1891 he knew all his major literary projects would be published in 1891

Neptune conjunct DESC (UNUSUAL events which lead to COOPERATION): 9/22/1914-12/15/14R-7/18/15-3/21/16R-4/30/16 = He was writing his *Memoirs* and was in a reflective, introspective mood. "In his poems of early 1915 WBY returned to the sense of his life as a 'past' woven into a pattern. ... the theme of memory pervades the poems."[10] He also now conceived the idea of purchasing his dream home Ballylee (the first home he ever owned – which he bought in 1917). But perhaps the "Neptuniest" event of this period was his Stopping-the-World:

> My fiftieth year had come and gone
> I sat, a solitary man,
> In a crowded London shop,
> An open book, an empty cup
> On the marble tabletop.
>
> While on the shop and street I gazed
> My body of a sudden blazed!
> And twenty minutes more or less
> It seemed so great, my happiness,
> That I was blessed – and could bless.

In a letter to Maud Gonne in 1927 W.B.Y. wrote: "I hate many things but I do my best, & once some fifteen years ago, for I think one whole hour, I was free from hate. Like Faust I said 'stay moment' but in vain. I think it was the only happiness I have ever known."[344]

Pluto conjunct IC (REVEALING events which strengthen the native's RESOLUTION): 6/26/87-11/14/87 R-5/14/88-1//08/89 R-3/26/89 = Corresponds to W.B.Y.'s move with his family from Dublin to London (which occurred in April 1887). At first he detested it: "this hateful London where you cannot go five paces without seeing some wretched object broken either by wealth or poverty."[59] It was this period that inspired his poem *The Lake Isle of Innisfree* about the joys of country vs. city living. But in the spring of 1888 the family moved to much better lodgings; and that fall his first book was published. He joined several fraternal organizations (of poets and mystics), and began to find his feet and make a reputation for himself. On a return to Dublin in the winter of 1887-88 he found it to be a small pond compared to London – he had outgrown that world (he didn't return to Dublin for three years).[73]

Pluto conjunct DESC (REVEALING events which elicit the COOPERATION of others): 10/05/1937-11/26/37 R-8/02/38-2/08/39 R-6/13/39 = The last year of his life (he died peacefully on 1/28/1939), which was a relatively happy time (after several years of illness and depression). He gave instructions that he wished to be buried in Sligo Ireland with "Just my name & dates & these lines: Cast a cold eye / On life, on death / Horseman pass by."[631] He wrote a play, *The Death of Cuchulain*, as an allegory for his own death; and he even began a new love affair during this period (with his wife's knowledge and acceptance). In the words of his biographer, "Like Cuchulain in his play, he prepared to face into the other world, attended by the women he most cared for."[649]

Turning Points

Much of our daily lives consists of schedules, bustling about, taking things for granted, and not paying much attention to what we're doing. Except for feelings of vague disgruntlement with how things are going or wistful yearnings for some goal we hope and imagine is just beyond the horizon, we rarely stop to take stock of ourselves, to ask ourselves whether we're on the right track and doing our best. Every now and again, however, an event occurs which jolts us out of our customary routines and forces us to consciously reflect on what we're about. These are the sorts of events symbolized by the transiting planets' changes of station (shifts in motion from direct to retrograde, or retrograde to direct).

Transiting changes of station are, quite literally, turning points: they symbolize a pause in our everyday routine in which our habitual modes of thought and action are suspended, and we become conscious of our true feelings, which we usually ignore or repress. The event symbolized by a station may be a major spiritual breakthrough or a minor memo from the cosmos to the effect that yes, things are okay, all is as it should be. Stations highlight a need to be fluid, to just relax and let go.

The days when transiting planets change station are times of great karmic flux for everyone in the world, but people who have planets in their natal charts on or opposite the point of the station are particularly affected. We will use orbs of plus or minus a day and a half in time, and plus or minus two degrees in longitude. In other words, the event produced by the station should occur within thirty-six hours of the exact time of the station (though it's much more likely to occur on the day before rather than the day after); and to be effective the station should fall no more than two degrees in longitude from the conjunction or opposition with a point in the natal horoscope (squares are sometimes effective; and three-degree orbs sometimes work too; but it's best to keep the analysis clear and simple).

The basic felicity or infelicity or the event seems to be more a matter of the condition of the natal planet being contacted rather than whether the station conjoins or opposes that planet. All transits (not just stations) to a natal planet dignified by sign or well-aspected will usually produce happy events; and all transits to a planet debilitated by sign or afflicted will usually produce difficulties.

There's a very slight difference in flavor between the two types of station (stationary turning retrograde, and stationary turning direct). Both types of station move you beyond something that was holding you back, but in a general way the retrograde station is unexpected (a new point of departure) whereas the direct station is long-awaited (gets you over a hump).

Whether the event produced by the station is of major or minor significance in your life, it usually gets you past a sticking point or hang-up. Dr. Marc Edmund Jones called this a "critical regrasp of experience" – blocked energies are liberated and you must let go of your habitual concerns and worries, and fly with your gut-level intuition. There is often a sense of relief or release of pent-up emotions. For example, you may get to tell someone exactly what's on your mind, as in those impassioned dialogues between lovers or spouses that go on all night long.

At the same time, stations propel you forward willy-nilly, move you beyond your limitations, force you to shift your plans or begin a new phase. For example, you may make a firm commitment to some new life direction, or you may meet someone for the first time who later turns out to be very important in your life. Indeed, it is often possible to predict the kind of relationships which will be affected by a station (or any transit) from the symbolism of the natal planet involved (e.g. sun symbolizes father, boss, husband, authorities; moon symbolizes mother, wife, employees; Mercury symbolizes children, siblings, neighbors, coworkers; etc.).

The retrograde stations can be significant as auguries or dress rehearsals for a long series of transits by a slow-moving planet to a natal body. The question arises, when there are multiple transits by a slow planet over the same point – direct, retrograde, direct; or even direct, retrograde, direct, retrograde, direct – which one or ones will better time the expected event?

There doesn't seem to be any hard and fast rule here; sometimes only one of the transits is effective, and sometimes all of them work as different stages in the unfoldment of a particular line of related events or relationships. In my own experience the retrograde transits are the least likely to be effective, but Colin James, for one, claims precisely the opposite. If one of the transits occurs at about the same time as a transit of Mars or a lunation, for example, over the same natal planet, then this may be the trigger that sets off the main event. Generally speaking, however, the first direct transit sets into motion forces or potentials which are consummated (or exhausted) at the time of the last direct transit. The point of this digression is that the events signified by a series of transits by a slow planet over the same natal point are often prefigured in some way by a retrograde station almost, but not quite, at the position of the natal body. So careful observation of the days when these stations occur may provide a clue to the events to come in the year or so following.

In the interpretation of the likely effect of a station, the transiting planet which is changing station symbolizes the impulse coming from without (the kind of event which might be expected); and the natal planet which it contacts symbolizes the feeling activated within the person (the emotional response). For keywords see the *Table of Keywords for the Transiting and Natal Planets* on page 118 and the tables of Detailed Interpretations given in the "Interpretation of Transits" essay. Quotations are from the natives' memoirs or biographies.

Mercury: ENCOURAGING – An event which changes your attitude, viewpoint, or self-image. You see yourself in a new light, in a new role vis à vis other people, and need tact, aplomb, and confidence in your own abilities.

Example: Winston Churchill – T Mercury SD conjunct natal Sun = 12/16/1899 (ENCOURAGING event which accentuates DETERMINATION).

(He had just escaped from a Boer prisoner of war camp, and was being hidden in a mine by a Mr. Howard, a British sympathizer). "On the 16th, the fifth day of escape, Mr. Howard informed me he had made a plan to get me out of the country. Wool was packed in great bales and would fill two or three large trucks. The bales could be so packed as to leave a small place in the center of the truck in which I could be concealed. Did I agree to take this chance?

"I was more worried about this than almost anything that had happened to me so far in my adventure. When by extraordinary chance one has gained some great advantage or prize and actually had it in one's possession and been enjoying it for several days, the idea of losing it becomes almost insupportable. I had really come to count upon freedom as a certainty, and the idea of having to put myself in a position in which I should be perfectly helpless, absolutely at the caprice of a searching party at the frontier, was profoundly harassing.

"However, in the end I accepted the proposal of my generous rescuer, and arrangements were made accordingly."

Venus: SOCIABLE – Encounters, gatherings, or events which play upon your affections. They may symbolize a poignant moment in a personal relationship, or creative, artistic expression.

Example: Anne Morrow Lindbergh – T Venus SR conjunct natal Mercury = 6/7/1932 (SOCIABLE event which accentuates UNDERSTANDING).

(Three months after her child's kidnapping, and a month after his dead body was found): Diary 6/6/1932: "Came back to find Skean and Bogy (her dogs) lost, gone since Saturday night, probably stolen. After our desperate efforts to avoid it by building a pen and keeping them in the house until it was finished. It was finished the evening they went off.

"I feel so hurt and terribly tired, terribly tired of perpetually trying to 'think of other things.' It is such a little thing, but completely in tune with my insecurity and lack of faith in *anything*. I am tired of fighting."

Diary 6/7/1932: "C. came in and handed me a note: 'Mrs. Lindbergh, the dogs are here.' Then Skean wriggled in, showing his teeth in a smile, rolling on his back on the floor."

Mars: FORCEFUL – Intense involvements with other people (though not necessarily conflictive). You have to take a position, stand up for yourself, be willing to fully commit yourself. Good day to confront or to tell someone off.

Example: Che Guevara – T Mars SR opposition natal Jupiter = 3/8/1967 (FORCEFUL event which accentuates FULFILLMENT).

(Fighting a guerrilla war in Bolivia): Diary 3/7/1967: "Four months. The men are becoming more and more discouraged, seeing that we are reaching the end of our supplies, but not the end of the trail. Food: three and a half birds and the rest of the *palmito*; from tomorrow on, only canned goods; then the milk, which is the end."

Diary 3/8/1967: "Inti and Ricardo dived into the water. Inti had difficulties and almost drowned; Ricardo helped him and they finally reached shore and disappeared. All afternoon went by and they didn't appear. I was very worried: two valuable comrades were exposed to danger and we didn't know what had happened to them."

Diary 3/9/1967: "About 16 hours, after a trying watch, (Inti and Ricardo) appeared. They brought back one pork, bread, rice, sugar, coffee, some canned goods, and fermented corn, etc. We had a little feast."

Jupiter: CHEERING – An opportunity to lighten up and take a positive, optimistic attitude towards your current situation in life; let go of worries and look at the bigger picture; join together with others and take a detached, generous, and conciliatory overview.

Example: William Butler Yeats T Jupiter SD conjunct MC opposition Mercury = 8/2/1912 (CHEERING event which gives HOPE and UNDERSTANDING)

"On 2 August he departed to (his beloved Maud) Gonne's Normandy house, exhausted by excitement and illness but determined to work on what he already conceived as 'a new volume of verse'. His fortnight there was spent in an intense frenzy of writing. ... his attempt to distance himself from his love for Gonne (by immersing himself in writing) was in the end confounded by her power to mesmerize and enchant."[467]

Saturn: CHALLENGING – Obstacles which have to be confronted directly. You cannot shrink from difficulties but must hold your ground and secure your position in life (good for making a new start after things have bogged down).

Example: Richard Nixon – T Saturn SD opposition natal Neptune = 9/27/1961 (CHALLENGING event which accentuates ATTUNEMENT).

(His decision to run for governor of California): "I was more convinced than ever that my first intuition was right: I should not run for governor in 1962. Hall said, 'Either you run or you're finished in national politics. Who will remember Dick Nixon? You can only win in '64 if you run and win for governor now.'

"My own political judgment at that point told me that Kennedy would be almost unbeatable in 1964. The real problem was that I had no great desire to be governor of California. Equally compelling was my knowledge of how strongly Pat felt against my running.

"Pat, as I expected, took a strong stand against it. We talked about it for almost an hour. Finally I went upstairs to my study and started to make some notes for the press conference, announcing that I had decided not to run for governor.

"Half an hour after Pat came in. 'I have thought about it some more,' she said, 'and I am more convinced than ever that if you run it will be a terrible mistake. But if you weight everything and still decide to run, I will support your decision.'

"After she had gone, I tore off the top sheet of paper and threw it into the wastebasket. On a fresh page I began making notes for an announcement that I had decided to run."

Uranus: SURPRISING – Unexpected (serendipitous or calamitous) events which shake you out of your ordinary routines and doldrums – a message to relax and go with the flow.

Example: Albert Einstein – T Uranus SD conjunct natal Jupiter = 11/8/1919 (SURPRISING event which accentuates FULFILLMENT).

(His theory of relativity had been confirmed, and the results announced to the international press the previous day): "Einstein awoke in Berlin on the morning of November 7, 1919, to find himself famous. The publicity was 'so bad that I can hardly breathe, let alone get down to sensible work.' Throughout the day Einstein was visited by an almost continuous stream of reporters. He genuinely did not like it. But he soon realized that there is a time for compromise as well as a time for standing firm. There was, moreover, one way in which the distasteful interest could be turned to good use. So there were no free photographs of Einstein; as one reporter later noted, 'These, his wife told me, are sold for the benefit of the starving children of Vienna.'"

Neptune: UNUSUAL – Odd, out-of-the-ordinary occurrences; strange vibrations and undercurrents. May provoke powerful attractions or repulsions on your part.

Example: Betty Ford – T Neptune SD opposition natal Jupiter = 8/19/1974; Jerry Ford – T Neptune SD opposition natal Venus and conjunct natal moon = 8/19/1974 (UNUSUAL event which accentuates FULFILLMENT <Betty>; INTIMACY and ASSURANCE <Jerry>).

(They moved into the White House): "A helicopter picks us up and takes us directly to the White House. It's the first time, and it's a very strange feeling.

"That morning, our house in Alexandria had been left in utter chaos, crates and cartons everywhere, chunks of our lives uprooted and labeled for storage. It'd been a very traumatic experience for me. That night we came back to new living quarters in perfect order.

"Our bed and bedding and pillows are in the First Lady's Bedroom, and the room usually referred to as the President's Bedroom has been made into a private sitting room for us. That night Jerry and I get into bed, and Jerry looks around and laughs. 'It's the best public housing I've ever seen.' he says."

Pluto: DECISIVE – Events of a disorienting, transformative nature. You have to take command, rise to the occasion, get on top of things.

Example: Timothy Leary – T Pluto SR conjunct natal Saturn = 12/21/1965 (DECISIVE event which accentuates DISCIPLINE).

(His baronial crashpad at Millbrook had increasingly become the object of police surveillance): "We agreed that we had gone about as far as we could go at Millbrook. The fun had stopped. The money, energy, able bodies, and utopian idealism needed to maintain a sixty-four room castle had been dissipated. I announced that I would close Millbrook and retire to Mexico to write the story of our adventures.

"On December 20, 1965, we turned off the water and power, locked the doors, and piled into the new leased station wagon heading for the Yucatan."

A Day of Reckoning

Solar return charts are cast for the birthday each year – for the moment when the sun returns to the exact spot in the zodiac which it occupied at the moment you were born – and for the place where you happen to be on your birthday. Supposedly, planets exactly conjunct angles in the solar return augur important events in the year to come; but I've only found this to work sporadically (e.g. Mars conjoined the Ascendant in Theodore Roosevelt's solar return for 1900, the year he acceded to the presidency). Nonetheless there is one aspect of the theory of solar returns which does work very well indeed.

The technique under consideration produces, in most cases, some important dates in the year after the solar return (the birthday). Moreover, the calculations involved are so simple that you can do them in your head. You don't need to know your exact birth time to employ this technique; you don't even need a horoscope – only an ephemeris for the current year. All you need to do is to observe the positions of the planets (other than the sun and moon) in longitude on your current birthday. Then, scan ahead in the ephemeris to see whether any of these planets, due to retrograde motion, will return to these same positions by direct motion in the months after your birthday. The day that a planet returns to the longitude that it held on your birthday that year there will usually be a noticeable event whose nature is symbolized by the planet involved.

For example, Theodore Roosevelt's 1900 solar return contained these positions:
Mercury = 27°SC51' and returned to this position on 12/10/1900
Neptune = 29°GE05' and returned to this position on 6/24/1901
Pluto = 17°GE25' and returned to this position on 6/20/1901

When a transiting planet returns to the same longitude that it held on your birthday, you usually will experience an unblocking of energies or a release of tension that has been bottled up. Emotions which have been held in check come to the surface. The event which occurs that day can be major or minor; oddly enough, in this technique, transiting Mars, Venus, and Mercury (respectively) tend to produce more important events than do Jupiter, Saturn, Uranus – probably because they occur more rarely. These transits bring a change in your normal state of affairs which forces you to reflect upon your purpose, or the meaning of your life. The events which occur on these days show you that you can't take things for granted; they strip away your confusion and doubts and reveal your underlying feelings and motives. These transits produce days of reckoning, in which things become quite clear, stand out in bold relief, and require objective thinking and decisive action.

When there are two transits to the birthday longitude by the same planet (i.e., the first one retrograde and the second one direct), then usually it is the last, direct transit which produces the event. However it is a good idea to note the date of the first, retrograde transit as well, since occasionally it has the primary role. Also, it can happen that Mercury or Venus return to their birthday positions in the month or two prior to the succeeding birthday. These dates are not significant: it is only the returns of Mercury or Venus within the month or two *after* the current birthday which produce noticeable events. Also, these transits should produce their effects on the exact date that they are due; or on the day before or after (in the cases of the three outermost planets, the effect may be two days off). The following examples are taken from the subjects' diaries or memoirs.

Mercury's return during the month or so after your current birthday to the longitude it occupied on your birthday usually brings you a new impetus to action. Often this is the result of an unexpected communication. For example, on his Mercury day on 7/22/1915 William Butler Yeats received his first message via automatic writing from his spirit guide, which occupied his attention for many years to come: "He asked me to write him a letter addressed to him ... giving all my doubts about spiritual things and then to write a reply as from him to me." Mercury's return may bring a complete shift in your plans or your outlook. You may see yourself in a different light, and have to exceed your normal expectations of yourself. On her Mercury return on 7/12/1935, Anne Morrow Lindbergh was visited by Harold Nicholson, who encouraged her to become a writer: "H.N. talks about writing and how if you want terribly to do a thing you probably have it in you. 'I can! I can!' pounds inside of me, so loud that I feel it is bursting out of me, and yet I feel I must not show it because it is unproved and untried. Caring about writing and not having proved anything is like being in love and not being able to show it. And all the time it is pushing inside of you – that giant." Mercury's return demands a new perspective on your affairs, a new approach or way of looking at things, a reordering of your priorities. You must give conscious consideration to what it is most important to you in life.

Venus' return to the position it occupied on your birthday usually brings encounters or meetings with friendly, like-minded people – people you really click with. Sometimes old ties are renewed; sometimes you meet people who become important later on in your life; and this can occur in the unlikeliest places. On my own Venus day on 10/21/1967, in the midst of the multitude gathered for the Peace March on Washington, I met a woman with whom I fell in love and later wound up living with for a year. Venus' return may also bring you a very poignant moment in an ongoing intimate relationship. It may bring help from other people, especially women. Anne Morrow Lindbergh's Venus day 8/18/1932 occurred two days after her second son's birth, which made a temporary lull of exaltation in the ongoing depression caused by her first son's kidnapping and murder the previous spring: "Slight reaction to elation; talk with Miss Cummings about case. I find that I have accepted, swallowed whole, one picture of it, and the slightest shift in that, the moving of a trifle, a different light, again makes it unbearable. The weather puts me back into last winter's mood and I realize, 'It is still there, it will always be with me.' Mother told me: 'If only he were here to see his little brother!' I love her for it and cried at such heartbreaking sweetness and understanding – cried and cried." The day of Venus' return brings with it spontaneous fellowship, warmth, and good feelings.

Mars' return to the position it occupied on your birthday occurs very rarely (once – or perhaps twice, spaced 2 years apart – every 14 – 15 years). Your Mars day usually calls for decisive action, or the need to deal with conflict or obstruction. William Butler Yeats' Mars return on 8/18/1922 occurred at the height of the Irish civil war, when the bridge by his home was blown up by rebels, flooding the ground floors of his house. His wife commented: "The men gave us 1½ hours warning. I consulted them as to where the safest place would be to bring the children & maids & they said half way up the tower. ... After two minutes, two roars came & then a hail of falling masonry. Since then we have both felt rather ill & our hearts both hopping & stopping." Sometimes the conflict stems from your own negligence or intransigence; thus self-restraint and caution are good counsel for the Mars day, since often some sort of resolution or modus vivendi can be worked out. Mars' return to its birthday position highlights a need for tact and reserve in your dealings with other people and the world around you.

Jupiter's return to the position it occupied on your birthday usually marks a very sociable time, when you join with others in some sort of endeavor. Anne Morrow Lindbergh's Jupiter day on 9/21/1924 was her first day at college: "The end of the first day! ... Such a wonderful feeling. I want to *hug* the room! I went to chapel this morning with Elisabeth and walked out arm in arm with someone! It was very nice. I love the walk past the President's, every morning." You may be presented with an opportunity to be helpful to others on your Jupiter day, or you may receive help from them such as pay raises, promotions, etc. Jupiter also favors travel and initiating new projects generally. On Richard Nixon's Jupiter day 3/13/1954 he delivered an important speech on Senator McCarthy: "This was not a speech I looked forward to writing or delivering. No matter how it was done, it was bound to alienate large segments of the party and large segments of the public. What it really involved was what Eisenhower himself had purposely avoided for two years: determining the administration's policy on McCarthy." After the speech was successfully delivered, "Eisenhower called me from Camp David, with his congratulations. ... My speech seemed to have buoyed him by giving voice to his own frustrations over McCarthy and by providing some focus for the administration's efforts."

Saturn's return to position it occupied on your birthday usually brings resistance or intransigence on the part of other people, especially Saturnine people – parents, employers, or older people generally. Saturn often brings frustration, or a feeling of being stressed and under pressure. Anne Morrow Lindbergh's Saturn day on 10/9/1928 was her first date with Charles Lindbergh: "It was *awful* – simply terrible – nothing that I expected. I feel so miserably unhappy and uncomfortable and angry – and flat. ... I had the feeling all the time that it was the most *hideous* bother for him, he didn't want to go, it was embarrassing for him. He was just doing it out of a sense of duty and not disguising it a bit. ... I feel terribly sorry for him – that he's in for me – and yet on the other hand a little insulted: I'm not used to being treated like a spoonful of medicine that's got to be taken!" Saturn forces you to break the habits or customs which put limits on what you can do; in many cases this means to submit and let things pass without protest, no matter how unjust the situation seems to you. On Richard Nixon's Saturn day 4/16/1974, special Watergate prosecutor Jaworski asked the U.S. District Court to subpoena the President's tapes after he had refused to turn them over voluntarily (which directly led to the president's downfall). On occasion, something apparently quite favorable or opportune comes along when Saturn returns to its birthday place, but usually nothing comes of it in the end, or its potentialities peter out over the next week or so. The best counsel for the day of Saturn's return is just to sit tight and let events take their course.

Uranus' return to the position it occupied on your birthday, often brings sudden crises: matters seem to boil over or come to a head. Sometimes this is positive, a heady sense of liberation or freedom: on Richard Nixon's Uranus day 7/27/1960 he was nominated Republican presidential candidate. However, Uranus can also cause a sense of disassociation, as if everything was going to pieces: Richard Nixon's Uranus day 10/8/1973 brought Vice-President Agnew's resignation. Uranus seems to force you to face up to the realities, and face up to them alone. The week before his Uranus day 8/6/1889 Theodore Roosevelt had been scourged by the press, and now he was called to answer charges he had made against the administration before President Harrison, who rejected him soundly: "'It was a golden chance to take a good stand; and it had been lost.' Roosevelt wrote bitterly."

Neptune's return to the position it occupied on your birthday usually marks a breakthrough in your current affairs which brings some of your innermost feelings to the fore. For better or worse, Neptune's return thoroughly transforms your frame of reference, facing you with new potentials as well as new uncertainties. On Richard Nixon's Neptune day 11/6/62 he lost the California gubernatorial election: "For sixteen years, ever since the Hiss case, you've had a lot of – a lot of fun – that you've had an opportunity to attack me, and I think I've given as good as I've taken. ... You won't have Nixon to kick around anymore, because, gentlemen, this is my last press conference." Neptune's return confronts you with a new world of possibilities in which your intuition and instincts come to the surface. On Theodore Roosevelt's Neptune day 6/5/1896 he had a showdown with a political enemy: "Roosevelt's face darkened to deep red, and beads of sweat stood out on his forehead as the maddening voice droned on, stinging him with insults that passed too quickly for retort. The two men stared steadily into each other's eyes, forgetful of other people in the room, obsessed by their struggle for supremacy. ... One of the items of agenda awaiting discussion was the new police revolver ... Reporters watched in fascination as (TR) absentmindedly fondled it, then, still talking, picked it up and shook it 'slowly and impressively' in Parker's face."

Pluto's return to the position it occupied on your birthday often brings a marked intensification or a heightened sense of urgency in your current affairs. Pluto may force you to come to grips with some of your fears; sometimes Pluto forces you to lower your expectations or take a step backwards. On Richard Nixon's Pluto day 10/03/1974, while hospitalized for treatment of phlebitis, he learned the House of Representatives had voted to slash by 75 % the funds he had requested for his transition to private life. On the other hand, Pluto's intensity is not always bad: it can also symbolize a triumphal breakthrough. On Theodore Roosevelt's Pluto day 6/23/1904 he was re-nominated presidential candidate by acclamation: "He met a congratulatory crowd of newsmen. He invited them in for 'an Executive session' and tilted back laughing in his big chair as they fired questions at him. Prophecies, jokes, reminiscences, and indiscretions poured out freely, enchantingly. Roosevelt asked that nothing he said be printed. And nothing ever was."

Lunations

Many of us find our everyday lives to be humdrum and boring. On the one hand, we do need the sense of security that our everyday routines give us; on the other hand, we too easily become the slaves of our customary moods and habits, allowing our lives to degenerate into a zombie-like existence.

In astrology, all habits – memory, everything in our lives that is familiar and routine – are ruled by the moon. When our moons don't function properly, we become "lunatics" – lost in a world where nothing is familiar any longer, where we can't recognize anything, because we can't systematically access a memory inventory to determine whether anything like what is happening to us right now has ever happened to us before. Newborns perforce deal with the world in this fashion, although even they are born with biological and racial memory (e.g., the urges to suck, cry, and be cuddled).

The aspect of everyday life ruled by the moon is the total of our customary moods (habitual feelings about ourselves and the world around us). For example, we might customarily walk around all day long feeling angry, or worried, or flighty, or grumpy and complainy, or serious, or devil-may-care, or whatever. The way we habitually feel about ourselves and the world is the glue that holds everything together for us; it is the source of our sense of security and stability in life (what W. B. Yeats termed *Will*). However, our customary moods are also the source of all our hidebound resistance to change: our laziness, inertia, and impulse to turn aside from anything new. They screen the true joyous impulses of our hearts and impair our sense of freedom.

The lunations – the new and full moons each month – are the points in time when the solar principle of decision can be brought to bear upon the lunar principle of memory. They are the epochs when we can most easily make a conscious decision to shake off stodgy habits and ways of feeling, and reach out to grasp a little joy. Although the times of new and full moons are significant for all beings on the earth, they have a particular importance for those people who have planets in their natal horoscopes located within a degree of conjunction or opposition to the point of the lunation.

In this analysis it doesn't make that much difference whether the lunation is a new or a full moon, nor whether it contacts a natal planet by conjunction or opposition. In a general sort of way, new moons symbolize new beginnings, whereas full moons symbolize a coming to completion or fruition. Similarly, oppositions may have more of a flavor of apparent conflict or estrangement to be overcome than do conjunctions. These effects, however, are not usually that important. Nor does it matter that much whether the lunation happens to be an eclipse (eclipses are traditionally more important in mundane astrology than in natal astrology – but see the essay "A Baffling Problem").

What is important, however, is the condition of the natal planet contacted by sign and aspect. The effect of a lunation is an impulse towards joy, so when the natal planet contacted is in an unfavorable sign or afflicted by other planets, the tendency will be to resist joy, to reject the opportunity outright, or else not to notice it when it occurs. If you list the events produced by lunations in your own life according to the natal planet contacted, you'll find that some natal planets work better than others: some produce uniformly important events, and others don't have much effect at all.

Because of the peculiar nature of the lunation cycle (as we shall see in connection with presidential elections later on), the distribution of points in the zodiac where lunations fall is not random, but tends to hit the same spots over and over. In other words, in a typical horoscope, some planets will be activated by lunations many times in the course of a life, whereas others may never be activated at all. And when the same planet is activated by lunations, the same types of events tend to recur.

In the horoscope of Prince Charles, for example, the natal Descendant was activated by the lunations preceding the birth of Princess Anne, the death of King George VI and accession of Queen Elizabeth, and the birth of Prince Andrew. In the horoscope of Queen Elizabeth II, the natal Mars-Jupiter conjunction opposite Neptune was activated by lunations preceding the births of Princess Anne, Prince Andrew, and Prince Edward.

Lunations which conjoin or oppose planets in your natal chart point to events which will occur sometime in the month following the date of the lunation; i.e., they don't signify vague themes or colorations of the time, but rather specific events whose nature is symbolized by the planet contacted in the natal horoscope.

Whether these events are major turning points in your life, or whether they are merely minor occurrences, depends largely on you and the state of your own psyche at the time. The more fluid you can be, the greater the importance of the events. If you cling obsessively to your accustomed moods and habits and are unable to open yourself to the feeling of the time, then the events will still occur, but without much noticeable effect. A stone dropped into a pond creates more ripples than a stone dropped onto ice.

If you go through the month following a lunation contacting your chart burdened down with your customary mindset, then nothing out of the ordinary will happen. If you try to protect yourself from feeling new feelings, then the lunation will have very little impact. But if you can lighten up a little and cultivate a hopeful, expectant attitude, then you will find that hardened situations and relationships open up for a moment, like clouds shifting briefly to let the sun shine through. If you don't fight against the time by screwing yourself down tighter, then you'll be able to pull yourself out of a rut, break through habitual moods that have been holding you back, and make a new start in a new direction.

The natal planets contacted often symbolize the types of people with whom you'll have to deal during the month following the lunation; e.g., lunations contacting the sun may involve you with your father, husband, superiors, or authorities; lunations contacting the moon symbolize relationships with your mother or employees; Mercury symbolizes children, siblings, neighbors, co-workers; Venus symbolizes women; Mars symbolizes men; Jupiter symbolizes advisors; Saturn symbolizes older or difficult people. The following interpretations give general indications for lunations contacting natal planets:

Sun: You have to stand up for yourself, take some decisive action on your own account, quit dilly-dallying around and make a firm commitment. You must be willing to trust yourself and take complete responsibility for your life direction. You may receive approbation, or be given a chance to shine.
Examples: Adolf Hitler = Munich beer hall Putsch (grab for power). Prince Charles = Coronation of Queen Elizabeth. Princess Diana =

Marriage. John F Kennedy = Proposed marriage to Jackie. Jackie Kennedy Onassis = Death of father.

Moon: You must be collected within yourself, marshal all your resources to get beyond wishful thinking and vague yearnings. Situations or relationships from out of your past may re-emerge in your present, putting your true feelings on the line. You have to give way, go along with others, or pick up loose ends in your life.
Examples: Mikhail Gorbachev = House arrest, coup against him. Elvis Presley = Discharged from army (resumed career). Jackie Kennedy Onassis = Election of JFK to presidency. Walt Disney = Mickey Mouse Club TV show began.

Mercury: You are alert, clear-minded, and able to embark upon new projects with self-confidence and dynamism. You may travel or find new interests and friendships. You may take up a new role which enhances your sense of competence and versatility.
Examples: Muhammad Ali = Second marriage. Richard Nixon = Birth of first daughter. Elvis Presley = Birth of first daughter; first big concert (start of success); Las Vegas opening (first stage show in years).

Venus: You are poised and assured regarding intimate relationships and creative, artistic endeavors. You may have social success or win other people over. It's a poignant and stimulating time for your affections, but you have to get past your usual defenses and let yourself be vulnerable to reach out to others.
Examples: Jackie Kennedy Onassis = Engagement to JFK. Frank Sinatra = Marriage to Mia Farrow. Prince Charles = Children's book published. Muhammed Ali = First Golden Gloves championship; recaptured world title from Frazier.

Mars: You have to take a decisive step forward to disencumber yourself of old patterns. You must seize the initiative, burn your bridges behind you, and fearlessly strike out on your own. There may be a powerful sense of release or relief.
Examples: Richard Nixon = Marriage. Frank Sinatra = Fistfight, teeth knocked out. Princess Diana = Birth of Prince Harry. Muhammad Ali = Inducted into army, refused, lost boxing license.

Topics in Astrology

Jupiter: You must go with the flow and expand yourself beyond your customary taken-for-granted assumptions. There may be some sort of "first", or you may get to do something which you've wanted to do for a long time. There are delightful experiences which heighten your optimism and enthusiasm.
Examples: Prince Charles = Birth of Prince William. Muhammad Ali = Reversal of five-year jail sentence. Frank Sinatra = Waldorf opening (first taste of big time). Elvis Presley = First job (as a theater usher).

Saturn: You must be willing to work hard, dedicate and discipline yourself, and be thorough and methodical. You may have to come directly to grips with something you dread, or undertake difficult responsibilities. You may need tact and self-control in dealings with others (define your own personal space and theirs).
Examples: Queen Elizabeth = Coronation. Frank Sinatra = Death of father. Elvis Presley = Wife left him for another man. John F. Kennedy = Inaugurated president.

Uranus: You must be ready for a major reevaluation of your previous thinking and plans – perhaps a complete reversal of what you stood for previously. There is a need for considerable flexibility and will on your part in order to triumph. It's a time to cut loose and fly with your impulses.
Examples: Jackie Kennedy Onassis = surprise marriage to Onassis. Walt Disney = Graduated high school, got first job. Frank Sinatra = First marriage.

Neptune: You must let go of your illusions and realistically address emotional issues and motives (yours and other people's). You may have unusual dreams or psychic experiences, and must attune yourself to subtleties and unspoken vibrations. It can be a dream come true, but it can also be a nightmare.
Examples: Albert Einstein = Fled Germany for U.S. Richard Nixon = Resigned presidency. Gerald Ford = Assumed presidency. Frank Sinatra = Divorced Mia Farrow.

Pluto: You must be detached yet unyielding; employ penetrating insight and unwavering determination in order to get a grip on your course in life. There may be a complete transformation, the necessity for you to take an entirely new approach.

Examples: Adolf Hitler = Invasion of Russia. F. D. Roosevelt = Pearl Harbor. Elvis Presley = Death of mother. Jackie Kennedy Onassis = Death of grandfather; birth and death of Patrick Kennedy.

The moon's Nodes and the Part of Fortune are of greater than normal importance in this analysis, since these artificial points are in one fashion or another derived from the lunation cycle. The Nodes are the points where the moon's orbit crosses that of the sun (i.e., the earth); and the Part of Fortune shows the moon's phase as measured in terms of house position. In practice, one finds that lunations falling on these points are even more effective (produce more significant events, with greater assuredness) than lunations which fall on natal planets.

North Node: A door opens. It can be like an answer to your prayers, a sense of help and encouragement from the universe or a feeling of being on the right track.
Example: Walt Disney = Released first Mickey Mouse cartoon (start of success).

South Node: A door closes. Be careful of the tendency to shut your eyes to where your true interests lie in the rush to grasp whatever life may dangle before your eyes now.
Example: Adolf Hitler = Surrender of German Army at Stalingrad.

Part of Fortune: Serendipity. Expect surprising opportunities that are fun and rewarding and seem to drop from heaven with no effort on your part.
Example: Prince Charles = First solo airplane flight.

ASC: You receive acceptance or approval from others. You may see yourself in a new light, recognize unsuspected capacities or prowess.

MC: This may signal a new career direction, group responsibilities and leadership, or an effectiveness in influencing authorities in your favor.

DESC: You join with others in common enterprises. You must be willing to adapt yourself to other people and the exigencies of the time.

IC: You may feel a need to withdraw from the usual hustle and bustle to go off by yourself to listen to your own inner voice.

By an interesting coincidence, the lunation cycle is roughly in phase with the cycle of U.S. presidential elections, so that if the new (or full) moon prior to an election falls on a candidate's natal planet, then the full (or new) moon four years later will fall opposite that planet. For example, the lunations preceding each of F. D. Roosevelt's four elections contacted his natal Saturn; both elections of Eisenhower were preceded by lunations contacting his natal moon-Uranus conjunction; both elections of Reagan were preceded by lunations contacting his Saturn; and both elections of George W. Bush were preceded by lunations contacting his Jupiter. Before jumping to the conclusion that the incumbent always has an "astrological edge", it must be noted that both Jimmy Carter's successful and unsuccessful bids for the presidency were preceded by lunations contacting his natal Saturn; and both of George Bush père's runs for the presidency were preceded by lunations contacting his natal moon.

When a lunation falls on a conjunction or opposition of several planets in the natal chart, it activates those planets as a combination. For example, the aspects of Jupiter and Saturn show high ideals and standards of conduct, and a deep moral courage. These natives are not interested in the latest fashions and buzzwords, but seek to make some positive contribution to the world. Thus a lunation falling on a natal Jupiter-Saturn conjunction or opposition will bring out the native's highest ideals. The full moon preceding Neil Armstrong's walk on the moon fell on his Jupiter-Saturn opposition; and lunations fell on Walt Disney's Jupiter-Saturn conjunction the month he got his first job doing animated cartoons, the month he married, and the month he opened Disneyland.

Lunations are also often useful in synastry (horoscope comparison). The new moon before the marriage of Jack and Jackie Kennedy fell on his moon and her Mars. The full moon preceding the birth of Charles Lindbergh, Jr. conjoined Charles Lindbergh Sr.'s Uranus and opposed Anne Morrow Lindbergh's sun-Jupiter conjunction; and the full moon before the baby was kidnapped fell opposite Charles Sr.'s Mercury-Venus conjunction (symbolizing children) and opposite Anne Lindbergh's Saturn.

All lunations contacting natal positions symbolize a break in your customary moods of everyday life. The trick at these times is to be loose and open to what you really want for your life. Regardless of whether the events produced by lunations are happy or unhappy, they always have an ultimate potential of hope and joy.

The Chance of a Lifetime!

They say that life begins at forty. As is often the case with such maxims, this one is based upon an astrological truth. Uranus' sidereal period of 84 years puts Uranus' opposition to its natal place somewhere between ages 40 to 43 in everybody's life. For most people, this is a new departure, even a rebirth. The Demi-Uranus Return, or DUR for short, signals a complete break with the past and the beginning of a new phase in the native's life. Often some sort of golden opportunity is clearly glimpsed and understood, or the irrevocable decision is made to pursue a goal. There is an undaunted spirit of daring, self-certainty, and command.

Uranus has been termed a malefic, but this is not at all true. It is merely disruptive. Uranus brings sudden, unexpected events which break us out of our customary moods and concerns. Sometimes these events are unpleasant – tense, conflictive, and highly stressful. This is particularly likely when there are negative concurrent transits or progressions. But most of the time transiting Uranus brings a heady sense of liberation – a lightening up and letting go.

The DUR in particular is – in the words of Carlos Castaneda – a cubic centimeter of chance. It is one of those moments in life when the wheel of fortune moves by itself and can make our dreams come true, if we have been doing the preliminary work necessary. The keyword is: BREAKTHROUGH, and as one might expect from Uranus, it often comes in a sudden and unexpected manner.

The DUR is often preceded by a time of great tension and frustration, as indicated by the symbolism of "Uranus" and "opposition." The indicated breakthrough may come as the result of complete desperation, or spiritual and emotional exhaustion. An example is Albert Schweitzer (DUR = 3/16/1915 – 7/30/1915 R – 1/17/1916), whose supreme intellectual breakthrough happened in typically Uranian fashion. The preceding year he had begun writing a long-considered book of philosophy, occasioned by his reaction to the outbreak of World War I. By the summer of 1915 he had reached an impasse in his thinking:

"For months on end I lived in a continual state of mental excitement. Without the least success I let my thinking be concentrated ... on the real nature of the affirmative attitude and of ethics, and on the question of what they have in common. I was wandering about in a thicket in which no path was to be found. I was leaning with all my might against an iron door which would not yield.

"While in this mental condition I had to undertake a longish journey on the river ... in September, 1915. The only means of conveyance I could find was a small steamer ... Except for myself, there were only natives on board. Late on the third day, at the very moment when, at sunset, we were making our way through a herd of hippopotamuses, there flashed upon my mind, unforeseen and unsought, the phrase 'Reverence for Life.' The iron door had yielded: the path through the thicket had become visible. Now I had found my way to the idea in which affirmation of the world and ethics are contained side by side! ... Now there stood out clearly before my mind the plan of the whole Philosophy of Civilization." This inspiration became the basis of his magnum opus *The Decay and Restoration of Civilization*, published in 1923.

In Schweitzer's natal horoscope Uranus is in the 10th house of career and life's work; it rules the 5th and it forms a grand square in fixed signs opposition SA, square MA and square PL; also it trines VE The grand square is a rather stressful, tense configuration to start with (although the native disguises his or her internal rage and turmoil with an outward friendliness and sociability); and when Uranus is one of its branches the internal tension is very much increased.

Uranus is a good planet to study since its transits tend to be highly localized in time. Because Uranus is disruptive in its action, its transits produce sudden events which can be associated with a date. By contrast, the effects of Saturn's transits tend to spread out over time. Saturn doesn't produce events per se so much as it informs a period of months or a year with a certain mood.

By concentrating our attention upon one single transiting aspect of one planet, we are holding other variables constant, so to speak. This allows us to examine some subsidiary astrological issues, such as:

> 1) When the transit occurs three times – first direct pass, retrograde pass, and last direct pass – when will the expected event occur?

2) When will the expected event occur in relation to the exact time(s) of the transit(s); what is the expected orb in time from the exact transit(s)?
3) According to astrological tradition, the nature of the expected event can be deduced from the house in which Uranus is posited, or the house which it rules – the house(s) with Aquarius on the cusp. Is this true?
4) According to astrological tradition, the nature of the expected event can be deduced from the aspects to Uranus in the natal horoscope; and from the houses in which the aspected planets lie. Is this true?
5) According to astrological tradition, if Uranus conjoins an angle in the natal chart, the expected event should relate to the meaning of that angle. Is this true?

At the risk of being anticlimactic, I will state at the outset that an informal survey of some fifty horoscopes of famous people and natives from my own files shows that the answers to questions 1) and 2) above are indeterminate; and the answers to the other three questions are that astrological tradition is wrong, or at least cannot be relied upon. We will comment upon these points as we go along (except for natives whose birth time is questionable).

In Schweitzer's case the expected event occurred in the middle between the retrograde and last direct transits. In other cases the events occur all over the lot – anywhere from a month before the first direct transit to a month after the last direct transit. In Schweitzer's case the house symbolism (10th house = career / life's work) is apropos, but we'll see in other examples that is not necessarily the case.

One common effect of the DUR is the native's being catapulted suddenly into power or fame. John F. Kennedy's DUR (9/21/1960 – 2/13/1961 R – 7/9/1961) coincided with his winning the presidency on November 1st, 1960; taking office on January 20th, 1961; and becoming embroiled in a number of difficult foreign entanglements. The worst of these was the Bay of Pigs fiasco in April 1961. JFK's natal Uranus is posited in and rules the 5th house, and it squares MA-ME-JU in the 8th; thus the house symbolism is not very apt. The principal event, taking office, occurred a month before the retrograde transit.

In Adolf Hitler's life the DUR (4/11/1932 – 12/18/1932 R – 1/7/1933) also coincided with a sudden rise to power. In March 1932 Hitler lost an election to Hindenburg, but since there was no majority new elections were called for April 10, 1932. Again Hitler lost, but he won more votes than previously. In an effort to appease conservative opinion Hitler decreed to abolish the SA and SS on April 14th. The rest of 1932 was a war of nerves with his rival. Finally on January 30, 1933 Hitler became chancellor of Germany; on March 23, 1933 he was given dictatorial powers.

In his natal horoscope Hitler's Uranus conjoins the ASC and is sextile SA in the 10th; Aquarius is intercepted in the 4th (it is interesting that Hitler and FDR, the two great protagonists of World War II, both had Uranus rising. Uranus rising gives a tough character – cold, hard, distant, indomitable). In this case the natal house and aspect symbolism are quite apropos (ASC – 10th houses); and the timing works pretty well also (three weeks after the last direct transit).

Teddy Roosevelt's DUR (1/18/1898 – 4/28/1898 R – 11/4/1898) also timed his rise from obscurity to national eminence. He was a minor secretary in the Navy department when the mysterious explosion of the *Maine* in Havana harbor on 2/15/1898 gave him the war against Spain which he had been campaigning for in his speeches. He resigned, used his political influence to secure a special commission, and recruited his own cavalry troop, the Rough Riders. He loved the reckless adventure of war, calling his attack at the battle of San Juan Hill, Cuba, on July 1st, 1898 "the great day of my life." On his return his heroism and panache catapulted him into national prominence. He was offered the New York gubernatorial nomination and he won the election on November 7th, three days after Uranus' last direct transit opposite its natal place. Here the astrological timing worked quite well; however in TR's natal chart Uranus is posited in the 12th, rules the 9th, and is unaspected. Thus the house symbolism doesn't work very well in this case.

Unaspected Uranus is interesting; it symbolizes Uranus in its purest form. Unaspected Uranus shows a native who is free-thinking, rebellious, and experimentative. These natives love risk-taking, are mischievous and conspiratorial, and delight in letting it all hang out. They have a true grit, a mettle which carries the day with its sheer audacity and cool determination. When their DUR's hit they really max out.

In the foregoing examples the DUR brought the natives prominence as a result of their immediate efforts. In other cases the DUR brings sudden prominence for work done many years previously. For example, Sir Isaac Newton published his magnum opus *Principia Mathematica* during his DUR (5/24/1687 – 12/4/1687 R – 3/9/1688). *Principia* includes Newton's laws of motion and gravitation, and is generally considered the greatest single contribution in the history of science. However the actual studies upon which *Principia* was based were done over twenty years earlier, between 1665 and 1666. The publication of *Principia* led to Newton's election to Parliament two years later and was the beginning of his public and political life.

Similarly, Albert Einstein's DUR (5/5/1919 – 7/9/1919 R – 2/14/1920) brought him international fame for work he had done fourteen years earlier. Actually this entire year was a big turning point in his life: he divorced his first wife 2/14/1919 and remarried 6/2/1919. He became a vocal convert to Zionism, and a pacifist and prosecutor of German crimes for World War I. Most importantly, on 9/27/1919 Einstein received word that the Eddington eclipse experiment in May of that year had vindicated Einstein's theory of relativity. "One of his students remembers how, as the two of them were discussing a book which raised objections to his theory, Einstein reached for a telegram lying on the windowsill and handed it to her with the words: 'here, this will perhaps interest you.' 'It was,' she has written, 'Eddington's cable with the results of measurement of the eclipse expedition. When I was giving expression to my joy that the results coincided with his calculations, he said, quite unmoved, "But I knew that the theory is correct," and when I asked, what if there had been no confirmation of his prediction, he countered: "Then I would have been sorry for the dear Lord – the theory is correct."'"

On November 7th, 1919 – the day before transiting Uranus changed station conjunct his natal Jupiter – a tidal wave of publicity broke and from one day to the next Einstein went from obscurity to world-wide fame. In his natal chart Uranus is posited in the 3rd, and rules and opposes JU in the 9th. In this case the house symbolism is pretty good (9th symbolizes fame for intellectual achievement), but the timing is off: the signal event occurred in the middle between the retrograde and last direct transits.

Sometimes the DUR is not the final triumph of the life but rather a dress rehearsal of it, a preliminary success or a glimpse of the final goal. In the case of Nelson Mandela (DUR = 8/3/1961 – 3/29/1962 R – 6/8/1962) he was forced to go underground to hide from the South African government. In January 1962 he left South Africa on an extended tour of African states and Europe to seek support and arrange for military training for recruits. This period away from South Africa was the first time in his life that he felt free "from white oppression, from the idiocy of apartheid and racial arrogance, from police molestation, from humiliation and indignity. Wherever I went I was treated like a human being." Upon returning to South Africa he was arrested on 8/5/1962 and sentenced to five years in prison with hard labor.

Another example of the Demi-Uranus Return being the forerunner or harbinger of ultimate triumph is Franklin Delano Roosevelt (DUR = 3/15/1924 – 10/29/1924 R – 12/24/1924), which brought about his return to politics after having been struck down by polio three years before. "To come back to politics was the greatest single decision Roosevelt ever made. This, if any one turning point can be chosen as the most vital of his whole career, was it. ... Instead of retiring to Hyde Park as a pleasant despot, a cripple who would be well cared for all his life, as his mother wished, FDR threw himself with full strength into the crossfire of the political arena, his disability ignored." FDR managed Al Smith's unsuccessful 1924 campaign for the Democratic presidential nomination, from which he learned valuable lessons for his own campaign eight years later. In FDR's natal chart Uranus rises and rules the 6th (illness), trining JU-NE in the 9th, which symbolism can be considered somewhat apt.

In some cases the meaning of the DUR is not so much public recognition or fame, but rather that the central idea or metaphor of the native's life comes to high focus. The DUR symbolizes the native's life purpose, the reason he or she was born, coming into conscious manifestation. Indeed, this is one of the most common meanings of the DUR; it was true of Albert Schweitzer and both Roosevelts, for example, and that's also how I would describe its effect in my own life. Another example is Oliver Wendell Holmes, whose DUR (10/1/1882 – 4/7/1883 R – 7/14/1883) coincided with a false start and then his grasping his destiny in a decisive fashion.

In September 1882, a few weeks before the first direct DUR, Holmes began teaching at Harvard Law School – a highly prestigious position, but about which he had doubts. His real heart's ambition was to be a judge, to have real power in the world rather than mere intellectual success and influence, which his writings on the law had brought him heretofore. He taught for three months, and then on December 8th he suddenly received word that he had been nominated to the state Supreme Court – if he resigned his professorship at Harvard.

Accordingly, he resigned the Harvard post and was appointed to the Court on December 15th, 1882; and he took his seat on the Court on January 13th, 1883. This was the beginning of Holmes' judicial career. "It was a stroke of lightning that in one second wiped out the past, changed his whole future." Holmes later comment on this subject can be considered a meditation on the nature of Uranus, "The place for a man who is complete in all his powers is in the fight. The professor, the man of letters, gives up one-half of life that his protected talent may grow and flower in peace. But to make up your mind at your peril upon a living question, for purposes of action, calls upon your whole nature." In Holmes' natal horoscope Uranus is posited in and rules the 5th; it conjoins SU and sextiles JU in the 3rd; hence the house symbolism isn't very apt. The principal events fell in the middle between the first and retrograde transits, so the timing isn't very good either.

Another common manifestation of the DUR is the sudden, unexpected love affair. Any Uranus transit can produce a burst of adrenalin; but in 40-something men who are bored with bachelorhood or marriage, it quite often brings a burst of testosterone as well. Thomas Jefferson's sudden love affair with his 14-year old slave girl Sally Hemings coincided with his DUR (8/4/1787 – 2/18/1788 R – 5/15/1788). Bachelor George Bernard Shaw met and fell madly in love with a young socialist socialite who later became his secretary during his DUR (2/21/1896 – 3/4/1896 R – 11/11/1896).

Another long-term bachelor, General Douglas MacArthur, had his DUR (4/13/1921 – 8/17/1921 R – 2/3/1922) while serving as superintendent of West Point. He met a socialite flapper at a dance and proposed to her the same night. Unfortunately she was also being courted by MacArthur's superior officer, General John Pershing, who sacked his upstart subordinate by transferring him to the Philippines. The wedding took place on St. Valentine's day 1922, two weeks after Uranus' last direct pass. Four months later MacArthur arrived at his new post and duty: to survey Bataan as a possible place for American troops to retreat and hold out in case the Philippines were ever to be invaded by Japan.

Another sudden, intense, Uranian romance was described by Bertrand Russell, who was quite tired of his sixteen-year marriage to Alys by the time of his DUR (3/6/1911 – 7/5/1911 R – 12/26/1911). En route to France he stopped for a visit at his old friends' Ottoline and Philip Morell, whom he had not seen for some time. "When I arrived there on March 19th, on my way to Paris, I found that Philip had unexpectedly had to go to Burnley, so that I was left *tete-a-tete* with Ottoline. During dinner we made conversation about Burnley, and politics, and the sins of the Government. After dinner the conversation gradually became more intimate. Making timid approaches, I found them to my surprise not repulsed. It had not, until this moment, occurred to me that Ottoline was a woman who would allow me to make love to her, but gradually, as the evening progressed, the desire to make love to her became more and more insistent. At last it conquered, and I found to my amazement that I loved her deeply, and that she returned the feeling. Until this moment I had never had complete relations with any woman except Alys. … I wanted to leave Alys, and to have her leave Philip. If I had known that he would murder us both (as Mrs. Whitehead assured me he would) I should have been willing to pay that price for one night. The nine years of tense self-denial had come to an end, and for the time being I was done with self-denial. … I told Alys that she could have a divorce whenever she liked, but that she must not bring Ottoline's name into it. She nevertheless persisted that she would bring Ottoline's name in. Thereupon I told her quietly but firmly that she would find that impossible, since if she ever took steps to that end, I should commit suicide in order to circumvent her. I meant this, and she saw that I did."

Although the timing of the decisive events in several of the foregoing romantic episodes comes close to one or another of the exact Uranus transits, in not one of these loves-at-first-sight does

Uranus occupy the natal 5th or 7th houses, nor aspect VE (in MacArthur's case Aquarius is on 7th cusp; albeit his and Jefferson's birth times are questionable). So much for astrological tradition.

While people who have a firm life purpose spring forward on their DUR's, people who are just drifting along, idly dreaming, living in their fantasies, get the same cosmic impulse; but they blow it. Uranus brings us gifts, but we must be clear and decisive in order to grasp them. If people don't really mean business, if they aren't prepared to give their all, then they won't reap much of Uranus' benefits, because Uranus demands and rewards complete self-dedication.

I've seen a lot of blown DUR's in my astrological practice. People wait most of their lives for their lucky break, but when it finally comes oftentimes they don't recognize it for what it is and they let it go. If people are living their lives haphazardly, with no particular plan or goals beyond materialistic and egoistic gratification; if their lives have no abstract purpose or meaning beyond their personal comfort and convenience; then the Uranus opposition to its natal place will bring a crisis – an unforeseen shake-up, which is threatening and disorienting.

What the people are supposed to do then is to reevaluate their life plan and goals; to take command instead of drifting along. If they choose not to do this, but instead try to pick up the pieces as best they can and go on as before, then they will have lost a real opportunity (perhaps their last opportunity in this life) to truly fulfill their destinies.

Isadora Duncan is an example of a blown DUR (3/2/1917 – 9/4/1917 R – 12/22/1917). February-March 1917 was the final break with her lover and chief financial backer, the heir to the Singer sewing machine fortune, who had been about to purchase Madison Square Garden to create an art center and school just for her. According to her autobiography, at a supper in her honor at which he had presented her with a fabulous diamond necklace, she deliberately insulted him by getting drunk and dancing a lewd tango with a "beautiful young boy who was present. Suddenly I felt my arm wrenched in an iron grasp, and looked round to find L. storming with rage." According to her biographer, her friends remonstrated with her, "'Do you realize what you've done?' we asked in a chorus of dismay. 'You could have had the school that was your life's dream, and now you have ruined everything.' 'He'll come back.' she said serenely. 'He always does.'" But he never did. She was left without any support and had to sell the necklace and other jewels and furs he had given her. "As I was now practically penniless, it would, no doubt, have been wiser to have invested the proceeds of the furs and jewels in solid stocks and bonds, but of course this never occurred to me and we all spent a pleasant enough summer at Long Beach, entertaining, as usual, many artists. ... After the pleasures of this summer, when we returned to New York, I found myself without any funds." In Isadora Duncan's case the house symbolism works because natal Uranus is in the 5th (lovers), rules the 11th (dreams), and forms part of a fixed grand square opposition MA, square MO opposite PL (inner warfare covered with a grinning, Cheshire cat smile).

Many people, like Isadora Duncan, miss the opportunity presented by their Demi-Uranus Return, and when the DUR is blown, it's blown. When that happens the rest of the life tends to be a downward spiral, just putting in the time until the Grim Reaper pays his visit. The Uranus DUR is the chance of a lifetime, and it knocks but once on the door.

Saturn Return Readings

No matter how grown up we may think we are in our twenties, life doesn't usually challenge us seriously until our Saturn return. We skip merrily through our twenties as if life were some kind of a picnic, as if we were charmed and invulnerable; and then suddenly, at age 29-30, a gauntlet is thrown down at us and we are forced to pick it up. Seemingly insuperable difficulties and obstacles pop up, everything we've been relying upon and taking for granted gives way, and we are faced for the first time with intimations of our mortality. It is a time of isolation and anguish.

Whether this sensation is pleasant (challenging) or unpleasant (oppressing), and which specific areas of life are affected, depend upon the condition of Saturn by sign, aspect, and house in the natal chart. But there is usually a sense that time is running out on us; we are getting older and still haven't even *begun* to get a firm grasp on life; and how we've been handling ourselves up until now just isn't going to cut the mustard. We are called upon to work hard, to truly dedicate ourselves, rather than to get by passing over our experience lightly and half-heartedly.

Life is serious business: decisions count, decisions can be irreversible. Life is like a vortex that can suck you down, down, down and trap you helplessly unless you take a stand. And the Saturn return is one of those times when we must take a stand and show life that we mean business. Something difficult, daunting, and oftentimes disagreeable has to be faced up to and dealt with. Of course, people have the option of ducking out of this responsibility and running merrily off to play; but if they do this, then they will spend their thirties – and perhaps the rest of their lives – adrift.

If the Saturn return is difficult, it is nonetheless also an opportunity. It calls for a *tour de force* – we have to go beyond ourselves, beyond what we thought we were capable of – and therefore it teaches us how to accept more responsibility for our lives and destinies. In forcing us to come to terms with our own limitations, Saturn teaches us the true meaning of freedom.

Finally, in the year or so after the Saturn return passes, a sign is given to us. We are shown that, yes, we *are* on the right track in life; yes, our suffering *does* have a purpose; yes, we *can* control the direction our life will take by using our own volition. We may have lost the nervous, eager expectations of our youth, but in their place we have discovered forbearance, discipline, and wisdom.

What each of the six people in the following examples had to do during their Saturn returns was to deepen – or seriously reexamine – their commitments. That's what the Saturn return is all about: deepening one's commitment to life instead of running off merrily to play. The examples are taken from their memoirs.

Miyamoto Musashi – samurai swordsman

"From youth my heart has been inclined toward the Way of strategy. My first duel was when I was thirteen. I struck down a strategist of the Shinto school, one Arima Kibei. When I was twenty-one I went up to the capital and met all manner of strategists, never once failing to win in many contests.

"After that I went from province to province dueling with strategists of various schools, and not once failed to win even though I had as many as sixty encounters. This was between the ages of thirteen and twenty-eight or twenty-nine.

"When I reached thirty I looked back on my past. The previous victories were not due to my having mastered strategy. Perhaps it was natural ability, or the order of heaven, or that other school's strategy was inferior. After that I studied morning and evening searching for the principle, and came to realize the Way of strategy when I was fifty."

Beverly Sills – opera singer

"The 1958 spring season of the City Opera would be devoted to contemporary American operas, sponsored by the Ford Foundation. The showpiece opera was to be *The Ballad of Baby Doe* by Douglas Moore.

"I loved the role (of Baby Doe). I read everything that had ever been written about her. I copied her hairdos from whatever photographs I could find. I absorbed her so completely in those five weeks of studying the opera that I knew her inside and out. I *was* Baby Doe.

"At every performance Walter Cassel, as Horace, made me cry. When Horace was dying he would look up at me and sing, 'You were always the real thing, Baby' and I would sing, in reply, 'Hush, close your eyes. Rest.' Then I would take him in my arms and howl like a baby. It was difficult to do the final aria after that scene. Walter and I lived those roles when we were on stage; there was never a moment during the performances when I didn't believe he was Horace Tabor. And even offstage he never called me Beverly or anything else, just 'Baby.'

"The morning after the opening night I grabbed the *New York Herald Tribune* away from Peter (her husband) before he had a chance to look at it. But there was no review on the regular review page. 'Look at that,' I said to Peter, 'they didn't even cover it, can you imagine?' 'Well,' Peter said, 'do you mind if I read the rest of the paper?' He turned to the front page and there – on the front page! – was the review.

"*The Ballad of Baby Doe* is one of the great contemporary American works. I will always be grateful to Douglas Moore for having written it and for the opportunity it gave me to play opposite someone like Walter Cassel. Baby became an integral part of my operatic experience; it was difficult to shake her off even after I left the opera house. If I have ever achieved definitive performances during my career this far, Baby Doe is one of them. The other three would be *Menon,* Cleopatra in *Julius Caesar*, and Queen Elizabeth in *Robert Devereux*. They have been the only times in my entire career when I have walked out of the theater feeling that I have done everything I wanted to do with a role and that nobody else could have done it better."

Charles Darwin – biologist

"During these two years (ages 28-30) I was led to think much about religion. Whilst on board the *Beagle* I was quite orthodox, and I remember being heartily laughed at by several of the officers (though themselves orthodox) for quoting the Bible as an unanswerable authority on some point of morality. I suppose it was the novelty of the argument that amused them. But I had gradually come, by this time, to see that the Old Testament from its manifestly false history of the world, with the Tower of Babel, the rainbow as a sign, etc. etc., and from its attributing to God the feelings of a revengeful tyrant, was no more to be trusted than the sacred books of the Hindoos, or the beliefs of any barbarian.

"But I was very unwilling to give up my beliefs; I feel sure of this for I can well remember often and often inventing day-dreams of old letters between distinguished Romans and manuscripts being discovered at Pompeii or elsewhere which confirmed in the most striking manner all that was written in the Gospels. But I found it more and more difficult, with free scope given to my imagination, to invent evidence which would suffice to convince me. Thus disbelief crept over me at a very slow rate, but was at last complete. The rate was so slow that I felt no distress, and have never since doubted even for a single second that my conclusion was correct. I can indeed hardly see how anyone ought to wish Christianity to be true; for if so the plain language of the text seems to show that the men who do not believe, and this would include my father, brother, and almost all my best friends, will be everlastingly punished.

"And that is a damnable doctrine."

Albert Schweitzer – theologian

"One morning in the autumn of 1904 I found on my writing table in the college one of the green-covered magazines in which the Paris Missionary Society reported every month on its activities. That evening, in the very act of putting it aside that I might go on with my work, I mechanically opened this magazine. As I did so, my eye caught the title of an article: 'The needs of the Congo Mission.'

"The writer expressed his hope that his appeal would bring some of those 'on whom the master's eyes already rested' to a decision to offer themselves for this urgent work. Having finished the article, I quietly began my work. My search (for a way of serving others) was over.

"My thirtieth birthday a few months later I spent like the man in the parable who 'desiring to build a tower, first counts the cost whether he have wherewith to complete it.' The result was that I resolved to realize my plan of direct human service in Equatorial Africa.

"My relatives and my friends all joined in expostulating with me on the folly of my enterprise. In the many verbal duels which I had to fight, as a weary opponent, with people who passed for Christians, it moved me strangely to see them so far from perceiving that the effort to serve the love preached by Jesus may sweep a man into a new course of life. They thought there must be something behind it all, and guessed at disappointment at the slow growth of my reputation. Unfortunate love experiences were also alleged as the reason for my decision. I felt as a real kindness the action of persons who made no attempt to dig their fists into my heart, but regarded me as a precocious young man, not quite right in the head, and treated me correspondingly with affectionate mockery.

"What seemed to my friends the most irrational thing in my plan was that I wanted to go to Africa, not as a missionary, but as a doctor, and thus when already thirty years of age burdened myself as a beginning with a long period of laborious study. And that this study would mean for me a tremendous effort, I had no manner of doubt. I did, in truth, look forward to the next few years with dread. But the reasons which determined me to follow the way of service I had chosen, as a doctor, weighed so heavily that other considerations were as dust in the balance."

Bertrand Russell – mathematician

"About the time that these lectures finished, when we were living with the Whiteheads at the Mill House in Grantchester, a more serious blow fell than those that had preceded it. I went out bicycling one afternoon, and suddenly, as I was riding along a country road, I realized that I no longer loved Alys. I had had no idea until this moment that my love for her was even lessening. The problem presented by this discovery was very grave. We had lived ever since our marriage in the closest possible intimacy. I had no wish to be unkind, but I believed in those days (what experience has taught me to think possibly open to doubt) that in intimate relations one should speak the truth. I did not see in any case how I could for any length of time successfully pretend to love her when I did not. I had no longer any instinctive impulse toward sex relations with her, and this alone would have been an insuperable barrier to concealment of my feelings.

"Although my self-righteousness at that time seems to me in retrospect repulsive, there were substantial grounds for my criticisms. She tried to be more impeccably virtuous than is possible for human beings, and was thus led into insincerity. She was malicious, and liked to make people think ill of each other, but she was not aware of this, and was instinctively subtle in her methods.

"During my bicycle ride a host of such things occurred to me, and I became aware that she was not the saint I had always supposed her to be. But in the revulsion I went too far, and forgot the great virtues that she did in fact possess.

"The most unhappy moments of my life were spent at Grantchester. My bedroom looked out upon the mill, and the noise of the millstream mingled inextricably with my despair. I lay awake through long nights, hearing first the nightingale, and then the chorus of birds at dawn, looking out upon the sunrise and trying to find consolation in external beauty. I suffered in a very intense form the loneliness which I had perceived a year before to be the essential lot of man."

Dylan Thomas – poet

Poem in October

It was my thirtieth year to heaven
Woke to my hearing from harbour and neighbor wood
And the mussel pooled and the heron
Priested shore
The morning beckon
With water praying and call of seagull and rook
And the knock of sailing boats on the net webbed wall
Myself to set foot
That second
In the still sleeping town and set forth.

My birthday began with the water-
Birds and the birds of the winged trees flying my name
Above the farms and the white horses
And I rose
In rainy autumn
And walked abroad in a shower of all my days.
High tide and the heron dived when I took the road
Over the border
And the gates
Of the town closed as the town awoke.

A springful of larks in a rolling
Cloud and the roadside bushes brimming with whistling
Blackbirds and the sun of October
Summery

On the hill's shoulder,
Here were fond climates and sweet singers suddenly
Come in the morning where I wandered and listened
To the rain wringing
Wind blow cold
In the wood faraway under me.

Pale rain over the dwindling harbour
And over the sea wet church the size of a snail
With its horns through the mist and the castle
Brown as owls
But all the gardens
Of spring and summer were blooming in the tall tales
Beyond the border and under the lark full cloud.
There could I marvel
My birthday
Away but the weather turned around.

It turned away from the blithe country
And down the other air and the blue altered sky
Streamed again a wonder of summer
With apples
Pears and red currants
And I saw in the turning so clearly a child's
Forgotten mornings when he walked with his mother
Through the parables
Of sun light
And the legends of the green chapels

And the twice told fields of infancy
That his tears burned my cheeks and his heart moved in mine.
These were the woods the river and sea
Where a boy
In the listening
Summertime of the dead whispered the truth of his joy
To the trees and the stones and the fish in the tide.
And the mystery
Sang alive
Still in the water and singingbirds.

And there could I marvel my birthday

Away but the weather turned around. And the true
Joy of the long dead child sang burning
In the sun.
It was my thirtieth
Year to heaven stood there then in the summer noon
Though the town below lay leaved with October blood.
O may my heart's truth
Still be sung
On this high hill in a year's turning.

Archie Goodwin's Horoscope

Archie Goodwin – gourmet and orchid-fancying detective Nero Wolfe's assistant, amanuensis, and biographer – was born in Canton, Ohio on October 23rd, 1914 (date from *Too Many Women* and *The League of Frightened Men*, by Rex Stout. Wolfe's birth date, unfortunately, is unknown).

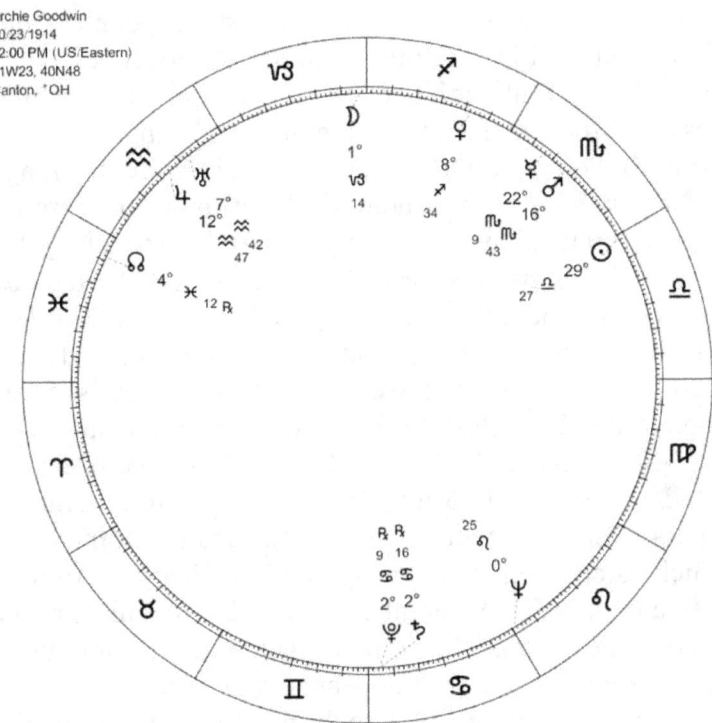

The three conjunctions describe Archie's personality quite well. The Mercury-Mars conjunction gives him his boyish charm and fondness for wisecracks. According to Charles Carter (*The Astrological Aspects*): "It is virile, aggressive, and satirical ... never lacks energy and courage, and it is entitled as a rule to respect for its sincerity and downrightness." In Scorpio this conjunction is the perfect position for a detective, as well as indicating a womanizer.

The Jupiter-Uranus conjunction gives Archie his humor, irreverence, and dry, ironic detachment. Charles Carter says of this aspect, "Too roving, independent, and turbulent to care for the beaten way. ... It tends strongly to the unusual and abnormal, not only in regard to its intellectual interests, but in a physical sense too." This conjunction is in a duet (sextile) with Venus, hence Archie has lots of love affairs, but never marries.

The Saturn-Pluto conjunction gives keen analysis, cunning, thoroughness, dogged tenacity. According to Robert Pelletier's *Planets in Aspect*, "Driving ambition ... determination and persistence ... an uncanny ability to understand people's motives, which serves you well in determining guilt or innocence." The moon opposes this Saturn-Pluto conjunction, which is another testimony to restlessness, violence, and love of adventure and danger.

Perhaps the greatest adventure in Archie's life, the long battle (through three books) with Arnold Zeck, criminal mastermind and Nero Wolfe's archenemy, is closely timed by transiting Uranus' conjunction with that natal Saturn-Pluto. In July 1949 (all dates from William S. Baring-Gould's *Nero Wolfe of West Thirty-fifth Street*) Uranus made its first pass over natal Saturn-Pluto, and transiting Saturn sextiled it, within two weeks of Arnold Zeck's ordering a machine gun squad to blast Wolfe's rooftop greenhouse. Luckily, Wolfe and Archie avoided a fight to the death on that occasion (*The Second Confession*); but in May 1950, when transiting Uranus made its final pass over natal Saturn-Pluto, Zeck made another attack on Wolfe which forced him to run away and hide, leaving Archie in the lurch for five months. In September 1950, when Archie's progressed Mercury conjoined natal Mars (thus repeating the configuration in his natal horoscope), Wolfe reappeared and together with Archie executed a bold and daring plot to bring Zeck down (*In the Best Families*). They triumphed (Zeck was killed) on September 8th, 1950, when Archie's transiting Mars exactly conjoined natal Mars.

Archie's progessed Mercury was conjunct its natal place (and transiting Saturn was exactly square natal Uranus) at the time of the adventure of *The Black Mountain* in March 1954, which took him and Wolfe on an extremely dangerous and clandestine foray into Communist Yugoslavia to bring back the killer of Wolfe's best friend. This climaxed in a shoot-out between Archie and three Russian agents in an old Roman fort on the Montenegro-Albania border on April 17th, 1954, within two days of transiting Mars' opposition to natal Saturn-Pluto.

Although Archie is a confirmed bachelor (and Don Juan), he has had a long-running affair with Lily Rowan, whom he met (and became involved with) in September 1938, when his progressed Mercury turned stationary direct; his converse progressed Venus was conjunct Mercury about this time also.

Close connections between horoscopic indications and the facts of a native's character and destiny are the final proof of astrology and our answer to skeptics. Archie Goodwin's horoscope is another good example of the undeniable veracity of astrology.

Theodore Roosevelt's Secondary Progressions

The system of secondary progressions is one of the most powerful predictive tools astrology offers. Where primary directions and transits refer primarily to "external" events in people's lives, secondary progressions refer less to happenings and more to emotional states: the ebb and flow of people's feelings; the pressures they face and the choices they must make in response; the "colorations" of periods of several months (or years, in the case of the outer planets). Of course, these sorts of emotional ups and downs are often triggered by external events in people's lives; but the important point is the inner realization which these events bring about. Secondary progressions indicate feelings to be felt and lessons to be learned – they arise from within the person (to a greater degree than primaries and transits, which seem more fortuitous).

In secondary progressions each day after birth (or before birth, in the case of the converse secondary progressions) is taken to represent one year of life. So, if you want to see where the progressed planets are on your 30th birthday, you count thirty days after you were born and look at where the planets have gotten to. If any progressed planets form an aspect with a planet in your natal horoscope (or with another progressed planet, in the case of progressed-progressed secondaries), then it's possible to predict the sorts of emotional currents that will be in the air then (at age 30, in our example). While converse progressed and progressed-progressed secondaries can be very effective (and should definitely be examined – although they are not usually as pronounced in their effects as are secondary progressions to the natal planetary positions), for the sake of brevity we will limit this discussion to simple progressed-to-natal secondaries. And while progressions to angles (ASC and MC) are often extremely powerful (and are indispensable in rectifying uncertain birth times), these will also not be examined here since they require an exact time of birth.

Expectation: Mercury's progressions aren't quite as effective as those of the sun, Venus, and Mars. The progressions of Jupiter, Saturn, and Uranus work very, very well indeed, but those of Neptune and Pluto are often indefinite (or perhaps spread out over so many years that the effect is difficult to gauge).

Orbs: I don't believe there's another area of astrological theory quite as fractious as the question of what orbs to take in secondary progressions. I don't want any arguments or letters to the editor here – the paragraphs below summarize my own experience, and all I can say is "take it or leave it":

Progressed moon – the expected event should occur exactly on the calculated date, or perhaps the day before (or after). These are relatively minor occurrences, but can be quite useful for making elections. For example, a Canadian client of mine who had been deported from the U.S. for working illegally here wanted to find a good astrological time to try to "sneak" back across the border. I saw that she happened to have P moon conjunct Jupiter coming up in 6 weeks, so I told her to cross on that day, during a lunar planetary hour (which rules moves). She took my advice and said later that she encountered no problem at the border whatever. Because the progressed moon's effects are so ephemeral, the lunar progressions in Theodore Roosevelt's horoscope won't be discussed here.

Progressed Mercury, sun, Venus, Mars – the effect should commence about a month following the calculated date (perhaps less in the case of Mercury) and go on for several months thereafter (perhaps more in the cases of sun and Mars).

Progressed Jupiter and Saturn – the effect should commence a couple of months following the calculated date and go on for a year or so thereafter.

Progressed Uranus – a sudden, unexpected event which turns the life topsy-turvy should occur within a year following the calculated date, and require a couple of years to sort out (though in the end resulting in much greater freedom than before).

Progressed Neptune and Pluto – these are usually subtler in effect, identifying periods of several years (beginning in the year or so following the calculated date) of greater necessity for ATTUNEMENT or CLARITY, respectively.

Progressed Stations: The Progressed Stationary Retrograde and Stationary Direct positions of the planets require what Dr. Marc Edmund Jones termed a "critical regrasp of experience": the natives are forced to stop in their tracks; take conscious stock of what they are about (instead acting on auto-pilot and taking things for granted); and then go on as before but with greater deliberation and awareness – more conscious control over this area of life (symbolized by the planet). Progressed changes of station get the native past some sticking point – something that was holding them up or back. The difference between the two progressed stations is that at SR the life becomes more personal, absorbing, and intense – it takes on a deeper meaning for the natives; whereas at SD they learn that they need not take things so personally – they can be more casual and relaxed about their affairs.

Progressed Sign Ingresses: These are subtle, indicating a change in direction or outlook, new horizons; or sometimes the close of one chapter in the life and beginning of a new one. If the progressed planet enters a sign it rules or in which it is exalted (e.g. P Mars entering Aries, Scorpio, or Capricorn), this indicates a favorable turn of events – new opportunities or a general lightening up; if the progressed planet enters a sign of its detriment or fall then what is indicated is a rocky road ahead for many years in the affairs symbolized by that planet.

Aspects: Only Ptolemaic aspects (conjunction, sextile, square, trine, and opposition) are considered in what follows. The particular aspect between a progressed and natal planet doesn't seem to be as important in predicting its effect as the symbolism of the planets involved (e.g. Mars-Saturn progressions are usually going to be nasty even if the progressed aspect between them is a sextile or trine; and Venus-Jupiter squares and oppositions can be quite felicitous). Note well the aspect (if there is one) between the two planets in the natal horoscope: if they are afflicted (square, opposition, or disharmonious conjunction) in the birth chart then a subsequent progressed sextile or trine will tend to bring out the underlying affliction (though it may have a felicitous outcome in the end); similarly the progressed square or opposition of two planets which are natally sextile or trine will bring favorable events, but these may seem conflictive at the start, or require considerable effort to bring to realization. In Theodore Roosevelt's progressions which are listed below the natal aspect between the two planets (if there is one) appears in parentheses following the progressed aspect (and before the calculated date).

Prediction: In a general kind of way, the progressed planet symbolizes the type of events which can be expected to occur; and the natal planet symbolizes your emotional response to these events (see the *Table of Keywords for the Transiting and Natal Planets* on page 118, which can be used also for the progressed and natal planets).

When there are several different progressions (plus transits and directions) all pointing the same way at about the same time, then more exact prediction is possible (such as a chain of favorable aspects by or to Venus, which would indicate romance or happy personal relationships). What follows is a list of all of Theodore Roosevelt's (non-lunar) secondary progressions to natal chart positions, from the time when biographers began recording his history up to his death. Entries marked with question marks ("?") don't correspond very well with astrological expectation, either because the astrological symbolism isn't especially appropriate; or because there is a lacuna in the biographical data available so it is not known (by this writer) what was happening in TR's life at that point.

P sun trine moon (wide trine) = 5/15/71 (DECISIVE event which heightens ASSURANCE): TR's asthma and general sickliness led his father to challenge him to "make" his body through a severe regimen of exercise: "He exercised throughout the winter and spring of 1870-71. Fiber by fiber, his muscles tautened, while the skinny chest expanded. ... Glorying in his newfound strength, he plunges into the depths of icy rapids, and clambers to the heights of seven mountains (one of them twice on the same day)."[61] TR also became interested in studying nature now: "This same summer, too, I obtained various new books on mammals and birds, ... and made an industrious book-study of the subject."[24]

P sun sextile Mars (wide sextile) = 7/7/72 (DECISIVE event which assists ADVANCEMENT): he received his first gun (a present from his father).[62] Also, he seriously took up boxing now "Having been a sickly boy, with no natural bodily prowess, and having lived much at home, I was at first quite unable to hold my own when thrown into contact with other boys of rougher antecedents. I was nervous and timid. ... Then an incident happened (late summer '72) that did me real good. (He ran into a couple of bullies his age). The worst feature was that when I finally tried to fight them I discovered that either one singly could not only handle me with easy contempt, but handle me so as not to hurt me much and yet to prevent my doing any damage whatever in return."[32] Also, around this time TR "got my first pair of spectacles, which literally opened an entirely new world to me. ... I had been a clumsy and awkward little boy, and while much of my clumsiness and awkwardness was doubtless due to general characteristics, a good deal of it was due to the fact that I could not see and yet was wholly ignorant that I was not seeing."[24]

P Mars enters Aquarius = 1/29/75 and P Mercury enters Sagittarius = 10/21/75 (ADVANCEMENT takes new direction and UNDERSTANDING takes new direction): In 7/75 TR took the Harvard entrance exams and did excellently;[76] and he entered Harvard in fall '76. Also this year he was falling in love with his childhood sweetheart, Edith Carow, and reached an "understanding" with her by summer '76 before leaving for college.[79]

P sun trine Neptune = 11/27/76 (DECISIVE event which heightens ATTUNEMENT): corresponds to TR's first semester at college (he had entered Harvard in 9/76).[85-6] Also at this time TR was insulted at political rally, which was his first involvement in politics (recall that in TR's case 10th house Neptune has a career / life's work significance). According to one eyewitness: "Every student there was profoundly indignant. I noticed one little man, small but firmly knit. He had slammed his torch to the street. His fist quivered like steel springs and swished through the air as if plunging a hole through a mattress. I had never seen a man so angry before. 'It's Roosevelt from New York,' someone said. I made an effort to know Roosevelt better from that moment."[82]

P Mercury opposition Uranus (quincunx) = 6/8/77 (ENCOURAGING event which leads to LIBERATION): End of first year college, went to the woods and later joined his family at Oyster Bay.[90] End July '77 TR published his first printed work (*Birds of Adirondacks*),[90-1] and by late summer he had decided to become a scientist: "My father ... told me that if I wished to be a scientific man I could do so. He explained that I must be sure that I really intensely desired to do scientific work, because if I went into it I must make it a serious career ... *if I intended to do the very best work that was in me*; but that I must not dream of taking it up as a dilettante. ... After this conversation I fully intended to make science my life work."[92]

P Mars trine Uranus = 6/16/78 (FORCEFUL event which leads to LIBERATION): TR's father had died four months previously and he entered a severe depression and illness. That summer he was recovering on a trip to Maine: "There I made life friends of two men, Will Dow and Bill Sewall (who became TR's mentor): I canoed with them, and tramped through the woods with them ... Afterward they were with me in the West."[34] This progression may refer to a fight he had with Edith Carow on 8/22/78, which "seems to have kindled some sort of rage in Theodore"[98] and which led to their break-up, thus paving the way for his eventual marriage to Alice Lee Saltonstall (whom he began seeing that fall).

P Mars square Mercury = 1/24/79 (FORCEFUL event which heightens UNDERSTANDING): Active in school, elected to Harvard's Hasty Pudding Club now; and he made his first public speech: "Thus, suddenly, in February of 1879, Theodore Roosevelt revealed that the political animal within him was at last beginning to stir."[109] "Although Theodore continued to dream of being a natural historian when he left college, he confessed that the prospect of three extra years of overseas study – a necessary academic requirement – made him 'perfectly blue.' Politics, on the other hand, was beginning to appeal to him so strongly that he asked Professor Laughlin if he should not perhaps make that his career instead."[110] Also, "Alice Lee did not relish the idea of Theodore becoming Professor or Doctor Roosevelt. ... Much later Theodore himself admitted that courting Alice 'brought about a change in my ideas as regards science.'"[110]

P Mars square sun (wide sextile) = 11/20/80 (FORCEFUL event which heightens DETERMINATION): TR was married the previous month, and now moved into a home in New York City and entered Colombia Law School.[137] The progression probably refers to the fact that in winter 1880-81 he began hanging out at the local Republican Club: "The men I knew best were the men in the clubs of social pretension and the men of cultivated taste and easy life. When I began to make inquiries as to the whereabouts of the local Republican Association and the means of joining it, these men – and the big business men and lawyers also – laughed at me, and told me that politics were 'low' ... and, moreover, they assured me that the men I met would be rough and brutal and unpleasant to deal with. I answered that if this were so it merely meant that the people I knew did not belong to the governing class, and that the other people did – and that I intended to be one of the governing class."[(55)]

P Mercury trine Saturn (wide square) = 6/10/83 (ENCOURAGING event which requires DISCIPLINE): From an acquaintance he met now TR got the idea of going hunting in Dakota, and on 9/3/83 he took his first trip west: "The romance of my life began."[214] He got the idea of going into the cattle business, and shot his first buffalo: "Roosevelt now abandoned himself to complete hysteria. He danced around the great carcass like an Indian war-chief, whooping and shrieking, while his guide watched in stolid amazement."[224]

P Mars square Pluto (wide trine) = 12/19/83 (FORCEFUL event which requires CLARITY): in the New York State Assembly, nominated for speaker but lost the election.[230] But this progression probably refers to the deaths of his mother and wife on 2/14/84 (the latter in childbirth),[243] which threw him into a deep depression (he emotionally abandoned his baby daughter since her presence was too painful to bear). Mars by primary direction was conjunct DESC now as well.

P sun enters Sagittarius = 5/6/84 (DETERMINATION takes new direction): involved in Republican politics as State Assemblyman, but his heart wasn't into it anymore – he wanted to move out west to forget his emotional loss. He returned to Dakota in June and found a perfect spot to build a ranch house, and bought it the next day.[278] This was the beginning of his ranching business (the happiest time of his life).

P Venus and P Saturn Stationary Retrograde = 6/13/85 (critical regrasp of INTIMACY and DISCIPLINE): TR spent the summer of '85 relaxing at Oyster Bay and hunting in Dakota – his first relaxation in two years.[304] The Venus station probably refers to early October '85 when TR fell in love with his childhood sweetheart Edith Carow; in November he proposed to her and she accepted.

P sun opposition Uranus (quincunx) = 10/31/86 (DECISIVE event which leads to LIBERATION): He was nominated for mayor of NYC but on 11/2/86 came in a disappointing third.<356-7> On 12/2/86 he married Edith Carow and honeymooned in England. However, the progression probably refers to his entire Dakota cattle herd being destroyed in the winter of 1886-87. Spring '87 he went to Dakota to survey his losses, and when he left Dakota to return to NYC he was emotionally and financially devastated.<373> He was now poor, with a bleak political outlook, and would have to make his money by writing.<374>

P Jupiter opposition Venus (opposition) = 7/22/87 (CHEERING event which accents INTIMACY) and P Mercury conjunct Venus = 10/31/87 (ENCOURAGING event which accents INTIMACY): On 9/13/87 TR's first son Ted was born.<381> In early 11/87 he took a trip to Dakota to hunt but there was no game.<382> TR became a conservationist now and on his return to NYC he founded the *Boone & Crocket Club* conservation association.<383> Vis à vis Mercury-Venus: on 1/15/88 TR began writing his magnum opus, *Winning the West* (which took him 7 years to complete).<387>

P Mercury opposition Jupiter = 9/21/89 (ENCOURAGING event which brings FULFILLMENT): TR's second son, Kermit, was born 10/10/89.<412> Also, "Roosevelt found himself something of a literary celebrity in the fall of 1889. His *Winning the West* was not only a best seller (the first edition disappeared in little more than a month) but a *succès d'estime* on both sides of the Atlantic."<410> Under Congressional attack now because of his work for the Civil Service Commission, he crafted a report which vindicated him: "President Harrison added to his sense of security by approving his report and recommending that the Civil Service's budget be increased."<413>

P Mars opposition Saturn and P Mercury square Neptune = 9/5/90 (FORCEFUL event which requires DISCIPLINE and ENCOURAGING event which requires ATTUNEMENT): TR's crusading for the Civil Service reform had met with severe attacks in Congress (since it threatened patronage), and in early October TR was rudely treated by President Harrison: "Damn the President! He is a cold-blooded, narrow-minded, prejudiced, obstinate, timid old psalm-singing Indianapolis politician."<426> Additionally, in January '91, TR's brother Elliott, who was drinking himself to death, announced that he was about to have a bastard son whose mother "threatened a public scandal if she did not receive financial compensation for her pregnancy. Roosevelt's reaction to this 'hideous revelation' was entirely characteristic ... If it ever got out that the Civil Service Commissioner was involved in blackmail payments, (his Congressional enemies) would annihilate him. But he saw no other way of protecting his family from a catastrophic scandal."[430-31]

P Neptune Stationary Direct = 5/18/95 (critical regrasp of ATTUNEMENT): He had been appointed New York City Police Commissioner the previous month, and he immediately began to shake things up in the police department, ousting the entrenched Police Chief[491] and – with Jacob Riis – investigating police negligence in nightly undercover forays throughout the city.[493] TR also called for strict enforcement of laws against drinking on Sunday, which made him universal enemies who attacked him from all directions (he even received a letter bomb in early August '95).[506] Note the Neptune symbolism of treachery (and his own delusions of grandeur, which brought it on); and that the matter at hand involved enforcing *liquor* regulations.

P sun trine Saturn (square) = 11/11/95 and P Mercury enters Capricorn = 11/25/95 (DECISIVE event which requires DISCIPLINE; and UNDERSTANDING takes new direction): After the landslide Democratic victory in New York City TR was abandoned by everyone (the loss was blamed on his crusading: "There could hardly have been a more crushing indictment of Reform in general, and Police Reform in particular. The contrast between local and state returns only emphasized Roosevelt's unpopularity in his native city.")[513] In a word, he was burnt-out now: "I have to contend with the hostility of Tammany, and the almost equal hostility of the Republican machine; I have to contend with with the folly of reformers and the indifference of decent citizens; and I have to contend with the singularly foolish law under which we administer the Department."[539]

P Mercury sextile Mercury = 1/19/98 (ENCOURAGING event which brings UNDERSTANDING): TR's sixth child (and favorite) Quentin was born on 11/19/97.[589] But this progression probably refers to the explosion on board the battleship *Maine* in Havana harbor on 2/15/98, which was just the excuse TR needed to launch a war against Spain which he'd been plumping for all along. TR exceeded his authority to order the Pacific Fleet into action during the absence of his boss at the Navy Department, "which (Admiral) Dewey later described as 'the first step' toward American conquest of the Philippines."[602] When the Spanish War broke out, TR used his political influence to finagle a position for himself (and his old cowboy buddies) in a special unit called "The Rough Riders."

P Mercury sextile sun (conjunction) = 1/26/99 (ENCOURAGING event which heightens DETERMINATION): TR's heroism at the Battle of San Juan Hill in Cuba the preceding July led to his being offered the New York Republican gubernatorial nomination, and he won handily on 11/7/98.[589] This progression refers to his first months as governor, exercising real power (and making powerful enemies of the "Bosses").

P Mars sextile Venus (semi-sextile) = 6/1/99 (FORCEFUL event which heightens INTIMACY): ? The reference might be to something going on in TR's private life which eluded his biographers. In TR's public life there was a reunion of the Rough Riders the end of June '99;[703] and TR spent this summer enjoying his celebrity and plumping for the 1900 Republican Vice Presidential nomination (the death of the sitting V.P. in November '99 opened the way for TR's nomination).[709]

P Mercury trine Pluto (opposition) = 11/9/1900 (ENCOURAGING event which requires CLARITY): The McKinley – Roosevelt ticket won an overwhelming victory on 11/6/1900. In January '01 TR took a hunting trip to Colorado (his first in years), and he was inaugurated Vice President on 3/4/01.[734]

P sun conjunct Venus = 5/11/02 (DECISIVE event which accents INTIMACY): TR's wife Edith was pregnant now (she miscarried late in June '02).[116] In July TR made his first inspection of the presidential yacht.[127-8] On the public front this summer there were riots in the anthracite coal fields, which TR defused with the help of an arbitration commission he appointed: "We were on the verge of failure, because of self-willed obstinacy on the part of the operators. ... (The operators) had worked themselves into a frame of mind where they were prepared to sacrifice everything and see civil war in the country rather than back down and acquiesce in the appointment of a representative of labor. It looked as if a deadlock were inevitable. Then, suddenly, after about two hours' argument, it dawned on me that they were not objecting to the thing, but to the name. ... I shall never forget the mixture of relief and amusement I felt when I thoroughly grasped the fact that while they would heroically submit to anarchy rather than have Tweedledum, yet if I would call it Tweedledee they would accept it with rapture; it gave me an illuminating glimpse into one corner of the mighty brains of these 'captains of industry.'"(367ff)

P Mars trine Jupiter = 2/16/03 (FORCEFUL event which brings FULFILLMENT): TR was on a political roll; the April '03 victory in Supreme Court decision on the Northern Securities anti-trust case was his "fourth political victory in fewer than four weeks."[219] In May he took a whistle-stop trip out west and made his first visit to California: "When I first visited California, it was my good fortune to see the 'big trees,' the Sequoias, and then to travel down into the Yosemite (on a camping trip), with John Muir."[260] And he was feted wherever he went: "Amid all the color and luxuriance, nubile girls in white waved prettily, to the President's obvious pleasure."[226]

P Venus square Neptune (square) = 1/31/05 and P sun opposition Jupiter = 2/12/05 (SOCIABLE event which requires ATTUNEMENT and DECISIVE event which brings FULFILLMENT): 2nd inauguration was 3/4/05. He was losing the sight in his left eye due to a recent boxing blow.[376] But the progression most likely refers to TR's offering to mediate the Russo-Japanese war in April '05, which resulted in his winning the Nobel Peace Prize.(422)

P sun square Neptune = 7/4/06 (DECISIVE event which requires ATTUNEMENT): ? In August '06 a group of Negro soldiers allegedly went on a rampage in Brownsville, Texas; TR's response was to (wrongly) cashier the soldiers, which greatly angered American Negroes.[467] This "Brownsville incident" – TR wrongly punishing Negro soldiers – was the "major mistake of his presidency."[535]

P Venus opposition Jupiter (opposition) = 5/30/07 (SOCIABLE event which brings FULFILLMENT): ? The stock market was crashing all this year (March, August, and especially October), and TR was blamed for having caused the slump because of his targeting big business.[495]

P Venus conjunct Venus = 4/18/12 and P Saturn conjunct Saturn = 5/2/12 (SOCIABLE event which accents INTIMACY and CHALLENGING event which requires DISCIPLINE): 6/12/12 was the Republican national convention Chicago: *"We stand at Armageddon and we battle for the Lord.*[716] Rejected by the Republicans, TR accepted the nomination of the new Progressive ("Bull Moose") Party in early August '12 and began barnstorming across the U.S.[720] The Saturn progression probably refers to TR's being shot on 10/14/12;[720] and on 11/5/12 he lost the election to the Democrat Wilson (but beat Republican Taft – his erstwhile protégé turned enemy – which was perhaps his main goal).[724]

P Mercury Stationary Retrograde = 12/28/12 (critical regrasp of UNDERSTANDING): ? TR was writing his memoirs, and in February '13 a magazine serialization of his autobiography began to appear.[724]

P sun enters Capricorn (the solsticial = decisive point) = 11/18/13 and P Mars enters Pisces = 11/21/14 (DETERMINATION and ADVANCEMENT take new directions): On 2/27/14 TR embarked upon a great adventure exploring the Amazon, which turned out to be a complete disaster: his crew ran out of supplies, TR was sickly with jungle fever the whole time and lost the sight in his eye. On 4/14/14 he finally arrived at a trapper's home and knew that he and his crew would be okay.[740ff] In the November 1914 elections the Progressive Party was defeated everywhere except California – a major setback – which made TR consider leaving politics for good.[740ff]

P sun sextile Mercury (conjunction) = 10/17/16 (DECISIVE event which brings UNDERSTANDING): ?

P sun sextile sun = 2/17/18 and P Mars square Uranus = 3/16/18 (DECISIVE event which heightens DETERMINATION and FORCEFUL event which brings LIBERATION): In February '18

TR entered the hospital for surgery, but this progression probably refers to the death of TR's son Quentin in battle in July '18.[740ff] TR was distraught and never got over it.[740ff]

    P Mars trine Mercury = 10/20/18 (FORCEFUL event which brings UNDERSTANDING): ? Severe illness, TR was in the hospital from 11/11/18 through 12/24/18. He died of a coronary embolism on 1/6/19.[740ff]

Topics in Astrology

Primary Directions for Beginners

Primary Directions are one of the most powerful predictive tools astrology offers. The most basic and important life events, such as births of siblings, major moves, deaths of loved ones, marriage, births of children, life and career changes, are more likely to be shown by primary directions to angles than by any other astrological technique. As directions are not so difficult to calculate, most anyone can learn how; and now there's software available that does all the work (see below).

The basic idea behind primary directions is that in the hours after birth, the diurnal rotation of the earth moves the planets clockwise around the chart, to positions where they cross (or aspect) the angles (the horizon and meridian) and each other. For example, in Theodore Roosevelt's birth chart (page 38) Mars is located in 18°04' Capricorn, on the 8th house cusp. In about 1.7 hours, the diurnal rotation of the earth will bring Mars down to the horizon (Descendant or 7th house cusp); and this 1.7 hours of real time is converted into symbolic time at a rate of approximately 4 minutes of real time = one year of symbolic time (so 1.7 hours equates to 25 ½ years of life - i.e., age 25 ½).

You can get a rough estimate of the time a primary direction to an angle will operate by taking the difference in longitude between the planet and the angle: for Mars conjunct Descendant d (direct), 18°04' Capricorn (Mars) - 25°41' Sagittarius (DESC) = 22°23'. This estimate falls somewhat short of the actual time (25 ½ years). Estimates of directions to the Midheaven and I.C. will usually be closer to exact than estimates of the directions to the Ascendant and Descendant (which vary depending on whether signs of long or short ascension rise; and also on how far north or south you are on the earth). With a little practice, you can do all these estimation calculations in your head automatically, as you look at a chart, without really having to think about it.

It is also possible to take converse primary directions. For example, in Theodore Roosevelt's horoscope, Saturn is in 11°40' Leo near the cusp of the 3rd house. About an hour and a quarter before birth Saturn had crossed the lower meridian (I.C.). Using our formula of 4 minutes of real time = one year of symbolic time, this means the direction Saturn conjunct I.C. c (converse) operates at about age 19. We can roughly estimate this by taking the difference between the longitudes of Saturn (11°40' Leo) and the I.C. (1°24' Virgo) =19°44'.

The theory of primary directions goes hand-in-hand with the theory of rectification of the birth time. In practice, the astrologer carries out both operations at once. Working from a list of prominent life events on the one hand, and a list of roughly estimated primary directions to angles on the other, a likely match-up is sought by trial and error. In particular, marriage is often shown by the conjunction of sun, Venus or Jupiter to the Descendant; moves and major journeys are often shown by conjunctions to the Ascendant or I.C.; career changes and new life directions are often shown by conjunctions to the Midheaven; births of children by conjunctions to the Descendant or I.C.; deaths of parents or spouse by malefic conjunctions to the Midheaven, I.C., or Descendant.

Here are some keywords for the sorts of events that might be expected when planets are directed to angles: sun (decisive); moon (emotional); Mercury (spontaneous); Venus (pleasing); Mars (dramatic); Jupiter (expansive); Saturn (final); Uranus (surprising); Neptune (elusive); Pluto (constructive); North Node (illuminating); Part of Fortune (serendipitous).

We note that TR's father died when the future president was 19 years old (which equates roughly with Saturn on the I.C. c); and that both his mother and his wife died (the same day) when Teddy was 25 years old (which equates roughly with Mars on the Descendant d).

The hypothesis that Saturn conjunct the I.C. c occurred at the time of TR's father's death leads to a rectified birth time of 7:49:11 P.M. LMT; and the hypothesis that Mars conjunct the Descendant d occurred at TR's mother's and wife's deaths leads to a rectified birth time of 7:49:30 P.M. LMT. In other words, the two hypotheses give the same rectified time of birth (within 19 seconds). The recorded birth time is 7:45 P.M. LMT, so the rectified time is only four minutes different.

Obviously, I've chosen an example horoscope in which primary directions to angles worked quite well. On the other hand, this is not at all uncommon. The trial and error of rectification should lead to a moment when everything goes "click" – when there's a convincing match-up between predictions and actual events.

Observe, however, that as with every astrological technique, primary directions work better in some horoscopes than in others, and at certain periods of a given native's life than at others. And even when they work well, they can still fail up to a third of the time. The power of primary directions lies not in their infallibility, but rather in their ability (when they do work) to pinpoint the most important events and transitions in a person's life.

Using an average rectified birth time of 7:49:20 P.M. LMT, we obtain a list of directions of planets to angles which occurred during Teddy Roosevelt's adult life:

Saturn conjunct IC c = 2/26/1878 => Father's death = 2/9/1878
Uranus conjunct ASC c = 9/18/1880 => 1st marriage = 10/27/1880
Moon conjunct ASC d = 10/20/1882 => moved into 1st home = 10/?/1882
Mars conjunct DESC d = 2/21/1884 => deaths of mother and wife = 2/14/1884
Pluto conjunct ASC c = 8/10/1898 => Battle of San Juan Hill = 7/1/1898; triumphal return to U.S. = 8/15/1898
Sun conjunct DESC d = 3/12/1900 => nominated V.P. = 6/20/1900
Mercury conjunct DESC c = 1/1/1901 => won V.P. = 11/6/1900
Mars conjunct MC c = 2/25/1901 => inaugurated V.P. = 3/4/1901
Moon conjunct IC c = 4/15/1902 => ??
Saturn conjunct ASC d = 5/16/1911 => ??
Mercury conjunct IC d = 4/20/1913 => ??
Sun conjunct IC d = 7/4/1914 => Amazon adventure (almost died) = 4/1914
Pluto conjunct MC d = 10/19/1916 => ??

The events with question marks can be considered dubious; either there was no major life event at the expected time, or else the life event doesn't make sense in light of the astrological symbolism (I happen to be pretty strict as compared to other practitioners of primary directions in requiring that directions to angles coincide with *major* events consonant with the planetary symbolism. As in TR's case, I, personally, have also experienced a "tailing off" of accuracy in the P.D.'s for my own life in recent years as compared with earlier in my life. Perhaps the assumption that the True Solar Arc in Right Ascension measure is incorrect – see further along). For the most part, however, there is a good correspondence between predictions and events, within reasonable orbs of time (a few weeks or months).

Events of secondary (usually) importance in the life are often shown by aspects (other than conjunctions) to the angles. To direct a planet to an aspect with an angle, just direct the aspect point to conjunction with that angle. For example, to direct Pluto to square MC converse, take the point 6°38' Aquarius (the square to Pluto = 6°38' Taurus) and direct this ecliptic (zodiacal) point to conjunction with the MC in the usual way. For example:

Saturn square ASC c = 9/1/1895 => NY police commissioner enforcing blue laws, created firestorm of anger and opposition (including letter bomb) = 8/5/1895

Sun square ASC d = 11/30/1902 => major accident, bodyguard killed, start lifelong knee pain = 9/3/1902

Jupiter sextile ASC c = 9/24/1907 => riverboat trip down Mississippi and bear hunt = 10/1/1907

Sign ingresses point to subtle but long-lasting changes in outlook, viewpoint, orientation, and direction which begin at this time and which endure for many years to come: the emergence of new horizons, ambitions, and life interests. For example:

0°Aries conjunct MC d = 8/12/1884 => retired from politics to run western cattle ranch = 8/1/1884

0°Leo conjunct ASC d 11/29/1897 => Sinking of the *Maine* (event which triggered TR's rise to glory) = 2/15/1898

What we have been describing here are technically known as zodiacal primary directions to angles equated to time with the True Solar Arc in Right Ascension measure – ascribed to Placidus – in which the Midheaven is moved forward (and conversely) at the same speed that the secondary progressed sun is moving in Right Ascension. There is nearly unanimous agreement amongst modern authors on the subject of primary directions on the validity of these primary directions (DeLuce, Jayne, Johndro, myself, et. al.).

However, there is considerable disagreement, over the long history of primary directions, about how to equate arcs of direction (difference in Right Ascension measured in the sky) into timespan in the native's life. When rectifying a horoscope with directions, it is necessary to bear in mind alternative options for timing directions, because different natives respond in different ways. For some natives, the simple radix One Degree-per-Year Symbolic Directions in Longitude (simple subtraction of planetary longitudes to produce arcs of direction, which are then equated to time at the rate of 1° of Arc = 1 year of lifespan, so that the planets advance uniformly in zodiacal longitude at a rate of about 5' per month in longitude) work very well. Other nativities (in my experience many, if not most) of natives for whom primary directions work at all seem to respond best to the Placidian True Solar Arc in Right Ascension method of equating arcs of direction into time. But there are other measures which have historically been used by other practitioners (Rumen Kolev's *Placidus* software explains and calculates these).

Because directions to angles work so well, it seems logical that it should be possible to direct planets to one another, as well as to angles. For example, after Mars by direct motion crosses the Descendant in TR's horoscope, it will some time later reach the position occupied by Venus (in the 6th house of the birth chart), which would form the primary direction Mars conjunct Venus direct.

Unfortunately, it is not possible to unequivocally perform these calculations, because it is not clear exactly how to define the word "conjunct" – where exactly in the sky Mars conjoins Venus (as opposed to knowing where Mars crosses an angle, which is unambiguous). Against what frame of reference do we measure that conjunction? What great circle on the celestial sphere are we projecting onto (the celestial equator, the prime vertical, the meridian, the horizon)? What is our point of view (the North Point on the Horizon, the North Celestial Pole, the North Ecliptic Pole)?

Renaissance thought (e.g. Morinus) favored a Regiomontanus approach to answering this question. Modern astrological thought on the subject is basically divided into three schools: the Placidians, the Campanians, and the Topocentrists. Various claims, some of them quite extraordinary, have been made by some of these practitioners for the validity of this or that method of calculating interplanetary primary directions (as opposed to directions to angles, on which they all basically agree).

I personally have spent twenty-odd years raking through the muck and investigating other astrologers' claims. At this point, I don't believe that there is a valid method of directing planets to one another, no matter how appealing that idea might seem; although Campanus-Regiomontanus directed interplanetary conjunctions and

oppositions can often be suggestive (in particular, check out comparing the two mirror-image direct/converse directions obtained by interchanging the promissor and significator in the direction, with corresponding events in the life). Otherwise, the only valid primary directions are those to angles (i.e., those described in this essay). However, if anyone wants to wade into the mire, they are advised to read my book *Primary Directions – A Primer of Calculation*, available as a free download from:
https://www.dropbox.com/l/scl/AADAM79RJoyiAuaiL1cBL7iiXTx4ZKfBvBw
https://www.dropbox.com/l/scl/AACqoT8RC-qRUQB14ztImNgetUqX3-TGrdU
https://www.dropbox.com/l/scl/AACzLtDlnnPfTuFtJU7zOHnGk8zeXi11aNo

Primary Directions calculations are easily done by Rumen Kolev's indispensable *Placidus* Primary Directions software, available from www.babylonianastrology.com.

Why Directions Sometimes Fail

I am a devotee of zodiacal primary directions to angles equated to time with the Placidian True Solar Arc in RA measure (the MC is moved in Right Ascension – both forward and conversely – at the same rate that the progressed sun is moving in RA. The Ascendant is dragged along at the same rate in Oblique Ascension). I've always found these directions to be pretty accurate, particularly the conjunctions, and therefore I've always been puzzled about why the converse direction of Neptune to my Ascendant in the fall of 1980 produced no event whatever.

About the only thing that was happening in my life then was that I was eleven years into an unhappy marriage which was progressively deteriorating (and would end nine years later), and I had a three-year-old son. Then an extremely attractive – Leo rising – single, hard-working and dedicated Scorpio woman, whose rising natal moon precisely conjoined my natal sun, moved into town.

Looking back it's kind of funny: my wife met her before I did and (being very psychic) immediately picked up the vibe – meeting this woman really raised her hackles. Anyway, from the beginning this woman and I were super turned-on by each other. She came onto me big-time and made little effort to conceal her feelings. I was torn to pieces, since although I would readily have dumped my wife in a second – even if this woman hadn't appeared – I couldn't justify to myself abandoning my son. It got so bad that I purposely avoided this woman whenever I could because being in her presence forced me to stifle impulses that were raging out of control. I have never had to clamp down upon myself so hard in all my life. Eventually, a few months later, she moved away and that was that. The marriage continued downhill, two more kids were born, and in the end we split up.

So, not much of an event that I can point to happened at that time to correspond to the Neptune direction to my Ascendant. But my spirit guides have told me that there is another probably reality (a "parallel reality" which branches off from this one whenever we make a decision) in which I did abandon my son and leave with this woman. According to my guides, we are not unitary beings who live our lives in linear sequence, but rather are infinitely ramified "waves" who can only remember one single line of personal history at a time. Thus to them this probable reality, in which I stayed with my wife and son, is no more nor less real than the probable reality in which I left with the other woman. And the birth horoscope is an indicator of all possible probable realities: the chart of the "me" who stayed with my wife is the same as the chart of the "me" who left with the other woman. So, if this is true, then at least the Neptune conjunct Ascendant direction worked in the probable reality in which I left (if not in this one, in which I stayed).

Then just today I was channeling to ask the question of whether I'd made the right decision in staying with my wife, since the thing fell apart in the end anyway. And this is what my guides told me: "It wouldn't have mattered. That's something you still haven't figured out – that there's no 'right' or 'wrong'; all there are, are different decisions, different lessons to learn, none of which ultimately matter in the least. That was a great sacrifice you made for your son (which he'll never understand or appreciate), but which definitely made you a far more selfless person – hence a better father and husband– and a more spiritual person. You lost a lot of selfishness on that one. And, if you'd left with K., it wouldn't have been any bed of roses either. That's what the Neptune conjunct Ascendant – which you've never understood – means. In some probable realities you left with K. In this one you made a tremendous sacrifice for the sake of another person, which put you squarely on the spiritual path. Or another way of putting it is: splitting with K. may or may not have destroyed your chances for spiritual advancement, just as leaving the ranch (a job I hated but which I sensed was a spiritual test), or leaving during the guerrilla war (another test: a situation in which I never knew from one day to the next who would show up to kill me, but which my guidance told me to stick out), might or might not have destroyed your spiritual aspirations. But sticking it out with your marriage – honoring the commitment you had made to your son (and wife) – definitely moved you forward on the spiritual path. Shirking your responsibilities and taking the easy way out would have left you right where you were. And that's what Neptune conjunct Ascendant meant."

The moral of all this is, that sometimes directions which we think have failed worked after all; it's just a matter of how you look at it.

Postscript: When I wrote *The Great Wheel* – a commentary on W.B. Yeats masterpiece *A Vision* – I began to look at the people I knew karmically. And it was only then that I understood that this woman wasn't for me. She is Phase 22 – a very conflicted phase – a person who is very dependent, a victim. Sure, her moon was right on my sun; and she was beautiful and sexy as hell; and fulfilled all my images ... but also we exchanged Nodes (she was born nine years after me); and her Saturn fell right on my South Node; so she was not good for me. I noted that at the time, but I didn't understand what it meant (because I didn't want to understand what it meant). Only when I wrote *The Great Wheel* did I understand (we're talking now about 30 years between when I knew this woman and when I finished writing *The Great Wheel*. I'm kind of a slow learner).

She didn't go out there to that remote Mayan village to start farming by herself. She was following her friend, a brassy Aries woman who led her. And, if I had united with her, she would have become my little love slave – which in a certain sense would have been hey nonny nonny ... but would also have been the death of my spiritual aspirations. She would have brought me down with her dependence. She was not for me. Not spiritually, anyway.

La Noche Triste

The following extract is from William Prescott's book *The Conquest of Mexico*, published in 1843:

(After the death of Montezuma, Cortes and his men were trapped in the heart of Mexico City, under siege by the Aztec population).

"There was no longer any question as to the expediency of evacuating the capital. The only doubt was as to the time of doing so, and the route. The Spanish commander called a council of officers to deliberate these matters.

"There was some difference of opinion in respect to the hour of departure. The day-time, it was argued by some, would be preferable, since it would enable them to see the nature and extent of their danger, and to provide against it.

"But, on the other hand, it was urged, that the night presented many obvious advantages in dealing with a foe who rarely carried his hostilities beyond the day.

"These views were fortified, it is said, by the counsels of a soldier named Botello, who professed the mysterious science of judicial astrology. He had gained credit with the army by some predictions which had been verified by the events. This man recommended to his countrymen by all means to evacuate the place in the night, as the hour most propitious to them, although he should perish in it.

"It is possible Botello's predictions had some weight in determining the opinion of Cortes. It is, however, quite as probable that he made use of the astrologer's opinion, finding it coincided with his own, to influence that of his men, and inspire them with higher confidence. At all events, it was decided to abandon the city that very night.

"At midnight the troops were under arms, in readiness for the march. Mass was performed by Father Olmedo, who invoked the protection of the Almighty through the awful perils of the night. The gates were thrown open, and, on the first of July 1520, the Spaniards for the last time sallied forth from the walls of the ancient fortress, the scene of so much suffering and such indomitable courage."

(After a terrible slaughter on this melancholy night, Cortes and the major part of his army succeeded in escaping the Aztec army, and returned a year later to lay siege to the capital and capture it. Botello was among those killed in the breakout.)

Nixon's Question

By the end of July, 1974, President Richard Nixon was at the end of his political rope. On July 24th the House Judiciary Committee began televised sessions on impeachment. From July 27th through July 30th, the Judiciary Committee voted for three articles of impeachment. In his *Memoirs*, Nixon wrote: "On the night of July 30 I could not get to sleep. After tossing and turning for a few hours, I finally put on the light and took a pad of notepaper from the bed table. I wrote the time and date at the top – 3:50 a.m., July 31 – and I began to outline the choices left to me. There were really only three: I could resign right away; I could stay on until the House had voted on the articles of impeachment and then resign if impeached; or I could fight all the way through the Senate. For almost three hours I listed the pros and cons: what would be the best for me, for my family, for my friends and supporters? What would be the best for the country?"

A horoscope erected for this moment can give us an answer to Nixon's question. Horary is the branch of astrology that seeks to reveal the answer to a question by means of a horoscope erected for the moment the question is put to the astrologer (an astrologer answering a horary question for him or herself uses the moment that it occurs to him or her to consult a horary chart for the answer; but as Dr. Marc Edmund Jones said, it's better to just wait until something happens which bears upon the question and then erect the chart for that moment). The analysis in horary differs from that in natal in that only those horoscope factors pertinent to the given question are taken into account – everything else is ignored.

Commentary by Bob Makransky:

The querent is the person asking the question, and he is represented by the planet which rules the sign on the Ascendant of the horary chart; and secondarily by planets in the first house and the Ascendant itself. In this case President Nixon is the querent, and his significator is the moon, ruler of the rising sign Cancer. We note that the moon is in her detriment, Capricorn, showing that the querent is in a helpless position, quite unable to influence the march of events in a constructive way. Had the moon been in Cancer, her own sign, or Taurus, her sign of exaltation, the querent could exert some control over the situation and might have turned the tide to his favor.

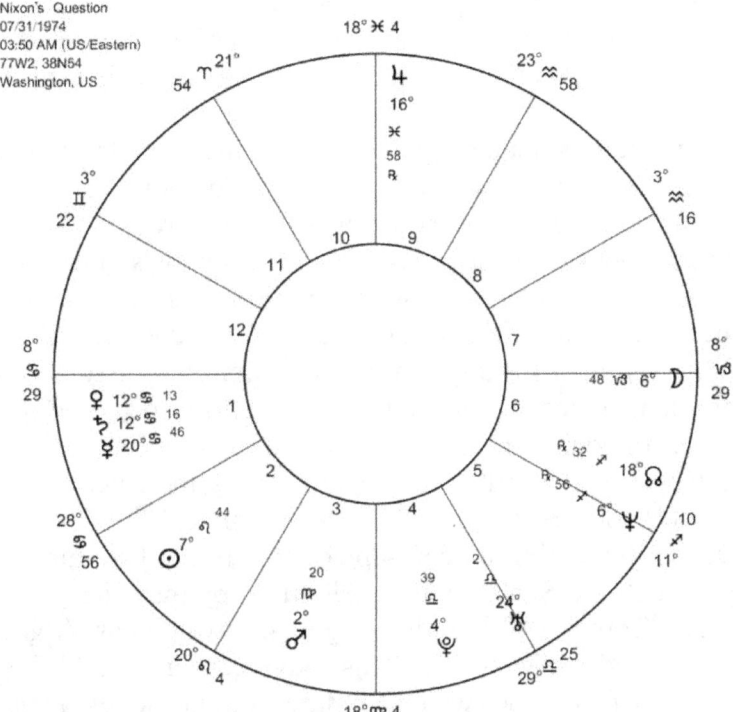

Note too that the Ascendant ruler moon occupies the 7th house of others, opponents, and open enemies, showing that the querent is very much in their hands

The quesited is the person or thing inquired about, and the significator of the quesited is the planet ruling the sign on the cusp of the house which rules the question (e.g. if a money question, then the significator of the quesited is the planet ruling the sign on the 2nd cusp; if a marriage question, then the significator of the quesited is the planet ruling the sign on the 7th cusp; and so on). In this case the quesited's significator is the ruler of the 10th house, representing Nixon's career, honor, and repute. Its ruler, Jupiter, is strong in his own sign of Pisces and at the Midheaven (because Jupiter is within 5 degrees of the 10th house cusp, it is considered to be a 10th house planet).

Note that President Nixon's natal Ascendant, 17 degrees of Virgo, is at the IC of the horary chart. Now if this were a 4th house question (about home or father) then this would be a favorable augury; but in the present 10th house question it is not a good indication for the querent. It suggests that the querent's honor and reputation probably cannot be salvaged no matter what course he adopts.

Now, there is not a single question being considered here, but rather three mutually exclusive options: immediate resignation, resignation after the House vote, or fighting through the Senate. Each of these options must be assigned a different significator, and each significator compared in turn with the querent's significator to determine which option will be most favorable to the querent.

The first significator, in this case Jupiter, is assigned to the most important option or the first option mentioned by the querent: in this case, immediate resignation. The second option, resignation after the House vote, will then be signified by the ruler of the 10th from the 10th, or the original 7th. The sign on the 7th house is Capricorn, so this option is represented by Saturn. The third option, fighting through the Senate, will be signified by the ruler of the 10th from the 10th from the 10th, or the original 4th, which has Virgo on its cusp and is ruled by Mercury. This may seem a bit odd, but it is standard horary technique (what Dr. Marc Edmund Jones terms "ring around the rosy"). For example, if a querent is thinking of taking a trip but can't decide between Europe or Hawaii, then the first option named (Europe) would be signified by the ruler of the 9th house (journeys) and the second option (Hawaii) by the ruler of the 9th from the 9th, or the original 5th house.

Since the actual outcome is known (the President did resign before impeachment), let us consider the two options not taken. The third option, fighting all the way through the Senate, is shown by Mercury, ruler of the IC. Mercury is disposed of by the moon (since it lies in Cancer which the moon rules), which indicates that this is the option the President would have preferred. Indeed, he stated that "In a subconscious way I knew that resignation was inevitable. But more than once over the next days I would yield to my desire to fight, and I would bridle as the inexorable end drew near." However the moon applies to a wide (14 degree) opposition to Mercury, showing that this is an option which the querent should reject; the moon and Mercury are in mutual reception by term and sign, indicating that not only President Nixon favored this option but so did his enemies in the Senate; however the opposition is such a divisive aspect that this mutual reception cannot override it. For example, in a love horary chart wherein the significators of querent (ruler ASC) and quesited (ruler DESC) are in mutual reception but also apply to square or opposition, what is indicated is that the two people love each other but circumstances will prevent their union.

The main criterion in deciding a horary question is whether or not there exists an applying aspect between the significators of the querent and quesited. Separating aspects don't count – they point to events that have already occurred and are over and done with. If the principle significators apply to conjunction, sextile, or trine, then the answer to the horary question is positive. If they apply to square or opposition, the answer is negative. Quite wide orbs (a whole sign, if there are other favorable testimonies) may be used in evaluation, but aspects shouldn't cross the line of a sign unless they are quite close (even then the crossing is significant – it may mean something like the whole matter at issue now will become irrelevant or have to be completely reconsidered in light of new developments).

If no aspect exists between the principal significators but Scorpio, Aquarius, or Pisces is involved; then Pluto, Uranus, or Neptune may be substituted as significator for Mars, Saturn, or Jupiter, respectively. If there is still no applying aspect between principal significators, then the horary answer is negative (there are other extenuating circumstances – such as translation of light – described in horary texts which can still yield a positive answer in the absence of an aspect between significators, but these tend to occur once in a blue moon).

Resort can also be made to other than the principal significators, i.e. to identify an applying aspect between querent's significator and the ruler of the house opposite or square to the quesited, but this dilutes the analysis unless other testimonies are present, such as good applying aspects by the moon to querent's or quesited's significator or the Planetary hour ruler, etc. Generally speaking, however, *if the thing is going to say yes, then it will say yes; and if it doesn't then the answer is probably no.*

In this question Mercury signifies fighting through the Senate, and Mercury in the horary chart not only widely opposes querent's significator but also narrowly (by little over one degree) opposes Nixon's natal sun in 20 degrees Capricorn, indicating that a fight through the Senate would do nothing for the querent's health and purpose in life, not to mention his honor and repute (the ostensible reason why he wanted to elect this option).

Now consider the second option, staying on until the full House had voted, then resigning if impeached. This option, and the House of Representatives itself, is signified by Saturn, ruler of the original 7th house (the tenth from the tenth), which is fittingly the house of open enemies. Saturn and the moon are in mutual reception – that is, each is in the ruling sign of the other – which indicates that both querent and quesited would relish this option: Nixon the beleaguered fighter vs. the crowd howling for blood. However, the moon applies to a six-degree opposition with Saturn, showing that the querent should reject this option as well. Saturn will very shortly conjoin Venus, ruler of Libra on the cusp of quesited's 11th house (that is to say, the original 5th house), so it is likely that the House of Representatives would realize its wishes in the matter and handily secure the vote of impeachment, so in no wise could the President be able to vindicate himself before this tribunal.

Finally, let us consider the first option, immediate resignation, signified by Jupiter. Jupiter is in his own sign and house at the Midheaven, indicating that this is a strong option, the dominant course of action. Jupiter is retrograde, and when any significator is retrograde it points to some kind of intransigence or immovability, which in this case points to the inevitability of immediate resignation. The clinching argument in favor of this option is the wide (= 10 degrees) mutually applying trine from moon to Jupiter. In spite of anyone's preference in the matter, the course of events inevitably points to resignation right away.

It might be supposed that since the moon applies to a good aspect with a strong Jupiter, that a wholly favorable outcome is in store, and the President would be able to stay in office. However, one must not lose sight of the question, which was "Should I resign right away?" The answer is yes, he should. Had the question been: "Should I fight the resignation?" then this favorable answer would indicate that he should fight; but that wasn't the question in this case. In retrospect we can see that immediate resignation – ending the thing as quickly as possible – was the best solution for all parties and the country.

In this particular horary only one of the three options was indicated by a favorable aspect between principal significators, so prognostication was easy. If several (or none) of the options had shown favorable aspects, then recourse would have to be made to other testimonies (or substitute significators) in the chart to determine which option was the *most* favorable. When all is said and done horary astrology has to be interpreted by feel, by psychic attunement to what the planetary symbols mean in this particular case.

The moon needs just over 10 degrees to perfect the sextile to Jupiter, so the resignation could be expected in about 10 days. The moon is in a cardinal sign, and both planets are angular; cardinal signs and angular houses usually indicate fastest timing; hence 10 days rather than 10 weeks or 10 years. The President actually left office on August 9th, nine days after the question.

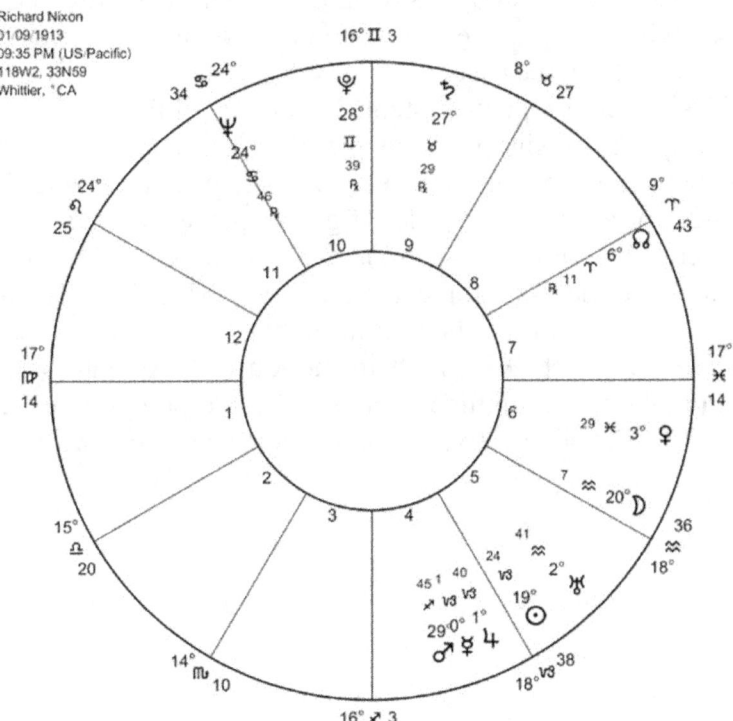

Commentary by Olivia Barclay:

"As the author says, one would choose the first named. Yet as a matter of fact; that is not the approach I would have taken. My immediate impression is, to fight or not to fight? The main significator goes over to the other side of the chart, giving in to the other, and Mars is weak. Mars, the fighting planet, is an important significator in this type of question. I was immediately reminded of the Prince Rupert chart on page 453 of *Christian Astrology*, where Lilly wrote, 'Let all the planets assist ... concerning war (fighting). If Mars himself, who is significator thereof, be unfortunate ... it is as good as nothing.' In other words, if Mars is weak, don't fight. I do think the chart shows that by his resignation and the mutual reception of moon with Saturn, he gained more sympathy than would otherwise have been the case.

"Using Lilly's point system, Nixon's significator moon is in mutual reception by sign (+5), in the 7th (+4), occidental (+2), not combust or under the sun's beams (+5), peregrine (-5), and slow in motion (-2) for a total of +9. The fighting planet Mars is in the 3rd (+1), direct (+4), not combust (+5), swift in motion (+2), occidental (+2), and peregrine (-5), for a total of +9. Nixon's opposition is shown by 7-ruler Saturn, which is in mutual reception by sign (+5), in the 1st (+5), direct (+4), swift in motion (+2), oriental (+2), not combust (+5), exactly conjunct Venus (+4), and peregrine (-5), for a total of +22. President Nixon's opposition was far more powerful than he."

The *Titanic*

The centennial of the *Titanic* disaster is a good excuse to take a look at the question of whether the rules of horary astrology, as laid down by Renaissance practitioners, are valid or not. William Lilly states, "Of a Ship, and Her Safety or Destruction: The Ascendant and the moon signify the ship and cargo; the lord of the Ascendant, those that sail in her. If you find a malevolent, having dignities in the 8th, placed in the Ascendant, or the lord of the Ascendant in the 8th in ill configuration with the lords of the 8th, 12th, 4th, or 6th, or if the moon be combust, and under the earth, you may judge that the ship is lost, and the men drowned. But if you find reception between the significators at the same time, the ship was wrecked, but some of the crew escaped; if all the preceding significators be free from affliction, then both ship and cargo are safe; and if there be reception, the more so. If the Ascendant and moon be unfortunate, and the lord of the Ascendant fortunate, the ship is lost but the men saved.

"But when the querent demand, of any ship setting forth, and the state of the ship ere she return, and what may be hoped of the voyage; then behold the angles of the figure, and see if the fortunes are therein, and the infortunes remote from angles, cadent, combust, or under the sun's beams, then you may judge the ship will go safe with all her lading. But if you find infortunes in the angles, or succeeding houses, there will chance some hindrance unto the ship. If the infortune be Saturn, the vessel will strike ground. If Mars, and he be in an earthy sign, he will signify the same, or very great danger and damage. But if the fortunes cast their benevolent rays to the place of Saturn or Mars, and the lords of the angles and of the dispositor of the moon be free, then the ship shall labour hard, and suffer damage, yet the greater part of the crew and cargo shall be preserved.

"If the signs afflicted by Saturn, Mars, South Node (and Uranus, if he be ill aspected) <n.b. evidently this is the editor's – Zadkiel's – interpolation, since Lilly certainly didn't use Uranus>, be those that signify the vessel's bottom or parts underwater <i.e. Taurus, Gemini and Cancer>, she springs a leak ... "

The question arises, which horoscope should we look at? *Titanic* was launched on May 31st, 1911; it began its maiden voyage on April 2nd, 1912; it left shore finally on April 10th, 1912; and it sank on April 15th, 1912. Let's look at the launch chart first.

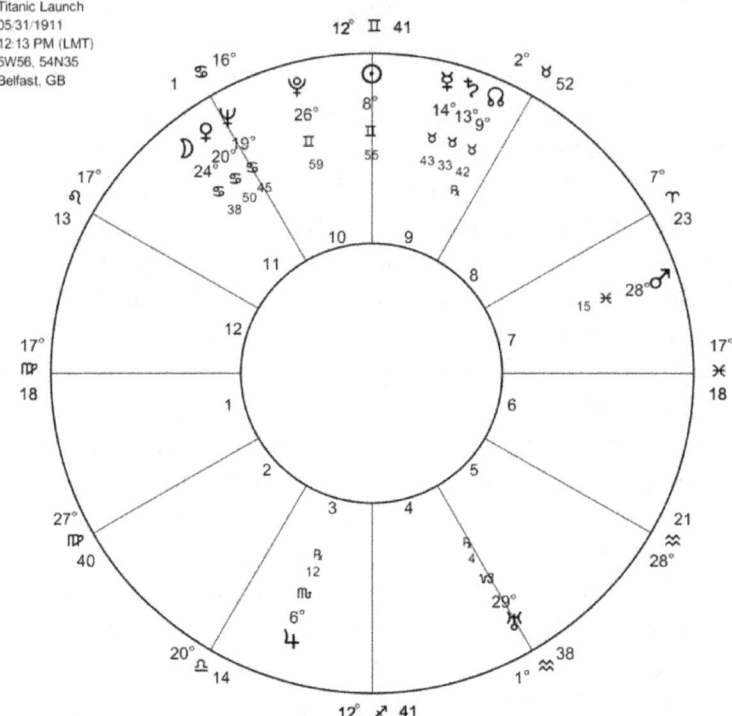

Titanic Launch – 12:13 pm LMT, 5/31/1911, Belfast: The Ascendant is 17°VI18', which receives good aspects from Venus, Neptune, Mercury (its lord), and Saturn. The moon is in her own sign, recently conjoined Venus-Neptune, albeit ominously applying to opposition with Uranus (sudden disasters). Mercury, lord of the Ascendant, is separating from conjunction with Saturn (ominous) but applying to sextile with its dispositor, Venus. Since none of the principal significators are afflicted, and the 8th house is uninvolved, then it would appear that both ship and cargo are safe (the more so since the moon disposes of Mercury by exaltation). The only apparent "chance of hindrance to the ship" is the moon's application to trine Mars in an angle (the seventh house). But this is a trine, not an affliction (although the place of Mars in the launch chart is quite close to the place of moon in the sinking chart); and since if "the fortunes cast their benevolent rays to the place of Mars, and the lords of the angles and the moon's dispositor are free" of affliction, which they are (Jupiter, lord of IC and DESC conjoins Fortuna), this would seem to imply there is not a major problem. In other words, Lilly's guidelines do not seem to implicate the *Titanic* launch chart as problematical.

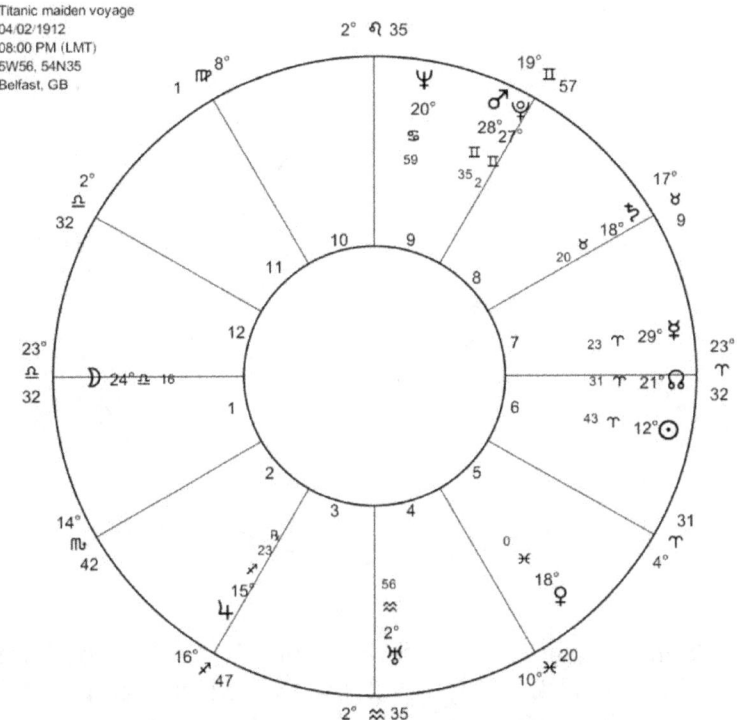

Titanic maiden voyage – 8 pm LMT, April 2, 1912, Belfast: the moon is rising, and moon and Ascendant receive squares from Uranus and Neptune and the opposition of Mercury; but are trine Mars-Pluto on the 9th cusp (voyages). Moon is with the South Node, which is quite ominous, but there is no relationship with the 8th house, or aspect to Venus (lady of Ascendant and 8th and dispositor of the moon). The moon is in an angle (conjunct the Ascendant), but the infortunes are remote from angles (except for Uranus on the IC). The main testimonies which perhaps point to a tragedy are that moon rising conjunct the South Node, and the lower culminating Uranus, both within a degree of exactitude. Interestingly, the IC in the maiden voyage chart is the ASC of the sinking chart; and the sun and Mercury in the sinking chart have advanced to opposition with the moon (and Ascendant) in the maiden voyage chart.

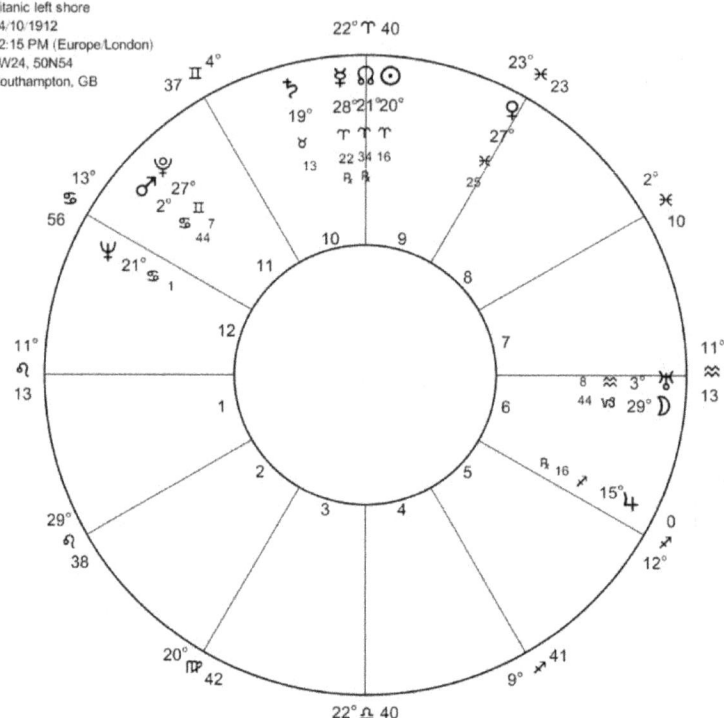

Titanic left shore – 12:15 pm, April 10, 1912, Southampton: the Ascendant is 11°LE13', ruled by exalted sun conjunct North Node on the Midheaven (according to Lilly, great success for the passengers; especially the Captain, E.J. Smith, whose Ascendant is 13° Leo!). Void of course moon is in its detriment, cadent, recently square Mercury and sun and recently opposed to Neptune. It is about to conjoin Uranus (disasters). All of this is ominous for the ship. The angles are free of affliction, except for Saturn in the 10th (but rather remote from the MC, and conjoined Fortuna). Although you can deduce that the moon's condition is bad, I don't think Lilly's criteria would enable you to predict disaster.

What have we learned here? That Lilly's criteria for ship sinkings are not all that useful, for one thing. Also, that trying to deduce the outcome of an event from the moment of its inception using the traditional rules of horary astrology is not exactly apodictic. Also, that perhaps we should look more at exact conjunctions with angles in horary charts (and making elections) – as the maiden voyage chart implies – rather than with traditional house rulerships. Also, that the most symbolical of the three charts – the maiden voyage, as opposed to the launch and leaving shore charts – is the most apropos. Perhaps it is as Dr. Marc Edmund Jones said: symbolism is more powerful than reality.

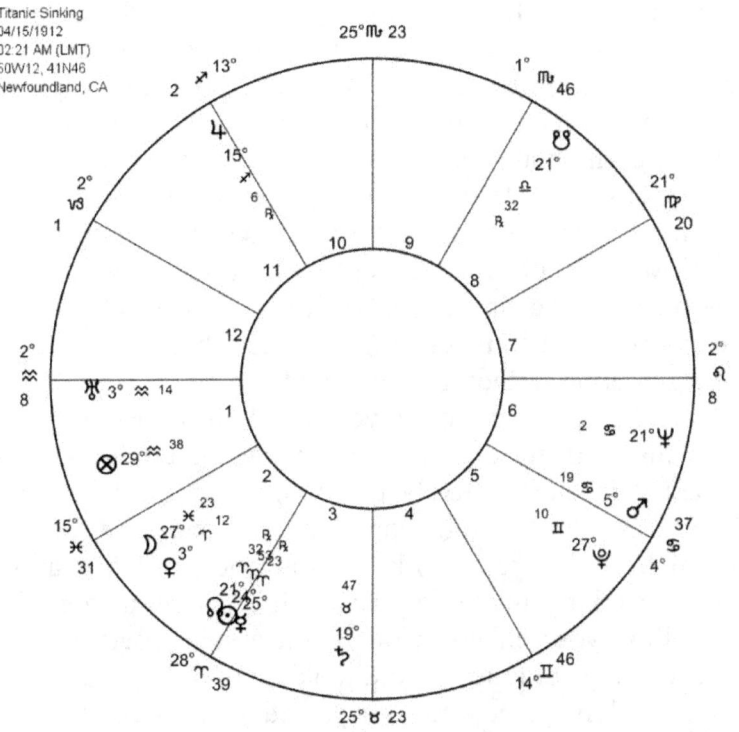

Picking Winning Lottery Numbers

The information which follows was channeled. Since I don't play the lottery myself (with South Node in my natal 2nd house and the 2nd house ruler Jupiter severely afflicted, why bother?), I certainly can't guarantee anything to anyone. I use these methods for electing propitious times to ask financial favors, to telephone my buyers, and to cast money spells, etc., rather than to play the lottery. I do find that in the hours and days after casting a money spell using these methods I usually receive new ideas on how to get some money (for information on how to cast spells, see my book *Planetary Hours*). However, later on we shall look at some charts of actual lottery winners listed in *AstroDatabank* to see how the given principles worked out in practice. Consider what follows to consist of tips and guidelines rather than hard and fast rules.

First off, you must look to your natal horoscope, to see if it is a winner's chart. If, for example, your natal sun conjoins or afflicts Saturn, then it is most unlikely that you are going to be winning many lotteries. Sun / Saturn combinations tend to have an inner attitude which prefers hard work, self-sacrifice, self-limitation; and which disdains taking any "free rides" in life. So no matter what you might be telling yourself consciously, on a subconscious level you will reject winning the lottery. And look at your 2nd house of money: if it contains malefic planets badly aspected, then forget it.

Also, you should only purchase one ticket per lottery draw, no more. Although mathematically it appears as though your chances of winning improve if you purchase numerous tickets; nonetheless, from the magical point of view this shows lack of faith – and it is faith that moves mountains (creates your reality). If the Spirit means for you to win, then you'll win; and if not, not. Purchasing lots of tickets isn't going to improve your chances with the Spirit one iota. On the contrary, your lack of faith diminishes your chances. The laws of luck are not the same as the laws of mathematical probability. In the world of humans you can hedge your bets; but when Lady Luck is seated across the table from you, you have to look her straight in the eye and bet your whole stack on one shot. Therefore, to enter the same lottery drawing more than once is to express bad faith and distrust in luck. It is being too pushy, too hungry, too needy. It's evidence of a losing attitude (although here and there, as in case # 7039 below, it has worked).

We are going to describe the system starting from its simplest elements to use in practice – techniques which even a beginning astrologer can easily apply. Fortunately, the simplest techniques are also the most important. Then, we will explain the more complex elements of the system (those which require some astrological expertise to apply). The most important part of choosing a good time to purchase lottery tickets – namely picking a good Planetary Hour – is not dependent upon your individual birth horoscope. Therefore, if you don't know your natal chart you can still use astrology to help. If you do know your natal chart, then it's possible to refine the analysis to a greater degree of complexity. However these operations don't improve your chances of winning any particular lottery; what they do is strengthen your *intent* to win the lottery (make it more likely that you will win the lottery *some day*). Again, the laws of luck – the way the universe really works – are very different than the logic of everyday society.

There is a general karmic flow to the universe. It's what Chinese philosophers termed the *Tao* – the way things really are and happen, as opposed to the way modern society teaches us they ought to be. People can either be in tune with the *Tao*, floating with the current; or they can be battling against it. Humankind in its primeval state was tuned in to this cosmic rhythm; but ever since it became a thinking and reasoning species (when it turned from hunting / gathering to agriculture) it lost its attunement to the way things are and happen. The way in which we moderns make things happen in everyday life is by thinking, and by trying to get other people to approve of our thinking. But this is not the way to get the universe to respond. We can only get the universe to respond by adapting ourselves to it, by flowing with it, rather than by trying to woo it and impress it (which is the way we get people to respond). We have to allow ourselves to be led, not try to impress the universe with our own self-importance (our feeling of how deserving we are).

Contrary to popular belief about the efficacy of magical techniques, you can only invite luck – not command it. You invite luck by strengthening your intent (your feeling that winning the lottery is important). If on a conscious level you are telling yourself that you want to win the lottery, but on a subconscious level you don't really believe you deserve to win, then there's no way you can be a winner no matter what elaborate motions you go through to improve your chances. On the other hand, the very act of ritualizing your entering the lottery (by using the more complex techniques based on your individual horoscope) tends to strengthen your intent to win, and at the same time weaken any subconscious opposing agendas. In other words, the effect of using more complex techniques is psychological and cumulative in effect; its purpose is to transform you into a winner by building up your confidence, and by erasing subconscious doubt that you are a winner. Any magical ritual (in this case calculating favorable days to enter the lottery based on your personal horoscope) which is repeated long enough, with as much sincerity as you can muster, will eventually bring about the desired result. Or at least, *a* desired result.

One way of adapting ourselves to the universe is to use astrology to time our actions according to the motions of the planets. To begin with, pre-selected lottery numbers are useless – e.g., numbers taken from number books or favorite people's birthdates, etc. All that matters is picking good astrological times to purchase your ticket. The ideal situation is to purchase your ticket on a day when there are good transiting aspects, for a draw which will occur when there are good progressed lunar aspects. At the moment when you purchase your lottery ticket, only *then* should you channel (go by hunch) which numbers to select (if it's that kind of lottery). The particular numbers chosen are of no importance whatever: all that matters is the astrological timing of the moment of purchase.

Lottery winners and winning numbers are not predetermined. The situation is in flux until the moment when the winning numbers are drawn; and at that moment the winners are "selected" from among those who entered the lottery at propitious times. Therefore, schemes for preselecting winning numbers are useless since it isn't the numbers themselves which matter, but rather the times at which those numbers were chosen. As mentioned previously, luck can be invited, but not commanded. By entering the lottery at a propitious time you are putting yourself in the best position for luck to "notice" you; and by surrendering your own power of decision at that moment (by choosing the first numbers that come to mind rather than preconceived ones) you are inviting luck to take you with it.

Planetary Hours

The most important astrological point is to purchase your lottery ticket during a favorable Planetary Hour, which – if you aren't going to use your own natal horoscope as a reference – means a Jupiter hour (since Jupiter symbolizes money and good fortune generally). The Planetary Hours are a system for electing propitious times to act based upon an ancient Babylonian technique which antedates the zodiac of signs. Even if you know nothing about astrology, you can still learn to apply this technique quite easily. For more information (and tables) see my book *Planetary Hours*.

As mentioned previously, however, the analysis can be refined based upon your own natal horoscope, by determining which are your strongest planets for success, and for monetary success in particular. To summarize the system briefly:

1) Purchase your ticket during a planetary hour ruled by your own money planet, or Jupiter. This is the most important point; and the easiest for a non-astrologer to apply.

2) Aim for a draw date which coincides with favorable progressed or converse progressed lunar aspects to your own money planet or to natal Jupiter; preferably when there are background (major) favorable progressed aspects to or by your money planet happening.

3) Purchase your lottery ticket on the day of a favorable transit by or to your own money planet or natal Jupiter (during a planetary hour ruled by your own money planet or Jupiter).

To summarize: purchase your lottery ticket during a favorable Planetary Hour; under a favorable transiting aspect; to bear fruit under a favorable progressed (usually progressed lunar) aspect. Favorable aspects are the trine and sextile; and also the conjunction between planets which combine harmoniously (see the *Table of Favorable and Unfavorable Planetary Combinations* on page 88).

Secondary progressions are also called "day-for-a-year" progressions. To progress your natal horoscope to the present time, just calculate a horoscope for as many days after you were born, as years you have lived. As an example, if 30½ days after you were born the moon in the sky reached the zodiacal position of Jupiter in your natal horoscope, then we would say your progressed moon conjoined natal Jupiter at age 30½.

You need to find a day within a day or two of a lottery drawing, when progressed moon favorably aspects your own money planet or your natal Jupiter. For complete information on how to calculate and interpret progressed and converse progressed aspects, see R.C. Davison, *The Technique of Prediction*, Fowler 1977; or Alan Leo, *The Progressed Horoscope*, Fowler 1969. For copious examples of how to interpret transits (using the horoscope of Theodore Roosevelt as the example), see the essay on "Mutual Transits".

Progressed lunar aspects usually operate on the very day they are mathematically exact (or on the day before or after). Converse progressed aspects can be as effective as progressed aspects. Progressed-to-progressed aspects (for example, progressed moon trine progressed Jupiter rather than natal Jupiter) are not as effective as are progressed-to-natal aspects. However, you have to use what's at hand; or else be willing to wait for years for favorable configurations.

Take a look at your chart and pick your strongest natal planets according to their aspects, sign positions, and angularity. In this analysis the strength factors are, in order of decreasing importance: unaspected; well-aspected; in ruling or exaltation sign; conjunct an angle. Avoid planets which are afflicted or in their sign of detriment or fall.

It has sometimes been said that speculation / gambling is a 5th house matter. However, it is best to go with any strong benefic planet in the natal 2nd house (the money house); or, if there's not one, then the ruler of the 2nd house (the planet which rules the sign on the cusp of the 2nd house in your horoscope), *if* it is strong by sign and well-aspected. Otherwise, choose (in descending order): Jupiter; Venus; sun; Mars; or Uranus. Avoid the moon; Mercury; Saturn; Neptune; and Pluto (unless one of them is strong and is ruler of the 2nd house, or located in the 2nd house). Call this planet (or these planets) your "own money planet(s)".

If you don't have such a money planet, then use Jupiter; and if Jupiter's no good either (because it is weak by sign or afflicted by aspect), then try Venus. If you don't have a money planet of your own; and if neither Jupiter nor Venus is strong by sign or house, or well-aspected; then probably the lottery won't be your ship coming in.

At the end of this selection process you should have a planet or two which you can use to find propitious times to purchase lottery tickets. There's no point in using weak, afflicted planets for something like picking lottery tickets. A weak, afflicted Jupiter is never going to bring you luck; but a strong, well-aspected Mars or Uranus *can* do so.

Visualization

You have to cooperate with the astrological process by projecting a future in which your desire is realized. You do this by the technique of Creative Visualization, which is essentially what prayer and casting spells are all about. It's best not to visualize yourself winning millions, but just enough to enable you to ... (fill in the blank with whatever your dream is). There's no reason to be greedy – it works better if you're not so greedy; and if other people are somehow benefiting from your wealth (it's not just about how much you will buy; or about you being waited on hand and foot). Visualize how you can help other people with your wealth. You can start with your loved ones – helping make their dreams come true; but also you should imagine yourself directly helping homeless people; or refugees; or starving people. Imagine how much delight you can bring to others with your winnings.

If you visualize yourself basking on your private yacht docked in front of the mansion on your private island, then the flow of luck comes to a dead halt. Being grabby is like breaking an electric circuit. But, if you visualize yourself being a *conduit* for luck – a Michael Anthony rather than a millionaire – then that's exactly what you will become: a channel for luck into the world. This doesn't mean that if you do win you have to give all your winnings away. But it does mean that you have to be psychologically prepared to do it if it comes to that. You have to visualize your winning the lottery making you a better, more generous person – not just a richer and haughtier one. You have to start loosening up your grasp of money in your everyday life – be freer in passing it out to people who need it; homeless people and beggars you meet on the street; etc., a*s if you were already rich.* You have to reach out to that probable reality, to feel it as if it were already true, to make it come true. Whenever you see or hear about another person's misfortune, imagine how happy you are that you can help that person *now that you're rich*.

This is not hard to do. Creative Visualization is similar to normal daydreaming but has the opposite intent. Where daydreaming stokes self-pity, Creative Visualization strengthens intent. In normal daydreaming you are actually pushing away whatever object you are daydreaming about into a future which never comes. In Creative Visualization you are actively drawing the object of your visualization to yourself by imagining it physically happening in the now moment, unfolding all around you. The difference between C.V. and normal daydreaming is that the former is a command of fulfillment and the latter is a command of lack. In normal daydreaming the focus is on yourself; other people serve only as mute witnesses to your own glory and vindication. In C.V. the focus is on the other people, and how happy they are (you have made them).

Creative Visualization is a matter of feeling, of longing, of reaching out for the object of your desire. Daydreaming is a matter of thinking, imaging, distancing yourself from the object of your desire. Daydreaming is actually reaching out towards self-pity, not towards the realization of your true desires. When you catch yourself daydreaming about wealth, switch it to C.V.

The future is not fixed. Rather, there are an infinite number of possible futures, termed "probable realities", which take off from the present moment (although some of these are more likely than others). In terms of lottery tickets, this means that every purchaser of a ticket for a given lottery turns out to be the winner of that lottery in some probable reality. There are as many possible outcomes as there are lottery ticket buyers. The basic astrological strategy, then, is to select the line of action which will propel you into the possible future in which you win the lottery; rather than into a future in which you don't.

Examples

Here are the only examples of lottery winners from *AstroDatabank* (http://www.astro.com/astro-databank/Main_Page) which include times and dates of ticket purchases as well as the winners' birth data (in tri-wheel charts the center is the natal chart; the middle ring is the progressed chart; the outer ring is the transiting chart):

AstroDatabank Lucky Lottery # 6780
Time of Purchase

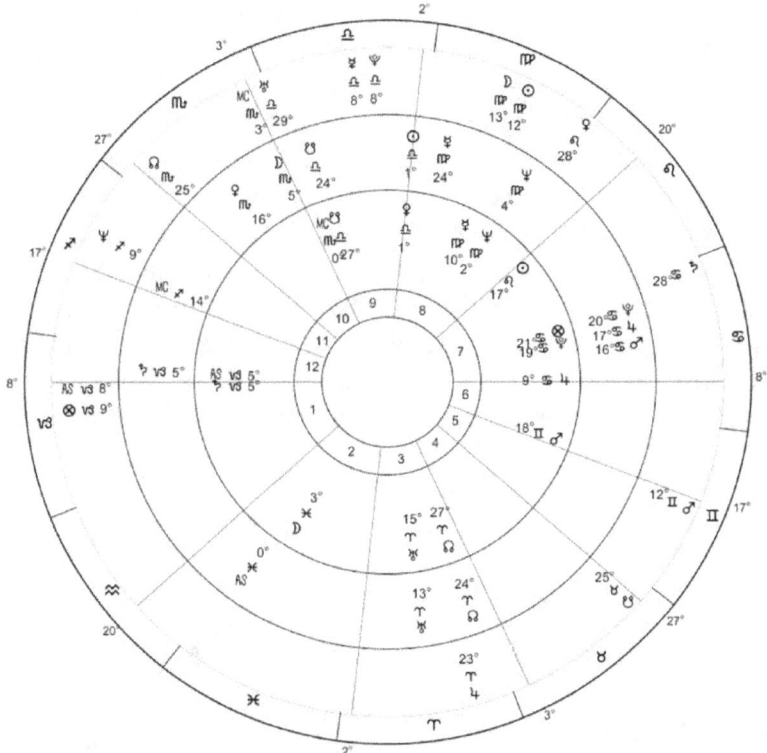

American lucky lottery winner of $50,000 in the Illinois state lottery on 9/18/1975 at 7:15 pm (born Aug. 10, 1930, 5:30 pm CDT, Chicago IL). He purchased the winning ticket on 9/05/1975, about 4:00 pm CDT.

The natal chart has Saturn ruler of the 2nd house (since Saturn is the ruler of Aquarius, which holds the 2nd cusp). Saturn is in its other ruling sign, Capricorn, exactly conjunct the Ascendant; sextile moon in the 2nd; opposing exalted Jupiter; and trine Mercury – Neptune. Saturn does square Venus in *its* ruling sign; but otherwise all the testimonies are excellent. Moon is located in the 2nd; trine and mutual reception (since each planet is in the other's ruling sign) Jupiter on the Descendant (this could imply that the native marries a wealthy person). Both Saturn and moon – as well as Jupiter – can be considered money planets for this chart; but Saturn is much more powerful than moon due to its being in its ruling sign and angular (conjunct the Ascendant).

Two points bear noting: a powerful Saturn *can* bring great fortune if it is strong enough in the birth chart. Secondly, an opposition to a powerful (exalted, angular, well-aspected) Jupiter is not bad; quite the contrary – i.e. oppositions are not intrinsically bad. Planets strong by sign and conjunct angles bring success, even when they are nominally malefic planets; or good planets in bad aspect.

The winning ticket was purchased with progressed moon a day past sextile natal Ascendant, and the win occurred two weeks later, when progressed moon was about to sextile natal Saturn. The purchase was made during either a Mercury or a moon hour (it's not certain which it was because the change from Mercury hour to moon hour occurred at 4:01 pm in Chicago on 9/5/1975). If it was a moon hour, then this bears out the theory, since the moon is a money planet here.

Time of Win

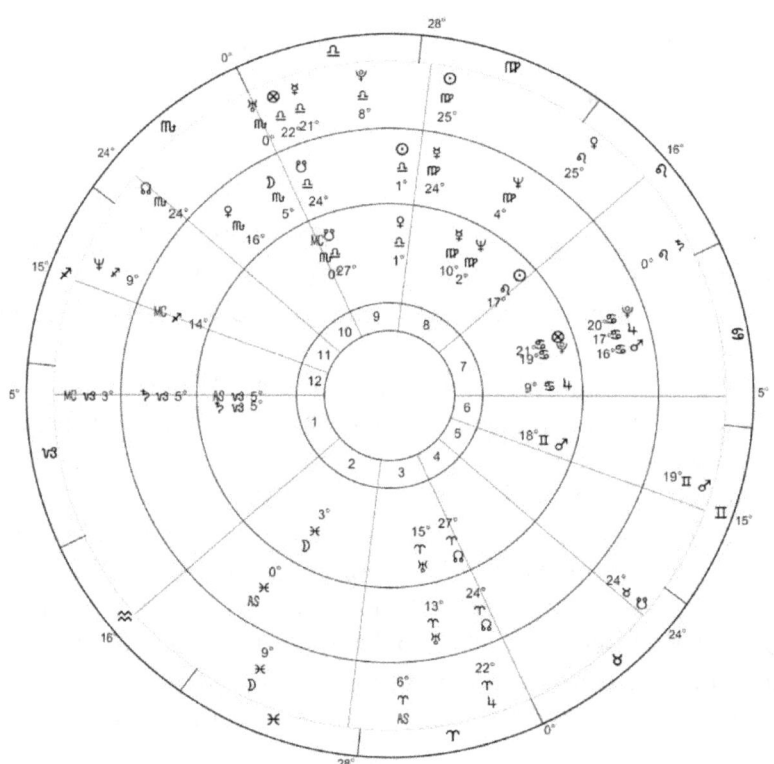

The win occurred 3 days before progressed moon sextile natal Saturn, which agrees with the theory espoused here – that the draw should coincide with a favorable progressed (lunar) aspect to the money planet (if you shade the orb on progressed lunar aspects a little bit – normally one expects them to happen within a day or two of exactitude).

Other important transits occurring at the time of the win are transiting Mars conjunct its natal place the preceding day (as we saw in the case of Theodore Roosevelt's transits this is often quite favorable); transiting Venus turned stationary direct trine the Node; the preceding new moon fell on natal Mercury; and, more importantly, transiting Uranus was 2 days from conjunction Midheaven (sudden, unexpected, radical shift in his honor / career / life's work). This is probably the precipitating influence – if he hadn't won the lottery, he would have experienced some other important and surprising life event which elevated his hopes and completely transformed his life direction.

Another very important background influence at this time was converse progressed Jupiter conjoining the Cancer point the preceding month. Beneficial progressed Jupiter aspects (including conjunctions with the Cardinal points) are so rare, that if you ever have one, you should purchase lottery tickets like mad.

AstroDatabank Lucky Lottery # 7039

American lucky lottery winner (born April 4, 1932, 3:00 am EST, Detroit MI) who bought two lottery tickets on 9/12/1984 at approximately 1:00 PM EDT in Washington D.C.; one of them was worth $1.7 million dollars.

This native's 2nd house is something else again. Above all, North Node (good karma and blessings) in the 2nd house means he'll always have enough money – it just flows to him. And the stellium of planets strong by sign and aspect (moon in Pisces trine Pluto; Mars in its ruler and conjunct the Aries point, no less, as well as sextile rising Saturn; sun exalted in Aries and trine angular Jupiter, which it disposes, since Jupiter is posited in the Sun's sign Leo). Anything this person does in life is going to bring him money – if he trips and falls, he'll land on money.

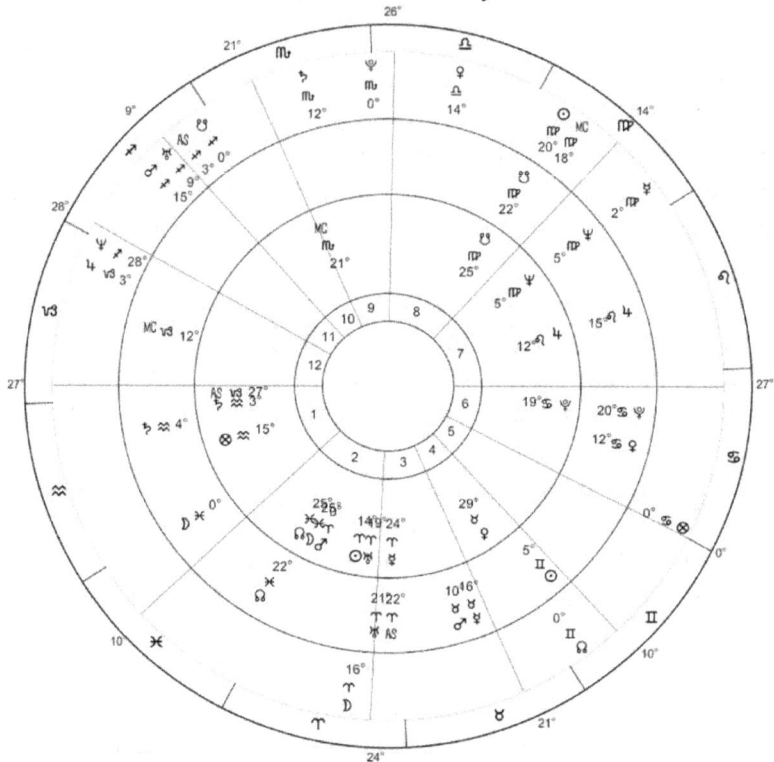

All of these planets are money planets for this native (though Mars, sun, and Jupiter are strongest). Really, the whole chart oozes strength and success (besides the 2nd house stellium, Saturn rises in its ruling sign Aquarius and Venus lower-culminates in her ruling sign Taurus).

The winning ticket was purchased during a sun hour. Since the sun is one of the money planets, this agrees with the theory. There are no important progressed or transiting aspects around the purchase date (except for transiting Mars trine natal sun the previous day. The preceding new moon fell on natal Neptune).

Lucky Lottery # 11398

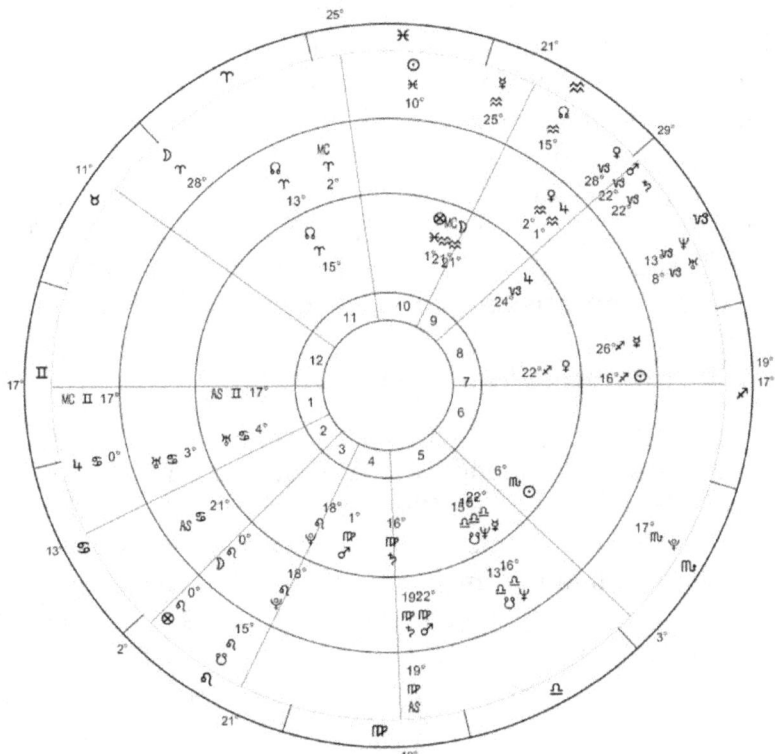

American lucky lottery winner (born October 29, 1949, 7:31 pm EST, Cleveland, OH). She bought the winning ticket 2/28/90, 7:00 pm EST, Parma, OH and received word the same evening that she had won the Ohio State Lottery.

In the natal chart moon rules the 2nd house (since Cancer is on the cusp); and moon is closely conjunct the Midheaven. Moon also receives favorable aspects from Venus, Mercury and Neptune (albeit also opposed to Pluto). Uranus is natally conjunct the 2nd cusp, and it receives a sextile from Mars and trine from the sun. Therefore, both moon and Uranus are money planets for this person. Uranus shows sudden, unexpected gains (and losses, but here more gains due to its favorable natal aspects).

Transiting Mars conjoined transiting Saturn square natal Mercury at the time of purchase; and it was purchased during a sun hour. None of this upholds our theory. Nothing in astrology (or life) is ironclad; all you can do is take your best shot. Nonetheless, this lottery win occurred within the context of converse progressed

Venus conjunct natal sun four months previously; and progressed sun conjunct Descendant a month later (no doubt the marriage benefited). The preceding full moon (lunar eclipse, actually) fell within a degree of opposition to natal moon.

Moreover, the native's transiting demi-Uranus return (DUR) – which always signifies a major life breakthrough – was two months previous; while transiting Saturn was coming to its first conjunction with natal Jupiter. In other words, there were some powerful beneficial background progressions and transits operating at this time, with particular emphasis on Uranus (sudden, unexpected, surprising, liberation).

AstroDatabank Lucky Lottery # 37457

American lucky winner (born October 29, 1932, 6:30 am EST, Cleveland, OH) along with her husband (born 3/27/1917, Cleveland OH) when he won the State Lottery of $21 million on 5/28/1986, 7:30 PM, Cleveland, OH. Mr. Swingle asked his wife to go to the store with him at approx. 7:10 PM where he bought $10.00 auto lotto tickets. Twenty minutes later they were $21 million richer.

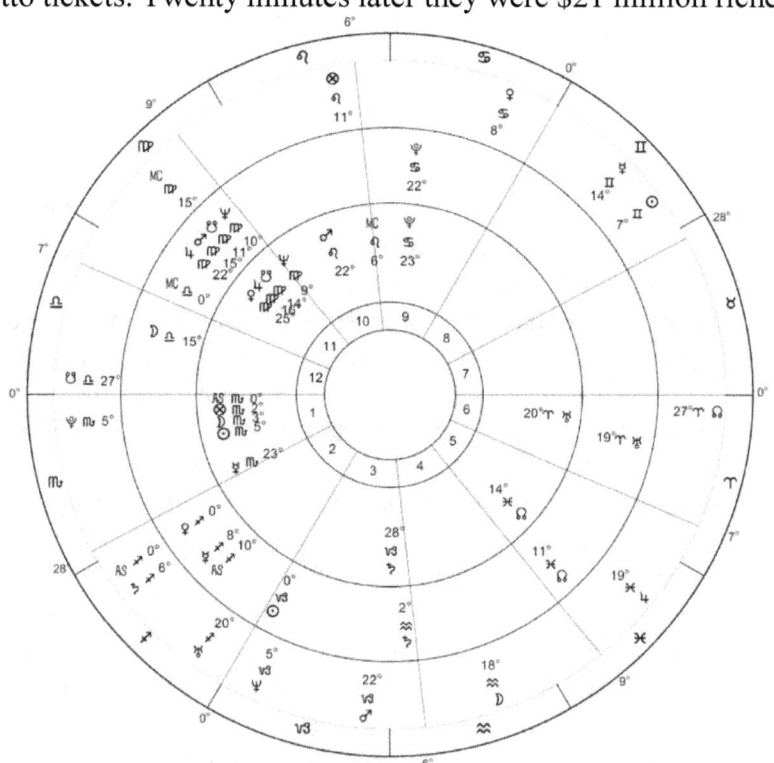

Mars rules Scorpio on the cusp of the 2nd house, and Mercury is not far from it, so both Mars and Mercury are money planets for this native. Converse progressed Jupiter sextile natal sun the previous year, and the native was still under the rays of this most favorable aspect (progressed aspects of the outer planets begin some months after the exact calculated time and go on for several years thereafter). Converse progressed Mars square Uranus the month of the win, which indicates some sudden, unexpected shakeup in the life; but since these planets are natally trine and Mars disposes of Uranus the ultimate outcome would be favorable.

Since the husband bought the winning ticket it is his chart which should be examined, but no birth time is given for him. He had converse Mars sextile natal sun and converse progressed Mercury sextile natal Mars about now; perhaps Mars was a money planet for him. His transiting Jupiter return occurred two months previously (this is a bit out-of-orb: one normally expects the Jupiter return to operate within a month following exactness). The winning ticket was purchased during a Jupiter hour.

A Baffling Problem

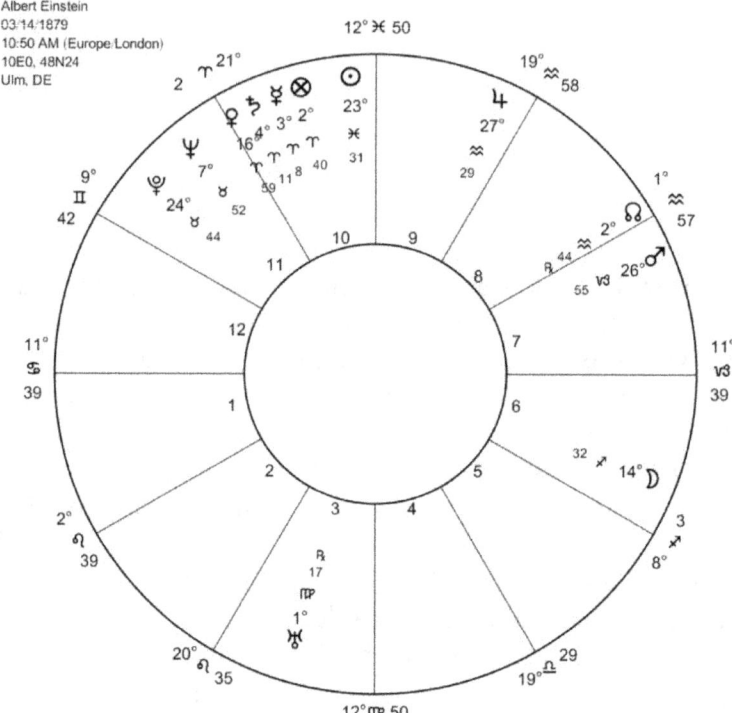

"During the total eclipse of May 29, 1919, A.S. Eddington and his colleagues made photographs of a field of stars close to the sun. The positions of the stars were shifted, demonstrating that light passing the sun was indeed deflected. It was a confirmation that helped to make Einstein famous." – Clifford M. Will, "Gravitation Theory", *Scientific American* 11/1974

This is the only historical instance of a solar eclipse having indubitably caused great changes in a native's life; moreover, the precise date on which those changes took place is known. Eddington required several months to measure his photographs, and it wasn't until 9/27/1919 that Einstein received word that Eddington's measurements had indeed confirmed his theory; and then it took until 11/7/1919 for the press and general public to learn that Newton's laws had been overthrown. On this latter date Einstein went from obscurity to worldwide fame overnight (date from *Einstein – the Life and Times* by Ronald W. Clark). Thus the "target date" which we wish to derive from the eclipse chart is 11/7/1919.

The first chart given above is Einstein's natal chart (data from the *American Book of Charts)*; the second chart below is that of the solar eclipse of 5/29/1919, erected for Berlin (where Einstein was residing at the time. If erected for Principe Island, where Eddington took the photographs, the angles only move back 4 degrees).

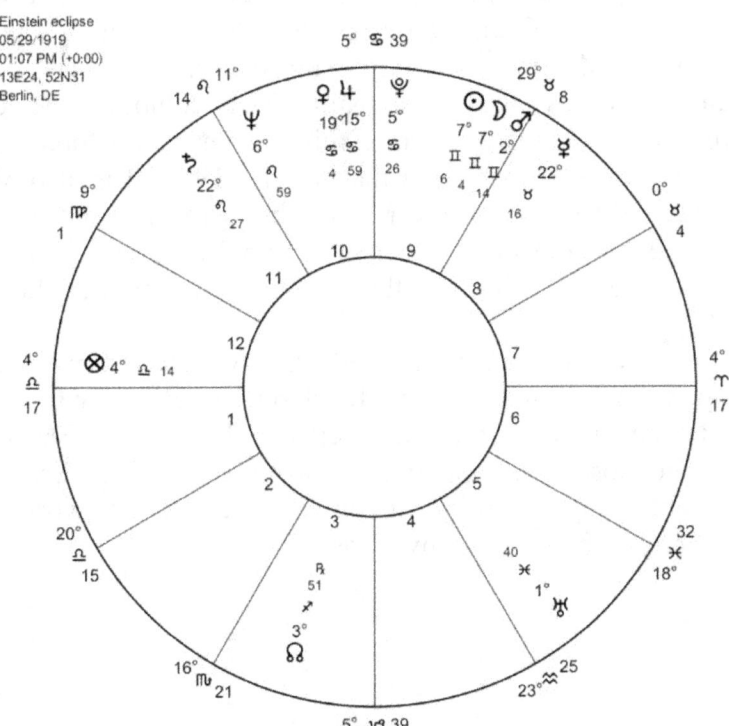

Mercury in the eclipse chart is 2 degrees from natal Pluto, and Uranus in the eclipse chart is less than half a degree from opposition to natal Uranus (DUR). But the only thing that is especially suggestive of imminent fame is the eclipse Descendant falling smack on Einstein's natal 10th house Saturn – Mercury – Part of Fortune conjunction. Okay, so given that we know what kind of event to expect, how can we time it?

As far as the target date is concerned, it must be noted that on 11/8/1919 transiting Uranus turned direct on Einstein's natal Jupiter, so this date is already demarcated without reference to the eclipse.

The only obvious eclipse referents are: 1) on 11/8/1919 transiting Mercury opposed the eclipse point, and 2) on this date also transiting North Node opposed the eclipse Mercury / natal Pluto conjunction. These scarcely seem to be powerful enough influences to have triggered the eclipse effect; and even if they are, who could have predicted it?

With regard to the other date, 9/27/1919, when Einstein received the news of Eddington's results, we have that the superior conjunction of Mercury with the sun occurred on the eclipse Ascendant on this day, and that transiting Mars conjoined the eclipse Saturn then also. However, while this date is more "predictable" from transits to the eclipse chart than is 11/7/1919, it is also of less significance. Einstein was never in doubt as to the validity of his theory, hence his receipt of the news from Eddington was not as important an event for him than the sudden fame which exploded on 11/7/1919.

Apart from transits, some authors have devised methods for predicting when the events symbolized by an eclipse will actually occur which depend upon the space between the eclipse ASC and the point of the eclipse (see Sepharial's *Eclipses*, p.83 ff for a summary of these techniques). However, none of these methods work in the present case. Anybody have any ideas?

Thatcher's Comet

In early July of 1861 the brightest comet in half a century appeared in the region of Ursa Major – the Big Dipper. It stretched for 100 degrees across the sky, with both head and tail visible simultaneously in broad daylight. At the time Thatcher's Comet was widely regarded as an evil omen: the *New York Herald* reported that people "regard it with fear, looking upon it as something terrible, bringing in its train wars and desolation."

Since Fort Sumter had been fired upon three months previously (although as yet no major battle had been fought), this interpretation required no great prescience. The question which arises for us astrologers is, that assuming that the comet indeed augured the American Civil War, what is its astrological correspondence with the United States? As is usual in such cases (where we have an indubitable coincidence between celestial and terrestrial events), nothing is very clear-cut.

To begin with, is it reasonable to suppose that Thatcher's Comet indeed corresponded with the American Civil War? Geoffrey Dean would argue no, that "such correspondences are quite unconvincing because the kind of events quoted (major disasters) occur every year somewhere in the world." And to assume, because we are Americans, that a major comet which appeared coincidentally with the beginning of the major tragedy in American history symbolized that tragedy, does seem somewhat chauvinistic. On the other hand, if ever a comet *did* portend a major national trauma, this one has got to be it (quite possibly there was also at this time a major upheaval in Fiji or some such place; or among the lemmings or something; but this doesn't contravene the theory. *If* comets have astrological effects there's no reason to suppose they will affect everyone on earth equally).

There are two points in a comet's path which are intrinsically demarcated: its perihelion and the point at which it becomes visible. Thatcher's comet reached perihelion on June 11th, 1861, in about 21 degrees of Taurus; it became visible the first week of July, while traversing the signs Cancer and Leo.

According to Alan Leo's *Mundane Astrology*, "Comets are regarded as invariably malefic. They bring trouble upon countries ruled by the sign of the zodiac in which they first are visible to the unaided sight." There is some question about which zodiacal sign rules the U.S.A., but Charles Carter, in his *Introduction to Political Astrology,* suggests that it is Gemini, not Cancer or Leo. Somehow, this does not seem like a very fruitful line of investigation.

With regard to the perihelion point, of 14 popular USA horoscopes listed by Richard Nolle in *Dell Horoscope Magazine* for July 1989 – including charts for the Declaration of Independence on 7/2/1776 and 7/4/1776; Constitutional ratification on 6/21/1778; Constitution in effect on 3/4/1789; and presidential inauguration on 4/30/1789 – none of these charts has any planet or Ascendant within 8 degrees of the perihelion point of 21° Taurus. Therefore, unless the actual horoscope is something other than one of these, the perihelion point of Thatcher's Comet provides no useful correspondence.

It may still be the case, however, that the comet has an extrinsic effect, i.e., by transit over a zodiacal point important to the astrology of the U.S.A. Obviously such a transit can't indicate the outbreak of the Civil War, since this occurred previously (4:30 am LMT on April 12th, 1861, at 79°W53', 32°N42'). In the chart for the firing on Fort Sumter, the planet closest to 21° Taurus is the moon in 16° Taurus. Ramus' ephemeris for Thatcher's Comet does not commence until the end of May 1861, so it cannot be ascertained where the comet was on April 12th, but it doesn't seem likely to have been near 21° Pisces (the Ascendant in the Fort Sumter chart).

Thatcher's Comet appeared during a lull, when war had broken out but both sides were still mobilizing, and no actual fighting had taken place (except for local riots here and there in the border states). The first major engagement of the war was the Battle of Bull Run, fought on 7/21/1861, when Thatcher's Comet was in 7° Libra, and moving about a half degree of longitude per day. Two of the charts listed by Nolle have Libra on the Ascendant – one a 7/4/1776 chart with 14° LI 35' on the Ascendant, the other a 6/21/1788 chart with 12° LI 15' on the Ascendant. These seem a bit off.

However, a Declaration of Independence chart for July 2nd, 1776 given by Julian Armistead in the same July '89 issue of *Dell Horoscope* as the Nolle article, has 10° Libra Ascendant, so for this chart at least Thatcher's Comet crossed the Ascendant within 3 days of a significant event. It might be worthwhile to give further study to this chart: Armistead gives a good argument in favor of it since the Declaration of Independence was passed by Congress on July 2nd; it was merely signed on July 4th.

Insofar as Thatcher's Comet is concerned, if there is an astrological correspondence involved it is not readily apparent. What could have (and perhaps *should* have, if there's anything to astrology) been a good example of the effectiveness of our technique has once again proved as nebulous as a comet.

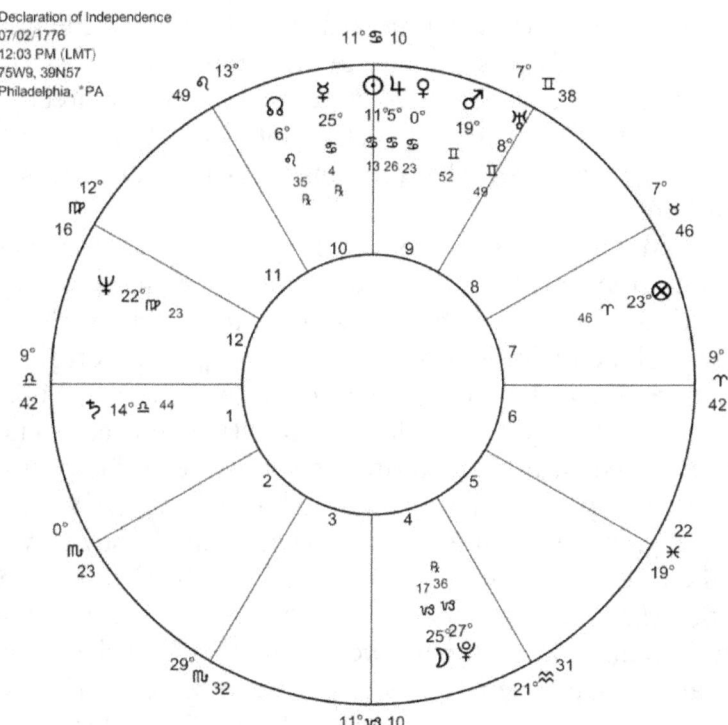

Mayan Astrology

The following is meant to be a brief introduction to Mayan astrology – a survey of the field rather than an in-depth discussion – largely because I don't believe that any in-depth discussion is possible. My experience of working with and interviewing Mayan priests with a view to classifying and trying to get an intellectual handle on what they are doing is rather frustrating, since most of the time you can't get the same answer to the same question from two different Mayan priests; nor the same answer from the same priest on two different days. This is because to them mind, intellect, has little to do with what is happening. They get their answers directly from the Spirit, and their astrology is just an intellectual armature which facilitates verbalization of what they channel (intuit directly, with no intellectual component).

Mayan priests are not only astrologers (diviners), but also healers and true priests – in the sense of being channels for information, guidance, and blessings from the spirit world. They don't just read a couple of books or take a couple of workshops and then hang out their shingles as astrologers or healers. First, they must be chosen directly by the Mayan spirits (which is not something that can be faked in a truly spiritual society – everybody instantly knows who the phonies are). And then, Mayan *Ajk'ihab* (day-counters) apprentice themselves for decades until they have truly learned their craft and can begin to practice on their own. Indeed, most of the Mayan priests whom I have had the privilege of meeting are humble maize farmers who were called to be priests by their spirits – and usually their spirits require enormous sacrifices from them in order to follow that path. One of my teachers, don Hermelindo Mas, lost a son and took two bullets himself from people who were trying to discourage his spiritual vocation. My principal teacher, don Abel Yat, was murdered by the curse of a black witch (or so his family told me).

Mayan astrology is not an astrology of planetary positions (although there is evidence that originally – before the Spanish conquest and book-burnings – Mayan astrology was indeed based upon planetary positions, since the Maya could demonstrably predict eclipses and Venus phases). At the present time Mayan astrology is based upon the *Chol Qij*, or "count of days" (note that *Chol Qij* is the

Kiché Mayan term for it; in Yucatec Mayan it is termed *Tzolkin*). The *Chol Qij* is a 260-day almanac which consists of twenty named days – or *naguals*. The twenty *naguals* can be considered to be roughly analogous to our zodiacal signs in the sense that they imbue persons born on the days they rule with certain personality traits. However the *naguals* differ from our zodiacal signs in that they are considered to be living deities who can protect their natives and advance their interests if those natives are scrupulous in remembering and respecting them. In particular, this involves carrying out certain propitiatory rituals every twenty days (when that *nagual* comes up again); and especially every 260 days when the birth *nagual* and coefficient coincide.

The Twenty *Naguals* of the Chol Qij

The twenty *naguals* are combined with numerical coefficients ranging from 1 to 13: thus 20 naguals x 13 coefficients = 260 days. The numerical coefficient modifies the meaning of the *nagual*: low numbers (1 – 3) are considered weak expressions of whatever the *nagual* symbolizes; and high numbers (11 – 13) are considered to be extreme manifestations of that *nagual*'s energy. Mayan numerals follow a dot (= 1) and bar (= 5) system; for example, one dot and two bars indicates the numeral 11.

Mayan Natal Astrology

Consider the Mayan horoscope for Albert Einstein, who was born on March 14th, 1879. This corresponds to the *nagual* 11 *Ajpu*, which means Lord, or sun. Much of the symbolism of the *naguals* has reference to the Mayan creation story as it is explained in the *Popul Vuh*, or book of the nation (the Mayan "bible"). The central tale in the *Popul Vuh* relates the story of twin brothers – *Junajpu* and *Ixbalankej* – who descended into the underworld to avenge the murder of their father. They tricked and defeated the lords of the underworld, and then rose into the sky to become the sun and moon. The *nagual Ajpu* refers to the older brother, who became the sun in the legend. And true to tell, *Ajpu* natives are very noble, spiritual people (Mary Baker Eddy and Sri Sathya Sai Baba are other examples of 11 *Ajpu* natives). Albeit kindly and a bit other-worldly, they are stout-hearted souls with superb intuition, and they make good Mayan priests. They are said to be "wise, valiant, good-hearted, friendly." The Book of *Chilam Balam* says that *Ajpu* natives are "Rich. Wise. Courageous, kind. Deaths of the children." (Einstein's first daughter died in infancy). Another Mayan source states that "People born on this day will be protected with personal power which, even if they themselves don't recognize it, will make them sources of new ideas for society." Note that 11 is a high coefficient, which indicates that Einstein is an extreme example of what *Ajpu* means: heroic, brave, humane, sagacious.

Note that by no means are all of the *naguals* considered to be as goody-goody as *Ajpu*; some of them (such as my own – *Ajmak* – "They're thieves, adulterers, short-tempered, and liars. ... This is not a very desirable day to be born on") are considered to be horrible. If this is your fate as well, don't take it too seriously. Just keep on propitiating.

The original birth *nagual* can be expanded into a 9-*nagual* diagram called *Ch'umilal* (our star in the universe) which is analogous to our horoscope chart. Each position in the diagram – which represents the human body – is obtained by adding or subtracting a certain number of days to or from the birth day, viz.:

Left arm	Head	Right arm
-14	-8	-2
Left waist	Heart	Right waist
-6	= birthday	+6
Left leg	Feet	Right leg
+2	+8	+14

In Albert Einstein's case, the 9-nagual diagram looks like this:

10 *Kemé*	3 *E*	9 *Tijax*
Death	Road	Blade
5 *Ix*	11 *Ajpu*	4 *Kemé*
Jaguar	Sun	Death
13 *Iq*	6 *Qanil*	12 *Ix*
Wind	Venus	Jaguar

Nine and thirteen are the sacred Mayan numbers: the nine *nagual* diagram reveals the connection between God (*Ahau*) and the earth as manifested in this person. That is, the diagram shows how the person fits into the cosmic scheme of things. The *nagual* of the birth day (in this case 11 *Ajpu*) is considered to hold the center position – that of the heart. The *nagual* 8 days before the nagual of the birth day is considered to be the person's head – what he or she has on their mind – which is the energy and force which directs the person's life (it's also considered to be the *nagual* of the day upon which the person was conceived). In Albert Einstein's case this is 3 *E*, which means Road: this is another good *nagual*, indicative of a good person who is a guide, who shows people the road of life. *E* in the position of the head indicates one who always has the welfare of others in mind: per the Book of *Chilam Balam*, "Wealthy ones, whose wealth is the community. Very rich, generous, not stingy. They take responsibility for the common good. Good people, very good fortune".

The right arm is the *nagual* 2 days before the birthday, which symbolizes the person's motivation and power; the force of his personality. In Albert Einstein's case this position is held by the *nagual* 9 *Tijax*, which means Obsidian Blade. This is a powerful *nagual*, associated with witchcraft (both black and white): "a curer, an active and intelligent person. More than a curer, he is a Mayan priest. ... Nobody can understand him." In Einstein's case having *Tijax* on his right arm gave him tremendous drive and force of will to accomplish his desires by cutting his way through (like an obsidian blade).

The left arm is the *nagual* 14 days before the birthday, and symbolizes that which impedes or weakens the person. Here it is 10 *Kemé* – Death – which indicates one who is staunch, strong-willed, and independent. It is said that "if they make sufficient offerings (to the gods) they can be successful in business and they can become important people, but they are destructive, they do damage without realizing it or caring what they do". Perhaps in Einstein's case he was impeded or weakened by being overly domineering (he divorced his first wife – a fellow-physicist and "equal" – to immediately marry a cousin who was utterly subservient to him).

4 *Kemé* is found at the place of Einstein's right waist (there are always doubled *nagual*s in the diagram). Both right and left waist symbolize duties and obligations: the right side is positive and the left is negative. On its positive side *Kemé* indicates patience and forbearance, especially in the face of danger, as well as verbal skillfulness, which qualities enabled Einstein to fulfill his duties and obligations when he was being assailed and rejected (he was in trouble with authority much of his life). Einstein's left waist is 5 *Ix*, or Jaguar, which is very distant, isolated, solitary, disliking company; indicating on Einstein's negative side a tendency to withdraw into himself (also to be unfortunate in love).

The legs symbolize the force which moves the person forward through life; some people take big, bold steps, others take small, cautious steps. The right leg is how the person initiates action, his enthusiasm. 12 *Ix* at his right leg indicates a person who is quite willing to dare and to go it alone to achieve his goals in life (12 is a high coefficient, indicating that Einstein didn't doubt for a moment that he was in the right: when asked by a student what he would have done had the Eddington eclipse experiment of 1919 disproved his theory of relativity, Einstein replied that he would have felt sorry for God; because his theory was correct).

The left leg shows obstacles in the person's road, and *Iq* (wind) is resolute, single-minded, strong-willed, confident and angry. Indeed, with the extreme coefficient 13, it indicates one who is quite pushy, violent-tempered, and inclined to go off half-cocked – which was one of Einstein's failings (e.g., his impatient meddling in left-wing and Zionist politics).

The feet show where the person is going: his destiny, the end of his life, and his death. *Qanil* is the *nagual* of the farmer, and it indicates one who is thorough, hard-working, dedicated, idealistic, but fickle – also given to illness (the latter point is not true in Einstein's case; he finished his life comfortably at the Princeton Institute of Advanced Studies).

This is a highly simplified explanation of how the diagram is interpreted; moreover, each practitioner adapts it according to his own (and his teachers') proclivities. E.g. the three *naguals* in the first column are considered to represent the material world; the *naguals* in the central column the social world; and those in the right-hand column the spiritual world. The first row is considered to represent ages birth to 13 years old; the middle row ages 13 to 35; and the bottom row age 35 onward. Any coefficients which are not represented in the diagram (in Einstein's case, the numbers 1, 2, 7, and 8 do not appear) show blocks / obstacles that the person has to overcome.

Mayan Mundane Astrology

The Maya don't have what we would call mundane astrology. The so-called "Mayan Prophecy for 2012" was just a bunch of New Age hokum, which in fact was invented by the same self-promoting phony-baloney who brought us the Harmonic Convergence a few years back.

The closest thing which the Maya have to a mundane astrology is a system for determining the quality of a year depending upon which one of four Year Bearers rules that year. In addition to the 260-day *Chol Qij*, the Maya use other calendar counts, including a civil year of 365 days called the *Haab*. The *Haab* consists of eighteen months of 20 days each, with an intercalary period of 5 days at the end (which is considered to be of ill omen). Since the *Haab* makes no provision for leap year, it slides back one day every four years as measured in our (Gregorian) calendar. At the present time (2016 – 2019) the New Year's Day – 0 *Pop* – of the *Haab* occurs on April 1st; from 2020 – 2023 it will occur on March 31st; and so on.

Because 260 and 365 have the common factor of 5, only four *naguals* of the *Chol Qij* can ever serve as New Years' Day (the initial day = 0 *Pop*) of the *Haab*, and these four days are termed the Year Bearers: *E*, *Noj*, *Iq*, and *Kej*. The Year Bearer for 2016 is *Noj*, since 4/1/2016 corresponds to 5 *Noj* of the *Chol Qij*. Similarly, the Year Bearer for 2017 is *Iq*; and the Year Bearer for 2018 is *Kej*.

It is said that the *E* years are good for business and health, since the Year Bearer *E* is quiet, calm, and enduring. The Year Bearer *Noj* is said to have a good head and many thoughts, and the years it opens are creative years, both for good and for evil. The Year Bearer *Iq* is very angry, and it brings violent rainstorms, or else no rain at all. Many people die in *Iq* years from being struck by lightning, from drowning, or from hunger. The Year Bearer *Kej* is also wild, and likes to trample people underfoot, causing many business losses and illnesses. The current year-bearer influences all divinations made from the *Chol Qij*; for example, a somewhat negative prediction made during an *Iq* year becomes extremely negative; whereas the same prediction made during an *E* year is somewhat ameliorated.

The Year Bearer is also taken into account in natal astrology: if natives of the *naguals E*, *Noj*, *Iq*, and *Kej* happen to be born under the same Year Bearer as their *nagual*, this is considered to be an extremely fortunate augury.

Mayan Horary Astrology

The *Chol Qij* is also used like our horary astrology, to divine for answers to specific questions such as: "Does my husband have another lover?"; "Should I do this business deal?"; "How shall I cure this illness?"; "What will be the outcome of this journey?"; "Should I marry this person?"; "Where is this lost object?"

When a Mayan priest is asked a horary question, he divines the answer by means of sortilege (casting lots). The priest takes his bag of 260 *tzinte* seeds (which look like bright red beans); prays over it; and then places the beans on a table. The client takes a handful of the seeds and places them apart. The priest then separates these into groups of four and counts how many groups there are. The remaining seeds at the end of the count lead to a *nagual* and numerical coefficient which – combined with the meaning of the *nagual* of the day on which the question is asked – yield an answer to the question. For more information on how the *Chol Qij* is used in divination, see Barbara Tedlock's *Time and the Highland Maya* (U. of New Mexico Press, 1992).

However, the sortilege operation serves mainly as an intellectual guide to help the priest put into words what is going on. The actual divination is done by means of feeling blood pulses in his veins and arteries: the interpretation depends upon the part of his body in which he feels the pulses; how many of them there are and how strong; and also up to which of the *naguals* he had counted in the sortilege operation when the pulses began (in relation to the *nagual* of the day upon which the divination was being done). The astrology part – the *Chol Qij* – merely serves as an intellectual framework to help to interpret the blood pulses.

Note that in the Mayan worldview, many of the problems with which people have to deal are consequences of ancestral karma – not only do people have to unravel their own karma (from past lives), but also bear the burden of karma created by their ancestors. So when a priest gives advice to a client with a view towards solving the clients' problems, this may involve some sort of propitiation or expiation of ancestral peccadilloes. A Mayan priest's usual answer to the question of "How do I resolve this problem?" is to hold a ceremony.

Mayan Ceremonial Astrology

Ceremonial invocations of the Mayan gods, spirits, and ancestors are the heart and soul of Mayan religious and astrological practice. We have nothing similar in our astrology to compare it to (except perhaps for some ritual forms of electional astrology such as *Picatrix*, in which celestial influences are invoked to charge talismans). Mayan ceremonies are held on certain days which are holy in the *Chol Qij*, particularly 8 Batz, which is the holiest day of all (8 Batz next occurs on March 21st, 2017, then December 6th, 2017, then August 23rd, 2018, then May 10th, 2019, etc.). Also, as noted earlier, special ceremonies can be held for specific purposes, such as to heal an illness; to bring prosperity in business or a suitable

mate in marriage; to fecundate a sterile woman; to win a lawsuit; etc. Certain *nagual*s are favorable for hunting, others for planting, others for asking a woman's hand in marriage, others for launching business enterprises. Initiating activities, as well as performing prayers or ceremonies to petition blessings for such activities, are done on the correct day. Mayan ceremonies are by no means solemn occasions (although they are serious in intent). On the contrary they are light and joyous. The accompanying marimba music is lively and animated. The *son* dance around the fire is a slow dance, but is carried out with élan and verve. The Mayan spirits are joyous, and they love it when people remember them and perform ceremonies to honor them; they shower blessings down upon all participants.

At the ceremony site the priest dons his uniform of office: bandana on his head, seashell necklace, wide cloth belt, ceremonial bag hanging by his side. An area is cleared around a shallow pit dug for the fire, and four large rocks are placed at the edge of the pit to mark the four cardinal directions. Then the cleared area around the fire pit is carpeted with pine needles and fragrant allspice leaves. First a circle is described in the pit with sugar, and the four quarters are delineated with a cross within the circle. On top of this 260 cylinders of incense are laid, and then a cross of many small candles, whose colors correspond to the four directions, is built in the center of the circle: red candles to the east, black to the west, white to the north, and yellow to the south. Chunks of *copal pom* incense are placed at the four corners, and more colored candles, dried herbs, cinnamon sticks, and cigars are arranged around the circle. The overall impression of the fireplace is quite decorative and colorful.

After the fireplace is laid out the priest makes offerings to the four cardinal directions in a sing-songy chant. The words sung-spoken by the Mayan priests aren't as important as the rhyme and rhythm, the hypnotic patter of the litany. Next the priest invokes the nine gods of the lower world (that is to say, the earth; as opposed to the thirteen gods or constellations in the sky). They are called the Creators – Formers because they fashioned the first humans from maize. Previously the gods had experimented with and destroyed two human-like races – the first made of mud and the second of wood. These attempts were unsuccessful because they lacked the intelligence and spirit to worship the gods. When the Creators – Formers made the first four humans they were a little too successful: these creatures were so clear-sighted and proud that the gods had to blow mist in their eyes to dumb them down a bit and make them more respectful. The first humans fashioned by the Creators – Formers were made of nine drinks of ground maize gruel: white maize made their bones, red maize made their blood, yellow maize made their skin, and black maize made their hair.

Then the priest invokes the earth god *Kawa Tzul Taka* (Lord Mountain-Valley), the principal deity of the *K'ekchi* Maya. The priest also calls for blessings from the 166 sacred mountains and ceremonial sites in Guatemala.

After the invocations are finished a handful of twenty small candles is given to each participant; and then the fire is lit by the client (the person who has commissioned the Mayan priest to perform the ceremony). The fire eventually ignites the other candles, incense etc. laid out in the fire pit, creating a large blaze which dances in the breeze. The flames are regarded as being alive, as representing the presence of *Kawa Tzul Taka*, and as such the priest watches the fire very carefully for omens throughout the five-hour long ceremony. The behavior of the fire in response to petitions (e.g. for health, or economic prosperity) made during the course of the ceremony is a sign of whether and how the wish will be granted. Sometimes during ceremonies the priest will stop and make a very specific prediction for one of the participants – apparently out of thin air (though it may be inspired by observation of what the flames are doing). For example, once during a ceremony my teacher don Abel Yat told me, "You are about to have a serious land problem." Sure enough, one week later, a huge dispute over land erupted which dragged on in the courts for the next twelve years, and cost me a boodle of time and money. Another time he told me that I was about to have a serious health problem (and I somehow understood it involved my legs); a few months later I began to experience pain in my left leg, which was later diagnosed as arthrosis of the pelvic bone which required a hip replacement surgery. On the last day of 2008 don Abel was doing a ceremony when he abruptly predicted that one of the half-dozen people there present would die in the coming year; and he died the following July.

After the fire is lit the head priest sacrifices a chicken. This payment is made to *Kawa Tzul Taka* to avoid illness and other troubles and to ask for blessings. The Maya are very much convinced that if blessings are to be petitioned and obtained, then the requisite payment must be made. In the Mayan worldview, there is nothing free in the universe. The priest first offers the chicken to the four cardinal directions (so that they know the payment is for them also), then he dances with it around the fire, with the chicken draped around his neck. Finally he kills it by hand by stretching the chicken's neck until the head tears off. The head is placed in the fire as an offering to *Kawa Tzul Taka*. Then the beating heart of the sacrificial chicken is torn from its breast by the priest, who hands it to the client to make a wish on until the heart stops beating, at which time it is offered to the fire.

Then the priest asks the participants for the names of all of their deceased antecedents; and as each ancestor is named he throws a candle into the fire and asks that ancestor's blessing (as mentioned previously, the Maya believe that one's ancestors are not only still present, but can guide and bless – or mess up – one's own life; and therefore they must be propitiated).

After the offerings are made to *Kawa Tzul Taka* and the ancestors, the order of the ceremony follows that of the twenty *naguals* of the *Chol Qij*. The twenty *naguals* are called upon in serial order to bless the "great-grandchildren," which is how the Maya refer to themselves. The first *nagual* is the *nagual* of the day the ceremony takes place. For example, if the ceremony is held on the day of *Batz* (ball of thread), then in a sing-songy litany the priest explains that time is symbolized as thread rolled up in a ball underneath the earth, and the unraveling of this ball of thread is the passage of time. *Batz* is the weaver of the family and community, the ties which bind people together. The priest asks this *nagual* that his client be able to roll up family, children, and wealth for the client and ceremony participants. At the end of *Batz* the priest counts up to thirteen for the thirteen powers (gods of the upper world): *jun* (1) *Batz*, *kwib* (2) *Batz*, *oshib* (3) *Batz*, *kayib* (4) *Batz*, *ob* (5) *Batz*, *kwakib* (6) *Batz*, *kukub* (7) *Batz*, *kwashakib* (8) *Batz*, *beleb* (9) *Batz*, *laheb* (10) *Batz*, *junlahu* (11) *Batz*, *kablahu* (12) *Batz*, *oshlahu* (13) *Batz*. After the count to thirteen is made for each *nagual*, the participants in the ceremony make a wish on one of the twenty candles they were handed at the outset and then throw the candle into the fire. The portion of the ceremony devoted to each individual *nagual* varies in length, but typically lasts five to ten minutes. At intervals there is ritual dancing of the slow *son* dance around the fire by the priest alone, and sometimes by participants as well. Participants are cued by the priest as to what to do next.

When a *nagual*'s turn ends the next *nagual* becomes "host" of the ceremony: after *Batz* comes *E* (road), and the priest sing-songs a litany about the road of life, and he asks this *nagual* to protect his client's journey, that no matter where he goes he should have no accidents and that he should have good roads, beautiful roads, level roads. During this invocation the priest and client journey (dance the *son* as they slowly circle the fire)

three times. The invocation of *E* ends with the count up to thirteen: *jun E, kwib E, oshib E,* etc. to *oshlahu E*; and then the participants make their wishes and throw a candle into the fire.

The *nagual Aj*, the maize plant, is then invoked. *Aj* symbolizes the maize plant in the house of the grandmother of *Junajpu* and *Ixbalankej* (twin heroes of the *Popul Vuh* legend). In the *Popul Vuh* story *Junajpu* and *Ixbalankej* journey to the underworld, but before leaving they planted two maize plants in their grandmother's house, saying that if these plants should dry up, it would mean they had died. When the plants dried up the grandmother was stricken with grief, but when the plants re-sprouted (when the twins were reborn from a fire in which they had perished) she knew they had triumphed in the end. The priest calls upon these twins (*Junajpu* and *Ixbalankej* – the sun and moon) to protect humanity. Where the great-grandchildren have forgotten their traditional ways, *Aj* reminds them of their inheritance and culture – how to count the days and to remember their forefathers and their past. Then the count is made to thirteen: *jun Aj, kwib Aj, oshib Aj,* etc. to *oshlahu Aj*, and the participants make wishes and throw candles into the fire.

Ix is the jaguar, who is the protector of the woods, the rivers, and the temples. The jaguar roams the earth and sees everything under his domain. *Ix* guides and protects the great-grandchildren and provides them with food and raiment. *Ix* represents strength and fertility, so clients seeking to have children might commission petitioning ceremonies on the day *Ix*. Then the count is made to thirteen: *jun Ix, kwib Ix, oshib Ix* … and candles are thrown into the fire.

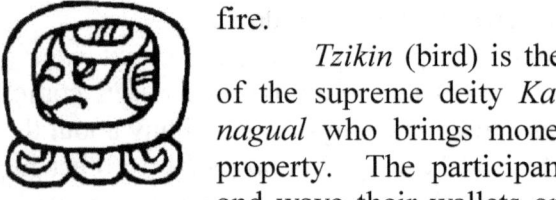

Tzikin (bird) is the guardian and messenger of the supreme deity *Kawa Tzul Taka*. It is the *nagual* who brings money, wealth, livestock, and property. The participants will approach the fire and wave their wallets or purses above it; and the priest asks this *nagual* for abundance for his client. After counting to thirteen this time the priest and participants each give the fire a handful of sesame seeds as an offering, since sesame is the food of

Kawa Tzikin; then they wish for prosperity and throw their candles into the fire.

Ajmak is the *nagual* of sinners. The priest and participants now kneel down around the fire and call upon *Kawa Ajmak* to forgive them their faults; to pardon wherever they have made errors, wherever they have committed sins, wherever they haven't done as they should. The priest and participants then prostrate themselves, touching their foreheads to the ground and kiss the earth, and humbly beg forgiveness. Then the count is made to thirteen *Ajmak* and candles are thrown into the fire.

Noj is the *nagual* of intelligence and wisdom. The priest asks this *nagual* to bless his client with wisdom and divine guidance. *Kawa Noj* is also asked to bless children who are studying in the *ladino* school system: at this point in the ceremony the children come forward and the priest blesses them by touching them with candles on the head (where ideas are born) and hands (with which they write), and then he throws the candles into the fire. Then the priest counts *jun Noj, kwib Noj, oxib Noj*, to *oshlahu Noj*.

Tijax represents the obsidian blade, and it is the *nagual* of danger. This day is used for rituals to avoid evil influences for people and sickness in domestic animals, and to remove curses. On the other hand, sorcerers use *Tijax* to perform witchcraft. After calling upon this *nagual* to protect his client from injury, the head priest counts to thirteen *Tijax*.

Kawok is the thunder. Its power is fire; its lightning illuminates the darkness. This day is used for ceremonies to cure sickness and to overcome conflicts and difficulties. The priest prays to the three lightning gods not to hurt the great-grandchildren, but to strengthen their spirit; then he counts to thirteen *Kawoq*.

Ajpu is the sun. This *nagual* refers to the *Popul Vuh* creation myth, in which the hero twins *Junajpu* and *Ixbalankej* journey to the underworld

Shibalba to avenge the murder of their father by the Lords of *Shibalba*. There they face many trials, even dying in a fire, but their cleverness and magic restore them to life each time. In the end they disguise themselves as impoverished dancers and perform a dance in which they cut men, and even each other, to pieces; and then they bring the dead one back to life again. The Lords of *Shibalba* are delighted by this performance, and ask the twins to do the same to them. The boys cut the Lords to pieces but don't restore them to life, thus they defeat their enemies and avenge their father's death. They then ascend into Heaven where *Junajpu* becomes the sun and *Ixbalankej* becomes the moon. Rituals done on this day are as powerful as the sun in banishing evil, sickness, and personal problems. Then the priest counts to thirteen *Ajpu*.

Imox is the rabbit. It guides and protects, particularly those who are crazy, confused, or have lost their way. Rituals are done on this day to help people with mental problems, to cure illness, and to pray for the return of a strayed or missing spouse. The invocation is completed with a count to thirteen *Imox*.

Iq is the wind. Rituals are done on this day to bless all that exists in nature and to give thanks for all of the Creators – Formers' works; and so that the wind will take away all suffering and evil influences. The priest petitions *Iq* not to blow troubles or illness the client's way; but to blow away what problems he does have. Then the count is made to thirteen *Iq*.

Aqabal is the dawn. Rituals are done on this day to give thanks to the light and to avoid calumny and lies. The priest gives thanks for our awakening each day, and invokes this *nagual* to give us good ideas and good thoughts. Then the count is made to thirteen *Aqabal*.

Kat is the net, like the net bags in which maize is stored. It is the day of payment to the ancestors. The priest invokes this Lord to bring the people together like nets bring together the ears of maize. Then he counts to thirteen *Kat*.

Kan is the snake, the plumed serpent (rainbow) which ties together the Heart of Heaven and the Heart of the Earth. Rituals are done on this day to ask for justice, wisdom, strength, equality and to avoid disequilibrium with Mother Nature. The priest petitions this *nagual* not to bite, not to send dangers. Then the priest counts *jun Kan, kwib Kan, oshib Kan, kayib Kan,* ... up to *oshlahu Kan*.

Kemé is the *nagual* of death. *Kemé* is conceived of much as we conceive of the grim reaper, except not as a metaphor  but rather as an actual being. Participants in the ritual who have come for a healing are now called forward one at a time. When healing someone the priest gives the person a handful of candles to hold and then stands behind the person with one hand on the person's shoulder and the other held above the person's head. The priest prays over the person, then he raises a bottle of *aguardiente* liquor, takes some into his mouth, and spit/sprays a forceful cloud of *aguardiente* over the person's body four times, once from each of the four cardinal directions, to burn away the person's illness. After the healings he has the person circle the fire, which he observes closely for information on diagnosis and cure. Then he counts *jun Kemé, kwib Kemé, oshib Kemé* ... up to *oshlahu Kemé*.

Kej is the deer. The priest petitions this *nagual* to bring strength to the great-grandchildren, to lift their legs and backs and heads, to give them the strength of a deer, to overcome weakness and tiredness, to grant them power and success. Then he counts to thirteen *Kej*.

Qanil is Venus. *Qanil* is the *nagual* of the farmer, the day to pray for a good harvest. The priest calls upon this *nagual* to bring forth bounteous harvests of grain and fruit to feed the hungry, and drink for the thirsty. The priest also petitions this *nagual* for good communications, reciprocity, and peaceful relations. Then he counts to thirteen *Qanil*.

Toj is jade, or payment. In the *Popul Vuh* the first humans were very cold and unable to cook their food, so they applied to

Tojil, the god of fire (and the principal deity of the *Kiché* Maya). *Tojil* demanded the torn-out hearts of sacrificial victims in payment for the gift of fire. This involved the *Kiché* in considerable conflict with their neighboring tribes, whom they raided to obtain sacrificial victims. The *nagual Toj* symbolizes offerings, the payment of what is due, and the leveling of justice. It's a day to seek peace with God and man. The priest begins the ceremony by offering payment (the chicken), and now he asks *Kawa Toj* to accept the tribute of candles, copal incense, etc. to protect the lives and roads (journeys) of his client and all the great-grandchildren. Then he counts up to thirteen *Toj*.

The final nagual is *Tzi*, the dog. On this day offerings are made so that negative forces won't triumph and so that the authorities will use wisdom and vision to administer justice. The priest petitions *Kawa Tzi* to influence and win over judges, lawyers, police, and the military on behalf of the great-grandchildren; to guide and protect them in the legal system and with all governmental authorities. Then he counts to thirteen *Tzi*.

After all twenty of the *naguals* have been invoked the priest thanks them for bringing the great-grandchildren together on this occasion, and asks them to bless everyone. Then all the participants are given a candle and instructed to kneel down around the fire and pray for whatever they desire; then the candles are thrown into the fire.

The participants stand and clasp their hands behind their backs, and everyone dances a slow, rhythmic *son* in a circle around the fire. The priest closes the ceremony as he began it, by thanking the four cardinal directions; then everyone breaks for a lunch of tamales. In all the ceremony lasts about five hours.

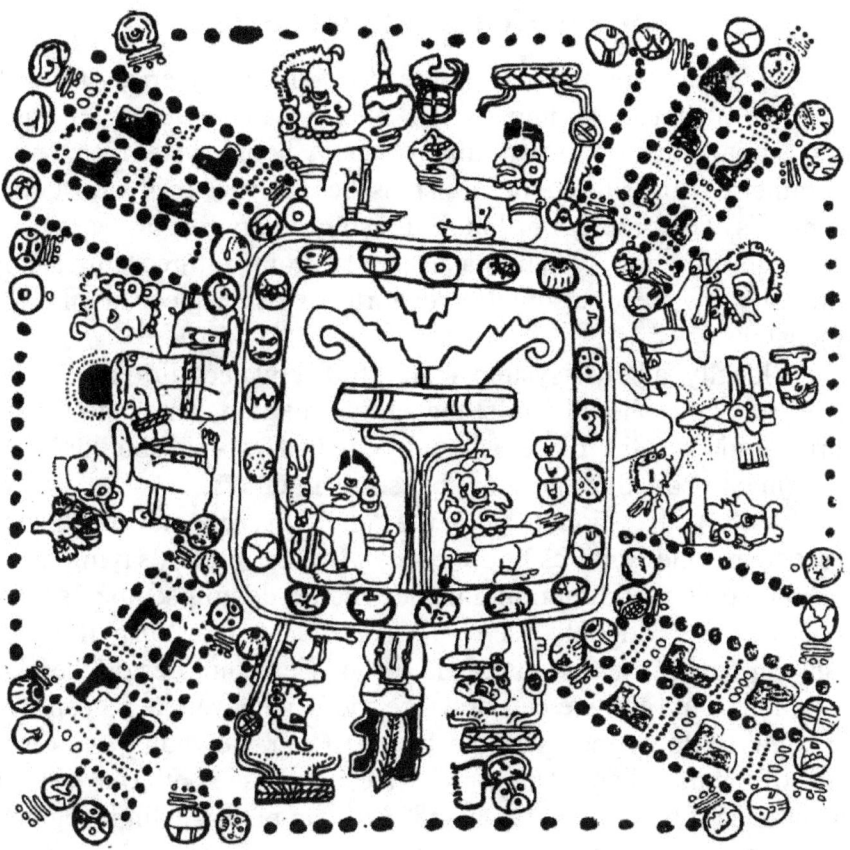

Mayan Calendar from *Madrid Codex*. Note *Chol Qij* glyphs in square surrounding the Tree of Life.

On the Domification Problem

The basic problem of house division theory arises from the fact that a house system is an attempt to represent a three-dimensional situation in two dimensions. A house system isn't a pie, but rather a tangerine. The divisions between wedges aren't lines, but planes. The problem of house division theory lies in the fact that certain information which makes sense from a three-dimensional point of view becomes highly distorted when squeezed into two dimensions.

Ideally, a house system should fulfill two conditions:

1) It should model the earth's rotation. That is to say, the diurnal motion of a planet should be constant – it shouldn't take more time to pass through some houses than others.

2) It should preserve the Ascendant, Midheaven, Descendant, and Nadir as house cusps. Another way of saying this is: both the horizon and meridian planes should delimit segments of the tangerine. We can only "see" the Ascendant as a cusp if we are "sighting down" the horizon plane (if our viewpoint lies on the plane of the horizon); and we can only see the Midheaven as a cusp if we are sighting down the meridian plane (if our viewpoint lies on the plane of the meridian). Therefore, we can only see both the ASC and MC at once if both the horizon and meridian planes delimit segments of the tangerine.

The basic problem of house division theory lies in the fact that these two conditions contradict each other; and all the different house systems known to man represent different people's ideas of how to resolve that contradiction.

In fact, there is no way to resolve this contradiction (it is mathematically impossible to resolve it). In practice what different house systems do is either ignore condition 1); ignore condition 2); ignore both conditions; or make a pretense of satisfying both conditions and end up satisfying neither of them.

Consider condition 1). In order for a house system to model the earth's rotation, the axis of the tangerine must be the earth's axis, and our point of view must lie upon it. We squash the tangerine down onto the plane of the equator (or some plane parallel to it). We are looking down from the viewpoint of the north celestial pole, so our viewpoint is stationary, and everything else rotates around us (at a constant rate). This is how the Meridian and Alcabitius systems are defined. The Meridian system is a perfect model of rotation. In Alcabitius, a body's rotation is constant east of the meridian, but at the meridian it "jumps the tracks" and rotates at a different constant rate west of the meridian. As we shall see later on, there is a similar discontinuity in rotation in the Placidus and Koch systems, except at the horizon. That is, in Placidus and Koch a planet passes through the houses above the horizon at a different speed than it passes through the houses below the horizon.

The Campanus, Regiomontanus, Sunshine, Horizontal, and Porphyry systems make no pretense of fulfilling condition 1), and therefore they are not good models of rotation. This is because the tangerine axes in these systems are not the earth's axis, and therefore as the world turns these models "wobble" (rotate at varying rates rather than smoothly at a constant rate). In these systems our point of view is not stationary, but is itself rotating around the earth's axis.

The Placidus system doesn't wobble per se because of a rather elegant geometrical trick. Placidus is the only house system in which the segments of the tangerine are not delimited by planes, but rather by curves. The edges of the tangerine segments are not flat, but have a wave to them, like potato chips. Because our line of sight along these edges "bends", it is possible to maintain a fix on both the ASC and MC at the same time. However, Placidus has the same rotational flaw as Koch: rotation is constant above the horizon, and rotation is constant below the horizon, but as a body crosses the horizon it either hits the accelerator or slams on the brakes.

Now, just as the first condition (that rotation be smooth and constant) requires that our viewpoint be looking down from the north celestial pole, so too does the second condition (that the angles be cusps) require that our point of view be looking south from the north point on the horizon (or vice versa). In other words, condition 1) implies that the axis of the tangerine is the earth's axis; whereas condition 2) implies that the axis of the tangerine is the line formed by the intersection of the horizon and meridian planes (this line cuts through right where we are standing, and runs due north and south across the floor). The two axes intersect at an angle equal to our latitude on the earth. This is the reason why conditions 1) and 2) contradict each other: each one requires a different point of reference.

The Equal House and Morinus systems resolve the problem by ignoring both of these conditions. In these systems the axis of the tangerine is the line joining the poles of the ecliptic (our point of view is the north ecliptic pole), so not only does the tangerine wobble, but also we can't sight down either the horizon or meridian planes in these systems because our point of view (the ecliptic pole), doesn't lie on either of these planes. The Equal House and Morinus systems, for these reasons, seem somewhat shameless in their pretensions to be considered house systems at all.

Only from the point of view of the south point on the horizon (squashing the tangerine onto the plane of the prime vertical), where we can sight down both the horizon and meridian planes, can both the ASC and MC be observed simultaneously. This is the viewpoint taken in the Campanus, Regiomontanus, and Sunshine House systems; and only these systems perfectly fulfill condition 2) while ignoring condition 1).

Some house systems ignore condition 2) altogether. For example, the ASC is not a cusp in the Meridian and Horizontal systems, and the MC is not a cusp in Equals (the way it is usually defined). Other house systems use some sort of trick or gizmo to pull both angles in as cusps.

The Porphyry system has a bit more shame than Equal House, but not much. It wobbles just as badly, but at least lip service is paid to preserving both angles as cusps. However the Porphyry system gives up on geometry and solves the problem by waving a magic wand and pulling the MC out of a hat.

The Koch system is the only house system in which the tangerine lacks a central axis. The planes which divide segments of the tangerine are tilted, so instead of intersecting in a line they intersect in a point at the center of the tangerine, forming a double cone (Figure 1). The Koch house cusps are not the planes which intersect the double cone at the lines, but rather are the planes which are tangent to the double cone at these lines (i.e. they delimit the double cone). Our viewpoint in the Koch system is the center of the tangerine – the point where all planes (lines of sight) meet.

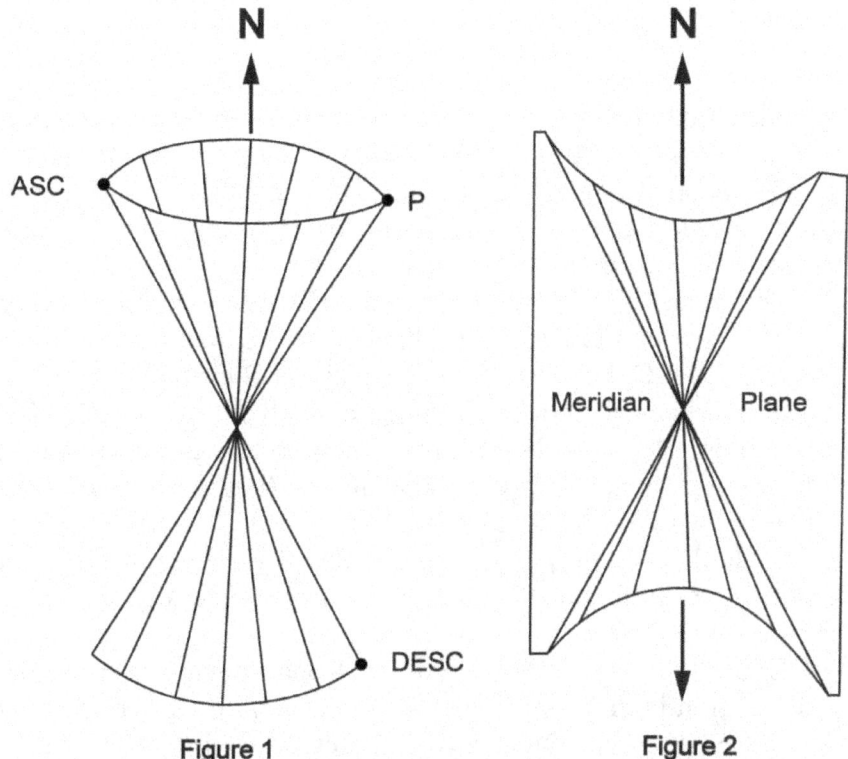

Figure 1   Figure 2

If left to itself, this double cone would rotate smoothly around the earth's axis (and hence be a perfect model of rotation, as the Meridian system is). Unfortunately what happens is that because all other house systems take a viewpoint located on the surface of the tangerine (the north celestial pole, north ecliptic pole, or north / south point on the horizon), we can "look down on" the whole tangerine at once. But if our point of view is the center of the tangerine, then we have to be looking either one way or the other – either up the double cone (north) or down it (south). We can't look both ways at once; so if we are looking at the ASC, we can never see the DESC. We *can* see the point P – the point on the double cone which lies directly across from the ASC, but this point is not the DESC (it's the antiscion of the Ascendant– it has declination opposite to that of the Descendant).

Nor can we ever see the MC or IC, since the meridian plane is not tangent to the double cone (it cuts through it, see Figure 2). So the double cone had to be "split" at the meridian into two half-cones.

Every time a body reaches the meridian, we have to shift our point of view from north to south (or the reverse) to keep it in sight. And at that precise instant, when we have to whirl around, we are able to steal a quick glance out to the side (down the meridian plane) and "see" the body transiting the meridian.

This is the basic problem with the Koch house system (apart from the logical contradictions it engenders) – it just doesn't make any sense. The Campanus, Regiomontanus, Sunshine, Meridian, Porphyry, Horizontal, and Morinus systems all make some kind of sense. There's a logic to them, flawed though it might be. Even the Placidus system makes sense at first glance (but falls apart under close scrutiny). In all of these house systems there's a fixed point of view. We don't have to be jumping about and waving our arms and looking this way and that. We can just sit there peacefully and watch the thing rotate.

One attempt to improve on the Koch concept of a double cone of rotation is the Topocentric house system, in which the cone is not a cone per se but rather a foil. Its cross-section isn't a circle, but a spiral; our line of sight is an Archimedean spiral which curls into the meridian, so we can see the IC as well as the ASC. The problem with the Topocentric system is that as the thing rotates our horizon keeps bobbing up and down, so we feel as though we are being tossed in a blanket (the angle between the earth's axis and the line beneath our feet north and south across the floor keeps fluctuating between zero and our terrestrial latitude).

In view of all these problems, it is not surprising that some astrologers eschew the use of houses altogether. Unfortunately for the theoretically-minded astrologer, the houses have a undeniable ability to work symbolically in the natal chart: e.g., Bill Gates has Jupiter-Pluto conjunct Regulus in the 2nd house, and so on. I would be interested in hearing about other people's experiences with progressions and directions to the intermediate Sunshine House cusps.

The Celestial Hourglass

Historically, the point of reference used in astrological measurement has been geocentric – i.e. assumes that the observer is located at the center of the earth. More recently, some astrologers have promulgated a heliocentric astrology, which assumes that the observer is located at the center of the sun (so the earth becomes a planet located 180° from the sun's natal zodiacal longitude in the geocentric chart). At the same time, there have been currents moving in the direction of a topocentric astrology, which assumes that the observer is located on the surface of the earth – which indeed is the case, and thus can be said to better model the astronomical reality than either the geocentric or heliocentric models do. In these topocentric models, it is noted that in the course of 24 hours the plane of the horizon sweeps out a double cone of rotation, which we shall term the Celestial Hourglass.

When we use the term "topocentric" (uncapitalized), we will mean "centered at the birthplace"; when we use the term "Topocentric House System" (capitalized) we will mean the house system devised by Argentine astrologers Wendell Pollich and Nelson Page, which was popularized by Alexander Marr in Germany, Geoffrey Cornelius and Margaret Millard in the UK, and Isaac Starkman in Israel. Unfortunately, the Topocentric House System is not a valid topocentric model, as we shall see later on.

The first historical move towards a topocentric house system was Walter Koch's Birthplace House System. Unlike other house systems in which the planes which divide space (delimit the houses) all intersect in a line (namely the axis of the house system), the planes which delimit house cusps in the Koch system intersect in a double cone (for a complete explanation, see the appendix to my book *Primary Directions*, available as a free download from:

https://www.dropbox.com/l/scl/AADAM79RJoyiAuaiL1cBL7iiXTx4ZKfBvBw

https://www.dropbox.com/l/scl/AACqoT8RC-qRUQB14ztImNgetUqX3-TGrdU

https://www.dropbox.com/l/scl/AACzLtDlnnPfTuFtJU7zOHnGk8zeXi11aNo

Although Koch believed that his house system was the only system which produced intermediate cusps valid for the birthplace (i.e. he believed that his system was topocentric), in fact the vertex of his double cone – the observer's viewpoint – is the center of the earth, *not* the birthplace.

Pollich and Page's Topocentric House System was a closer step towards a true topocentric model. Although the Topocentric House System was supposedly first derived from empirical observations (of primary directions to house cusps) and only later was the geometry conjured up to support the empirical results, there is considerable reason to doubt the truth of this claim (see my *Primary Directions*, p 81ff). Moreover, the geometrical model described by Pollich and Page has several serious mathematical flaws.

I am going to describe a correct topocentric double cone model for a house system. It must be borne in mind that this is not the only way such a system could be constructed; however, I believe it represents the general idea towards which Koch, Pollich, and Page were groping.

The observer (birthplace) is the *topocenter*. The line passing through the topocenter and the north celestial pole is the *topocentric axis*. To an observer at the topocenter, the entire firmament appears to rotate around this axis in twenty-four hours (see the illustrations on page 175 of Geoffrey Dean's *Recent Advances in Natal Astrology*, Astrological Assoc. 1977). This is the chief attraction of a topocentric house system: it is a much better model of the actual physical reality than either the geocentric or heliocentric models are. During twenty-four hours, the plane of the horizon will sweep out a double cone of rotation, with its vertex at the topocenter. Since the angle between the horizon and the north pole equals Φ, the terrestrial latitude of the topocenter, then the angle between a cone element and the topocentric axis must also equal Φ.

A true topocentric house system must needs be finite rather than infinite. It is not possible to mathematically formulate an infinite topocentric house system. Koch's Birthplace House System is geocentric and infinite; the Topocentric House System is topocentric and infinite, but the way in which Pollich and Page work out this contradiction is by changing the rules of spherical trigonometry.

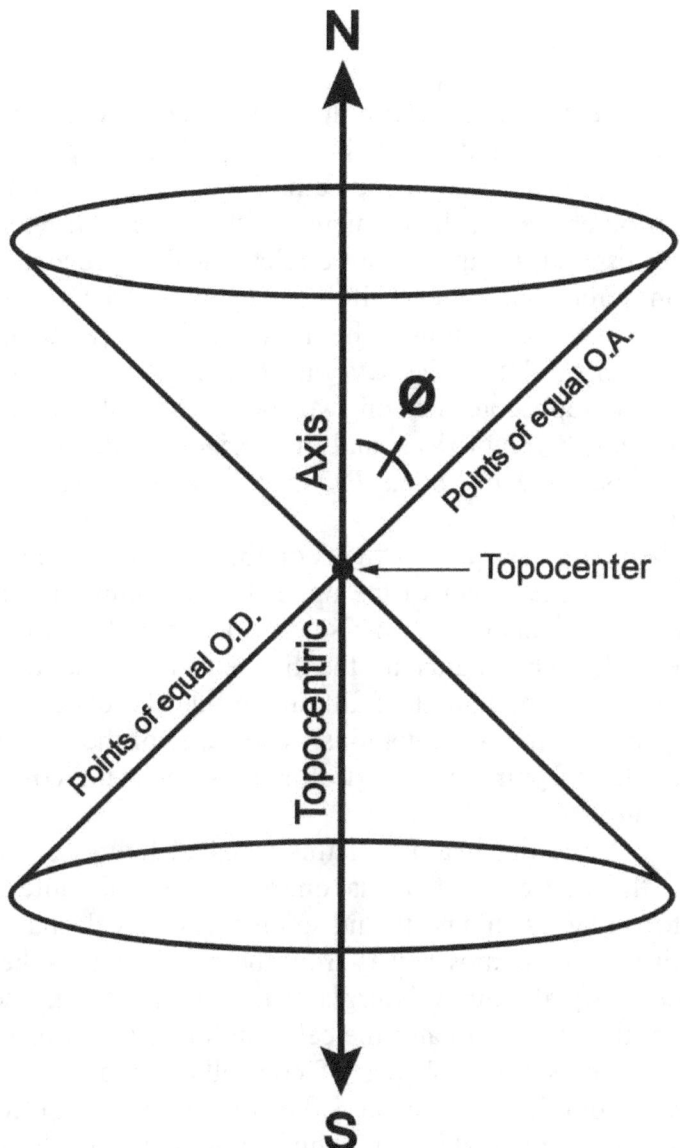

A finite double cone model of the firmament resembles an hourglass. The vertex of the hourglass is the topocenter (birthplace). A point in the sky with declination less than the co-latitude of the birthplace is projected onto the surface of the hourglass at a distance from the vertex equal to its declination. Thus, the entire celestial equator is projected onto the vertex. In the northern hemisphere, the elements of the cone consist of points which have equal Oblique

Ascensions (i.e. which all rise in the east at the same Sidereal Time) north of the vertex; and points having equal Oblique Descensions (which all set in the west at the same Sidereal Time) south of the vertex. In other words, the elements of the cone in the topocentric model correspond to ascension circles in the geocentric model (ascension circles are great circles tangent to the diurnal – or declination – circles through the north and south points on the horizon. Every point in the sky with declination less than the co-latitude of the topocenter lies on two such circles: the horizon circle at the moment the point rises, and the horizon circle at the moment the point sets. See my book *Primary Directions* page 71 for an illustration).

  The hourglass has two "lids" on the top and bottom: the north celestial pole is the center of the upper lid (assuming observer is in the northern hemisphere) and the south celestial pole is the center of the lower lid. The radius of the lids equals the latitude of the birthplace, so circumpolar stars fall on the lids at a distance from the center equal to their co-declinations. The edges of the lids, therefore, are the circles of points whose declinations equal the co-latitude of the topocenter.

  The interesting feature of this celestial hourglass is that the shape of the hourglass depends on the terrestrial latitude of the topocenter: at the earth's north and south poles the celestial hourglass is a flat disk. As you move away from the poles towards the equator, it becomes a squat, stubby hourglass; then a tall, skinny hourglass; and then at the earth's equator the celestial hourglass turns into a line through the poles. The shapes of constellations also alter as you move away from the poles towards the equator, changing from wider and flatter to taller and skinnier. Thus, photographs of the sky taken at different terrestrial latitudes wouldn't be congruent. Nonetheless, this model does make sense in that it is true that at the earth's poles nothing rises or sets; and on the earth's equator the horizon is the meridian (ascension circles are hour circles).

Orion at the North Pole

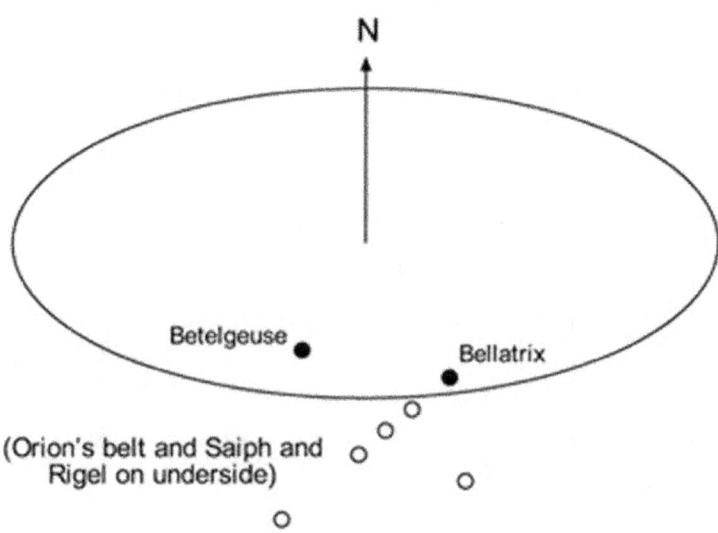

Orion at 50° North

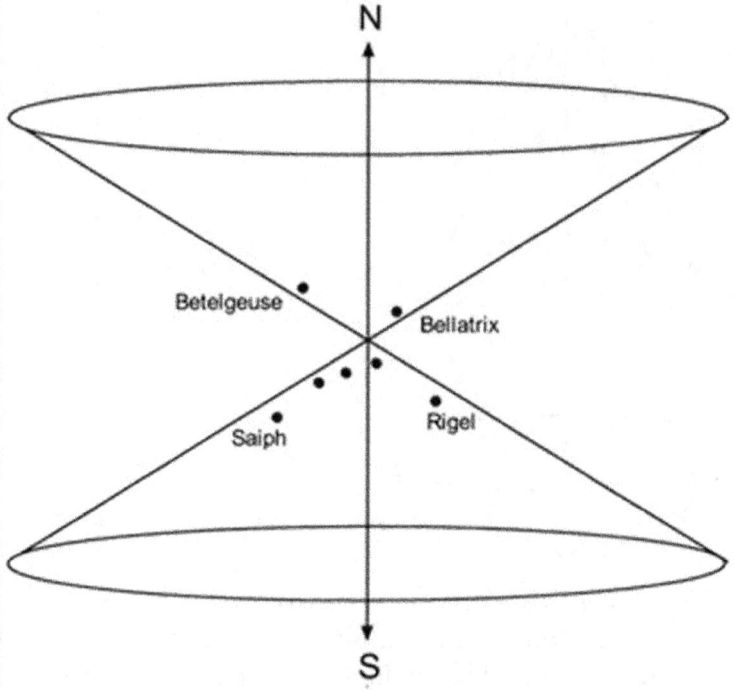

Orion at 25° North   Orion at Equator

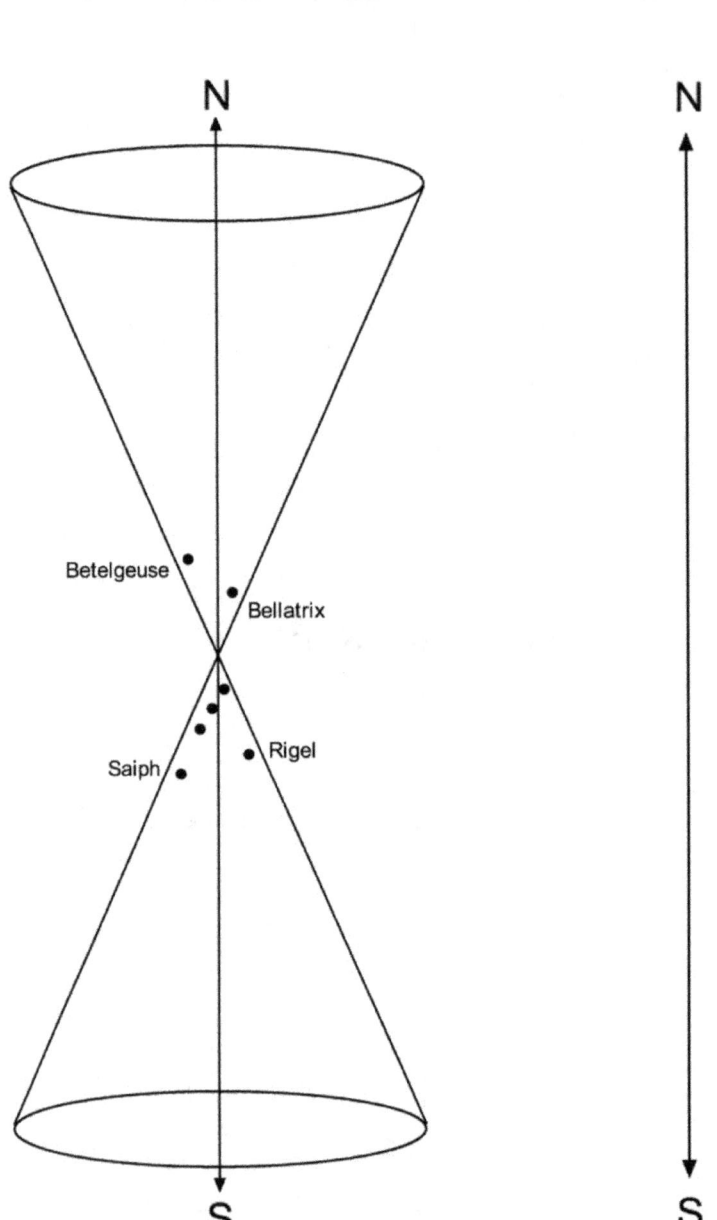

The *arc of direction* between two planets (or a planet and angle) in this system is the amount of time elapsed between the moment when the following planet of the pair rises over the eastern horizon, minus the moment in time when the leading planet rises over the eastern horizon. Thus the arc of direction equals the difference between the two planets' *Oblique Ascensions* – their *Right Ascensions* minus their *Ascensional Differences* = RA - arcsin(tan declination x tan Φ). This arc of direction is converted to time by one of several theories, such as those of Ptolemy, Naibod, Placidus, or others. In most of these theories the arc of direction is converted into years of life at the rate of roughly a year of life per degree of arc of direction.

Now, the foregoing model of a celestial hourglass assumes that the linear distance measured along a radius from the centers of the lids (for circumpolar stars); or from the vertex along a cone element (for non-circumpolar stars); varies linearly as the stars' declinations. This is the simplest assumption we can make, but it's by no means the only assumption we could make.

In the double cone model promulgated by Pollich and Page, a much more complex (and highly arbitrary – one might even go so far as to characterize it as absurd) function was used to assign distances of stars along cone elements from the vertex. The important point is that in any finite model – which includes cylinders as well as cones – we are faced with the problem of assigning units; and any such assignation is necessarily going to have to be highly arbitrary. This problem doesn't arise with the geocentric model precisely because it is infinite (the radius of the earth is taken to be zero). Thus, while a topocentric double-cone model is appealing in that it takes a more correct view of the actual physical reality than a geocentric spherical model does, there is no intuitively obvious way of definitively formulating such a model.

Geodetic Equivalents

Our choice of which house system to use not only determines how we should calculate horoscopes, but also how we should calculate primary directions, Arabian parts, and astrolocality maps as well. By the same logic, our choice of house system also determines how we should calculate geodetic equivalents. In this essay I will describe two theories of geodetic equivalents which have been propounded by previous authors (Sepharial and Johndro), as well as a new approach to the question.

Sepharial's Method

Astologers (like most people) like things simple and clear-cut. They don't want to know that there are a myriad of different possible ways of performing the same calculations, and that there is no a priori reason for preferring one way over another. For example, they use Placidus houses because until very recently those were the only kind of house tables available, which was the result of a decision made by some ignoramus several centuries ago. Similarly, they use Sepharial's method of calculating geodetic equivalents because Sepharial was the first to publish a book on the subject, and he calculated them the way he did because he didn't know (or care) enough about mathematics to calculate them any other way.

In Sepharial's method the terrestrial longitude of a place east of Greenwich is equated to zodiacal longitude. For example, the terrestrial longitude of Berlin is 13°E23', so its zodiacal longitude is taken to equal 13°AR23'. For locations west of Greenwich, the terrestrial longitude is first subtracted from 360, and then equated to zodiacal longitude (e.g. the terrestrial longitude of Washington equals 77°W01'; 360 − 77° W01' = 282°-59' = 12° CP59'). The zodiacal longitudes of place obtained in this fashion are considered to be Midheavens; a table of houses is consulted with this Midheaven and the terrestrial latitude of the place to obtain an Ascendant (e.g. Berlin's latitude = 52° N30', so its ASC = 6° LE10'; Washington's latitude = 38° N53', so its ASC = 23° AR11').

Sepharial's method is the most popular one in use among earthquake predictors (see e.g. articles by Jim Haynes in *Considerations* vm. VI no.2, and Ann Parker in *Mercury Hour*

25/X/39). However, from a mathematical point of view, this method is a mish-mash for the following reasons:

1) Terrestrial longitude corresponds to right ascension in the sky, *not* zodiacal longitude (since both terrestrial longitude and right ascension are measured in the plane of the earth's equator, whereas zodiacal longitude is measured in the plane of the ecliptic). To impose an ecliptic measurement on the earth's equator is to badly jumble the geometric symbolism.

2) To then derive an "Ascendant" from such a "Midheaven" is a completely fictitious calculation: you can plug numbers into it and get numbers out of it, but it's GIGO – it isn't a valid geometrical model because it doesn't describe anything that's actually going on out there in an astronomical sense.

3) The choice of the Greenwich meridian baseline (Greenwich = 0 degrees Aries) is wholly arbitrary and unfounded, again because it doesn't model any geometrical or geophysical reality.

Johndro's Method

A correct method of calculating geodetic equivalents is the same as a method of calculating astrolocality maps for a universal house system for a given Sidereal Time. A universal house system is one in which the projection poles don't depend upon a given place of birth. There are two such house systems: Meridian (which includes Alcabitius as a subset), which projects from the north pole (of the earth or sky); and Morinus (which includes Equals and Porphyry as subsets) which projects from the ecliptic pole (of the earth or sky).

The Johndro method of calculating geodetic equivalents is the same thing as a Meridian astrolocality map, for one of two fixed Sidereal Times. In the course of his career Johndro advocated two possible Sidereal Times, switching back and forth as he discovered that neither one of them worked very well (see Geoffrey Dean, *Recent Advances in Natal Astrology*, page 193). Johndro's pyramid baseline system uses an ST = 1h 56m 40s on the Greenwich meridian (in 1930; or ST = 1h 59m 52s in 1992). This method puts the Aries point on the earth's equator at 29 degrees 58 minutes west longitude in 1992. Supposedly the Aries point was located on the meridian of the Great Pyramid at the time it was built, and has receded westward in the interim due to precession. Later Johndro switched from the pyramid baseline to an ST = 0h 0m 0s at Greenwich (which doesn't move due to precession).

Using the pyramid baseline, the right ascension of a place on earth is equal to 29° 58' (in 1992) plus the terrestrial longitude of the place east of Greenwich. For example, the terrestrial longitude of Berlin is 13°E23'; 29°-58' + 13°-23' = 43°-21', which is taken to be the RAMC of Berlin. From a table of houses for the latitude of Berlin (52° N30') we find that this RAMC corresponds to an MC of 15° TA49' and ASC of 27° LE40'.

Using the Greenwich baseline, the right ascension of a place on earth is equal to its terrestrial longitude east of Greenwich. Again, a table of houses is consulted for the latitude of the place to obtain values for the MC and ASC (in the case of Berlin, an RAMC of 13°-23' at 52° N30 yields an MC = 14° AR32' and an ASC = 6° LE55').

Although Johndro's method (unlike Sepharial's) is based on a correct astronomical model, the use of a Greenwich baseline is wholly arbitrary and unfounded; and the use of a pyramid baseline, while not unfounded (since it does align with an actual feature on the earth) is still arbitrary. Why not use Stonehenge; or the Potala Palace; or Disneyland? Also, the notion that the baseline moves along the earth's equator due to precession is an arbitrary and unfounded assumption.

Moreover, in deriving his Ascendants Johndro employed geocentric rather than geographic latitude, which is manifestly incorrect. Geographic latitude should be used in all celestial sphere calculations (see Robert Hand, *Essays*, page 49; or my book *Primary Directions*, page 9, for a refutation). It is not surprising, therefore, that Johndro could not obtain satisfactory results from either of his systems.

Zodiacal Method

The other universal house system is that of Morinus, which gives rise to the Zodiacal method of calculating astrolocality maps, and which can be used in turn to obtain a system of Zodiacal geodetic equivalents once we specify a Sidereal Time. In this case, however, we do have one obvious baseline at our disposal which is not wholly arbitrary and unfounded.

In Zodiacal astrolocality maps we project from the north ecliptic pole, which is located at a terrestrial latitude of co-obliquity (about 67 degrees north) and which sweeps around the 67th parallel in the course of 24 hours. If we place the north ecliptic pole on the meridian of the north magnetic pole, then we've got a system of geodetic equivalents which makes some kind of logical sense (which is not to say that it would work in practice).

The earth's magnetic poles move over time; in 1992 the north magnetic pole was located at 104° W18', 78° N24'; and the south magnetic pole was located at 138° E42', 64° S42'. In 2001 the north magnetic pole was located at 110° W48', 81° N18'; and the south magnetic pole was located at 137° E52', 64° S32'. The rather rapid movement of the magnetic poles leads to rapid changes in the zodiacal longitude of a place on earth over time (see last two columns of table below for 1992 and 2001 figures, respectively).

To calculate the Zodiacal longitude for a given place on earth, we identify the longitude of the north magnetic pole with an RAMC of 270 (which is the RAMC of the north ecliptic pole). In other words, we use the Zodiacal Longitude of Place Algorithm (on page 136 of the appendix of my *Primary Directions* book) with a birthplace longitude of 104° W18' (1992) or 110° W48' (2001) and an ST = 18 hours. To project with the south magnetic pole, we go into the Zodiacal Longitude of Place Algorithm with a birthplace longitude = 138° E42' (1992) or 137° E52' (2001) and an ST = 6 hours.

The main theoretical objection to this system of geodetic equivalents is that the north and south magnetic poles do not lie exactly opposite one another on the earth; and neither one lies on the 67th parallel (though they're close to it).

It has been suggested by Bob Wachtel (co-author of the *Occidental Table of Houses*) that average values of the magnetic poles be computed by "smoothing out" the locus of points equidistant from the two magnetic poles to make a great circle on the earth.

It has also been suggested that the north magnetic pole be used to calculate Zodiacal longitudes for places on earth in the northern hemisphere, and that the south magnetic pole be used for places in the southern hemisphere; presumably one would split the difference for points on the equator.

Unlike the Sepharial and Johndro methods, the Zodiacal method yields only one Zodiacal longitude for each place on earth, rather than two (an "MC" and "ASC"). Here is a table for several places on earth, with zodiacal longitudes computed according to each system (in the case of the Sepharial and Johndro methods, only the "MC"s are given, not the "ASC"s):

Place	Sepharial	Johndro Greenwich	Johndro Pyramid	Zodiacal 1992	Zodiacal 2001
London	29°PI54'	29°PI53	2°TA02'	6°TA49'	11°TA26
Paris	2°AR20'	2°AR32'	4°TA34'	6°TA50'	11°TA35'
Berlin	13°AR32	14°AR32'	15°TA49'	16°TA51'	21°TA54'
Moscow	7°TA35'	9°TA59'	9°GE14'	4°GE42'	9°GE00'
Beijing	26°CN24	24°CN29'	24°LE03'	2°LE28'	7°LE30'
Tokyo	19°LE45	17°LE18'	18°VI49	22°LE37'	27°LE55'
Melbourne	25°LE00	22°LE39'	24°VI31'	29°VI04'	4°LI54'
San Fran.	27°SC34	29°SC45'	27°SG44'	1°SG05'	11°SG10'
Chicago	2°CP21'	2°CP09'	0°AQ08'	28°CP45'	8°AQ53'
Washington	12°CP59	11°CP56'	10°AQ30'	12°AQ50'	21°AQ31'

What Do We Mean by "Strength"?
(Some Notes that Got Left Out of *Planetary Strength*)

There is probably no term in astrology so fundamental and so vague as "strength" – that this or that criterion (ruler/exaltation; angular; conjunct a fixed star) makes a planet "strong". Many systems of analysis, such as the Vedic Shad Bala and the Church of Light's astrodynes, have been promulgated to precisely measure the strength of each planet, or to identify the "dominant" planet(s) in a horoscope. But nowhere is the term "strength" defined in such a manner as to provide an inkling of what the devil it is that we are trying to measure here.

In the first place we must distinguish between "strength" (meaning power) on the one hand, and good / bad, dignity / debility, harmonious / disharmonious, beneficent / maleficent, on the other. It is clear that the definition of "strength" can be laid upon the "good / bad" dichotomy: a planet can be "strongly good" or "strongly bad". If a planet is posited in a sign it rules, we say that it is "strong", meaning powerful for the good. If it is located in its detriment, we say it is "weak", meaning powerful for the bad. A planet in bad celestial state (detriment) is as powerful as a planet in good celestial state (ruler), but its strength is for the bad rather than the good. Only when it is in a sign in which it has no essential dignity at all (neither good nor bad) is it truly "weak" – lacking in power for neither good nor ill.

The dichotomy of good / bad, harmonious / disharmonious, have reference to the dichotomy of material / spiritual. What is good in pursuit of material ends is bad in pursuit of spiritual ends, and vice versa. Most of our clients come to us astrologers in pursuit of material ends, so we quite arbitrarily label criteria which symbolize material gain as "good". With our occidental values and outlook we label anything which means comfort, success, leisure, back-patting as "good"; and anything which entails work, challenge, sacrifice, and discipline as "bad". However Vedic astrology, which values the spiritual good more highly than the material good, reverses our "good" / "bad" nomenclature. Thus, for example, in occidental astrology retrogradation is considered to be a debility, whereas in Vedic astrology it is considered a dignity.

Therefore it is clear that the distinction "good" versus "bad" is wholly arbitrary, and the labels "good" and "bad" could just as easily be interchanged by shifting our point of view.

Having once decided what it is we mean by "good" (in this case, good for material things), we can now try to define what we mean by "strength". By "strength" we will mean focalization along some previously determined line of interpretation – in other words, a planet is considered to be "strong" if it calls attention to itself once we have decided to pay attention to it.

To consider a planet as angular, or retrograde, or conjunct a fixed star, is to pay a certain kind of attention to it, to place certain expectations on it, to see it in a certain way. And it either fulfills those expectations, disappoints those expectations, or doesn't give a damn one way or the other. Astrology, like the materialistic sciences, is a mirror: it will reflect back at you whatever you are looking for or seeking to find in it. What we call "strong" is a "strong" reflection of what we seek to find. Thus the term "strength" in predictive astrology means "predictability" – do important events run to a type consonant with the planetary symbolism involved?

One way of looking at "strength" is as a species of conservation of energy: angular planets, well-aspected planets, and essentially dignified planets show energy that is conserved and deployed wisely; whereas cadent, afflicted, and essentially debilitated planets show wasted energy – more energy being expended than is necessary. This definition of "strength" is a measure of effectiveness, smoothness, naturalness, effortlessness, cleanness of planetary action.

What we mean by "strength" is precisely the same thing that we mean by "strength" or "greatness" in art. The vivid emotional quality which makes Beethoven's music or Rembrandt's paintings or Faulkner's novels "strong" is the same quality we are measuring when we speak of planetary strength. Although this sort of strength is wholly subjective, nonetheless there is a consensus of people knowledgeable in the field to agree on what is "strong" and what isn't. The strength conferred upon a planet in its ruling sign has a very different flavor to it than the strength conferred by angularity, just as Rembrandt's art has a different feeling to it than van Gogh's art; but they are both *strong*.

But since basically what we are measuring is strength of feeling, there is no way it can be reduced to numbers. The temptation to try to calculate overall "strength" totals for the planets has led to various pseudo-mathematical attempts to quantify this mysterious quality, such as Shad Bala in Vedic astrology; astrodynes in the Church of Light methodology; and even my gurus J.B. Morin and Dr. Marc Edmund Jones promulgated methods for numerically measuring overall strength of each planet.

But I don't believe that this is a fruitful endeavor. About the best we can hope for in the way of pinning "strength" down to something measurable is to impose the dichotomy "good" / "bad" over it. That is, if we consider strength to be like a vector, we give up all hope of measuring its magnitude and content ourselves with measuring its direction.

Observe that the good / bad dichotomy also underpins the definition of "strength", even in the case of factors which are nominally neutral, such as conjunctions. A conjunction is not normally considered intrinsically good or bad, but it is still generally considered to be the strongest aspect.

Conjunction with a critical degree is generally regarded as enhancing a planet's strength – and whether this is good or bad is wholly a matter of viewpoint. Conjunction with a critical degree is definitely good for spiritual concerns and bad for material concerns. Of course, this assumes that you look at critical degrees in the first place, since as mentioned previously wherever you look – whatever you put your attention on – thereby becomes important. And in astrology, susceptibility to analysis can always conjure up some interpretation to fit (worry not: the materialistic sciences as practiced in academia are in the same fix. So we astrologers are not the only ones who don't know what the hell we are talking about).

There is a modern tendency within astrology to attempt to define "strength" statistically – that a given horoscope factor is considered to be "strong" if it can be shown to statistically correlate with an identifiable population. Of course, Gauquelin has been the spearhead of this movement. The chief limitation to this approach is the difficulty of finding identifiable populations; that is to say, the information which a horoscope gives us about a native is not often information which can be correlated with an isolable population group. Angularity, however, can be analyzed in this fashion, as

Gauquelin showed, because what it symbolizes (success) can be measured objectively (after a fashion) – there are objective criteria of success which can be used to identify and isolate a statistically analyzable population.

Gauquelin's work showed only a correlation between angular planets and eminent professionals – had he tried it with all (eminent and obscure) professionals he would have found nothing. And, luckily, eminence is something which can be measured statistically.

It should also be possible to obtain a correlation between afflicted horoscopes and people who are indubitably struggling (e.g. prison and refugee camp inmates, bankrupts, etc.). But a list of members of posh country clubs wouldn't necessarily correlate with well-aspected charts. Although you could probably get a sample of people who don't receive much social validation, it would be difficult to get a sample of people who do, since what we are measuring are psychological, emotional, attitudinal factors which only rarely will correlate with some recognizable (isolable) segment of the population.

In other words, if we define "strength" to mean "that which can be shown to be statistically significant" we are on solid ground from a materialistic point of view, but we are limited to considering only a tiny fraction of the information contained in a birth chart.

But generally speaking, what a horoscope shows cannot be directly correlated to specific populations which could be pulled out of a database. It's dubious that essential dignity could ever be measured statistically since what it indicates is a sense of style, grace, and artistry; but this doesn't mean that essential dignity doesn't "strengthen" planetary function in some definable way – it just means that that definition is not amenable to statistical analysis.

BOOKS BY BOB MAKRANSKY:

Bob's Amazon.com book page =
amazon.com/author/bobmakransky

* * * * * * * *

Intermediate-level Astrology textbooks:

Planetary Strength – a commentary on Morinus

An essential contribution to natal horoscope interpretation. Taking as its point of departure *Astrologia Gallica* by Jean Baptiste Morin de Villefranche (1583 - 1656), *Planetary Strength* explains the differences between the strengths conferred upon planets by virtue of their sign placements (celestial state); house placements (terrestrial state); and aspects (aspectual state). A detailed system of keywords is augmented by insightful "cookbook" interpretations for each and every planetary combination. The depth and quality of the analysis – as well as the hundreds of practical examples and tips – make *Planetary Strength* an essential reference work which both neophyte and experienced practitioners will consult every time they read a horoscope.

"The book is beautifully written. With Makransky, whether you agree or disagree is not the issue - you will always get a good read. It is clear. He has done his homework. He makes the genius of Morinus accessible to English speakers. He shows us how to 'think astrologically'." – Joseph Polansky, *Diamond Fire* magazine

"What's fascinating about Planetary Strength *is that the author is using his own prose to describe the planets' conditions. In the introduction, he advises readers to study Morinus, but clearly Makransky's efforts are the better source. ... Try them in practice and compare these interpretations to what you might otherwise think about a planet. It may just sharpen your ability to make accurate statements about character, a person's history, and even to make predictions. And what more do you ask of astrology?"* – Chris Lorenz, *Dell Horoscope* magazine

"This is certainly an interesting addition to reading and interpreting the translations of Morinus' original work. It is detailed and considered, and the author's knowledge and experience are evident throughout." – Helen Stokes, *AA Journal*

"Presenting a mixture of discussion, detailed cookbook offerings and chart examples as well as keywords and tables, this fascinating book also addresses the fixed stars. ... This fascinating book assumes a fair knowledge of astrology as well as some experience in preparing charts." – Margaret Gray, *ISAR*

"This is a book that every beginner as well as advanced student of astrology would do well to possess. The author is extremely perceptive in his descriptions of the planets in their various strength and weaknesses ... this book would be a helpful aid to the researcher, as it would point him in the right direction." – Wanda Sellar, *Correlation*

Planetary Strength – 130 pages – paperback –
Price = £ 11.99
http://wessexastrologer/product/waps001/

*   *   *   *   *   *   *

Planetary Combination

Planetary Combination picks up where *Planetary Strength* left off, explaining how the planetary influences combine in aspects and configurations to paint a picture of a person and his or her life. Descriptions of planetary configurations such as Grand Trines, Grand Squares, T-Crosses, Wedges, Fans, Rectangles, Kites, and Trapezoids provide overall schematics of people's psychological dynamics. Then, detailed interpretations for the conjunctions, sextiles / trines, squares, oppositions, parallels / contraparallels, and Mutual Receptions between the individual planets enable the practitioner to see clearly how these dynamics work out in a particular horoscope. An illuminating chapter on planetary conjunctions with the moon's nodes reveals the underlying karmic influences at work. An indispensable reference you'll consult every time you read a chart.

"While this book is nominally a series of explanations about aspects between the traditional planets, the degree of character description for each planetary pair is extraordinarily precise. An entire personality is captured within these aspects. In the same way that the author provides highly detailed character sketches for each planetary duo, he gives the same attention to configurations. In addition to the most common shapes, he also provides several pages on shapes that are not found in any other astrology text. An unusually terse and bold reference, Planetary Combination *transcends psychological mumbo-jumbo to give you the bare-naked reality of the adult Western psyche."*
– Chris Lorenz, *Dell Horoscope magazine.*

"You are entering a world of verbal complexity and conceptual subtlety. There will be plenty you have not seen anywhere else. You may find Makransky's approach to astrology insightful, delightfully unconventional, or just plain weird. I applaud Bob Makransky and his publisher Margaret Cahill at Wessex Astrologer for having produced a work of originality and complexity and befuddlement, astonishment and inspiration and irritation."
– Joseph Crane, The Astrology Institute

*"*Planetary Combination *is an excellent and comprehensive summary of all the relevant chart factors. ... One has to search hard to find such material! But this is all presented, as is all of Makransky's work, with vigour, wisdom and accessibility. ... Much of the book is taken up – as we might expect – with a very generous coverage of the astrological aspects. I looked up a few of my own and they were spot on. ...* Planetary Combination *fills a gap in the current state of astrological literature. It manages to retain both a sense of firm tradition whilst feeling utterly new and fresh."* – James Lynn Page, author of Everyday Tarot, Celtic Magic, The Christ Enigma and The New Positive Thinking.

"This is one of the best books on aspects out there. He not only deals with aspects themselves, but goes deep into chart morphology. It is one thing to analyze aspects and quite another to look at the 'pictures' - the forms - that the aspects make. Most books on aspects deal with the aspects of longitude. But he also includes the parallels and contra-parallels. He has an interesting discussion

of orbs, values (strengths of an aspect) and mutual receptions. A student would have to read many books from many authors to get the information that is given here. As always with Bob Makransky's work, the book is interesting and well written, not for a beginner or casual reader, but fascinating nevertheless - especially for a serious student." – Joseph Polansky, *Diamond Fire* magazine

Planetary Combination – 232 pages paperback
Price = £ 17.50
http://wessexastrologer/product/wapc001/

* * * * * * *

Planetary Hours

Planetary Hours are an ancient astrological system for selecting favorable times to act (and avoiding unfavorable times), by assigning planetary rulers to the twenty-four hours of the day. **Contents:** instructions for finding and interpreting your birthday and birth hour rulers; electional astrology – how to use the Planetary Hours to find lucky times to act (to ask for money; to ask someone on a date or to marry; to go on a journey; to begin a new business); how to cast spells; the Firdaria, an ancient astrological prediction system; Tables of Planetary Hours for any day of the year, and for anywhere on earth from the Equator to 58° North and South latitudes.

"Bob Makransky's new book ably taps the rising vogue for traditional astrology, though eschewing the fatalism often assigned to so-called 'magical' ancient approaches. He describes Planetary Hours (PH) as the "astrology of luck" and a method of finding empowering life moments for the proper exercise of freewill – to be yourself and not an enslaved cog of convention. ... As an introduction, this book is highly accessible." – *AA Journal*

"Bob Makransky has written the definitive book on Planetary Hours. It's the best book on the subject out there. It will be read and studied by future generations of astrologers. Its not just something

that you read and discard. You want it in your bookshelf to refer to again and again." – Joseph Polansky, *Diamond Fire* magazine

Planetary Hours – 130 pages – paperback
Price = £ 11.00
http://wessexastrologer/product/waph001/

* * * * * * * *

Bob Makransky's Introduction to Magic Series:

"In this series, not only do we get an author who knows his subject inside out, but also a directness of approach often not seen in works of this kind. Not for Makransky the wishy-washy approach that attempts to soothe and reassure the reader with false promises of magical success - something about which many customer complaints arise on the Amazon website - but, rather, an honest and uncompromising study of what Magic really entails. – James Lynn Page (author of *Celtic Magic, Everyday Tarot* and *The Christ Enigma*)

What is Magic?, the introductory book on witchcraft, can be sampled and purchased at:
paperback $19.95: http://www.amzn.com/1499279418
ebook $9.95: https://www.smashwords.com/books/view/132491

Magical Living, the second volume about paganism, can be sampled and purchased at:
paperback $16.95: http://www.amzn.com/1499279337
ebook $9.95: https://www.smashwords.com/books/view/22860

Thought Forms, the third volume about cognitive psychology and the Mercury cycle, can be sampled and purchased at:
paperback $24.95: http://www.amzn.com/1499267444
ebook $9.95: https://www.smashwords.com/books/view/22859

The Great Wheel, the fourth volume about reincarnation and the lunation cycle, can be sampled and purchased at: paperback $24.95:
http://www.amzn.com/154416355X
ebook $9.95:
http://www.smashwords.com/books/view/306020

Volume I of Bob's Introduction to Magic series:

What is Magic?

Magic is a spiritual path which is not very well understood in our society. This is because the theory and practice of magic have never before been explained clearly and convincingly, in a way that makes sense to intelligent and thoughtful people. Written in a sassy, irreverent style, *What is Magic?* discusses how such otherworldly concepts as demons, casting spells, and bewitching are just the hidden underside of everyday society – the skeletons in everybody's closet. *What is Magic?* answers the questions which all serious spiritual seekers, no matter what their spiritual path, ask at one time or another, but can never find satisfactorily answered:

1) What is the difference between faith and fooling yourself?
2) What is the relationship between altered states and normal, everyday life?
3) If you lose your desires, as many spiritual paths advocate, what zest or spice does life have left?
4) If the world is an illusion or dream, as it's said to be, then why does it seem so real?
5) Where does the world of magic – the shaman's world – take off from the world of everyday life? What and where is the interface?
6) Why is it so difficult to achieve real, permanent spiritual growth?

Contents: Spirits, Intent, The Nature of Reality, Spells, Charms & Rituals, Science Debunked, Demons, The Nature of the Self, Bewitching, Magic & Money, Death, Black Magicians & Vampires, Power Places, The Magician's God, Magical Time, Magic and Morality, Dreaming & Stalking, Magic and Sex.

"Bob is daring, willing to be offensive with his truths, and wise in the ways of words and magic. ... Bob Makransky, I feel, has written a great treatise on magic. I urge you to enjoy it as much as I have." from the foreword by Michael Peter Langevin, publisher of *Magical Blend* magazine.

"There is a certain no-nonsensical feel to his presentation that is both refreshing and a bit disconcerting. Makransky's writing

style is very different from other New Age authors, and that alone should appeal to readers looking for a bit more substance in their study of magic" – J Byrne, *Psychic Magic* magazine

What is Magic? paperback $19.95:
http://www.amzn.com/1499279418
ebook $9.95: https://www.smashwords.com/books/view/132491

*   *   *   *   *

Volume II of Bob's Introduction to Magic series:

Magical Living

Winner of the Reader Views Reviewer's Choice Award; the Sacramento Publishers' Association Awards for Best Nonfiction and Best Spiritual book; and Mind-Body-Spirit Finalist in the National Indie Excellence Awards and the USA Book News Best Books Awards.

Contents: How to channel spirit guides, communicate with plants and nature spirits, develop your psychic vision; together with inspirational essays on managing love relationships, handling oppressive people, and dealing with hurt.

"*I love this little book! ... Carry this book with you, read and reread the essays, and connect with joy.* " – Kathryn Lanier, *InnerChange* magazine

"*He writes beautifully, clearly, elegantly ... he is incapable of an unoriginal thought.*" – Joseph Polansky, *Diamond Fire* magazine

"*I could not get enough! I actually read some of the essays 2 to 3 times and discovered new insights each time. ... Magical Living by Bob Makransky is an easy to read little book with a lot of surprises. A great book to revisit more than once!*" – Susan Violante, *Reader Views*

"*It's a beautiful little book to carry around for when you just want something to read at odd moments, but I suspect that, for some, it will be a book that's picked up over and over again. At times, I find myself ruminating over something I read or glance at the contents*

page to have something jump out at me that's relevant to the moment. I highly recommend this book to anyone with an open mind and a real willingness to look at themselves and their surroundings."
– J Byrne, *Psychic-Magic* magazine

Magical Living: paperback $16.95:
http://www.amzn.com/1499279337
ebook $9.95: https://www.smashwords.com/books/view/22860

* * * * *

Volume III of Bob's Introduction to Magic series

Thought Forms

Contents: Astronomical and astrological explanations of Mercury's synodic cycle – its cycle of phases as it circles the sun, with tables 1900-2050; explanation of the astrological / magical view of mind (the theory of thought forms): what consciousness is, how it arose, and whither it is going; basic course in white magic with detailed instructions on: how to channel and banish thought forms; creative visualization; how to banish the black magicians in everyday life; how to cast out demons; how to use tree spirits.

"Bob Makransky is a knowledgeable, purposeful and entertaining writer." – Paul F. Newman, *The International Astrologer*

"*Steady* Diamond Fire *readers are well acquainted with the genius of Bob Makransky. Highly recommendable.*" – Joseph Polansky, *Diamond Fire*

"Considerations *readers have become familiar with [Makransky's] fresh insights into different facets of astrology. In this book* Thought Forms *he is especially provocative and I strongly recommend its purchase and study.*" – Ken Gillman, *Considerations*

"Thought Forms *is both highly readable and highly informative, and is very definitely worth checking out.*" – Kenneth Irving, *American Astrology* magazine

"*I will fully agree with the statement that 'You've never read a book like this before!' The material is fresh and woven very skillfully*

to conclusion. I look forward to his next installment of the trilogy."
– Marion MacMillan, *SHAPE*

Thought Forms paperback $24.95:
http://www.amzn.com/1499267444
ebook $9.95: https://www.smashwords.com/books/view/22859

* * * * *

Volume IV of Bob's Introduction to Magic series

The Great Wheel – *a commentary on the System of W.B. Yeats'* **A Vision**

Contents: connecting with your true purpose in this life; how to run past life regressions, probable reality progressions, and recapitulation of present life memories; interpretations for the 28 phases of the moon in the natal horoscope; Mind and Memory, Waking and Dreaming, Change, Familiarity, and the Akashic Records.

"This new work in Bob Makransky's excellent and thought provoking 'Introduction to Magic' series ... is a fascinating and illuminating take on the meaning of the Moon. It's truly a Moon book unlike any other and is guaranteed to alter your perception of yourself and the world." – Paul F. Newman, author *LUNA: The Astrological Moon*

The Great Wheel paperback $24.95:
http://www.amzn.com/154416355X
ebook $9.99 from: http://www.smashwords.com/books/view/306020

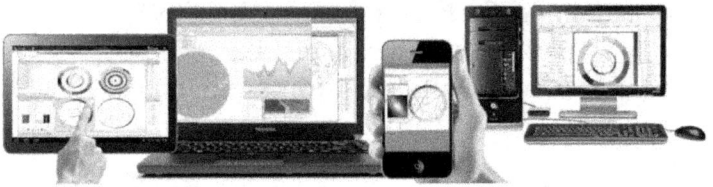

AstroApp is the first professional Astrology software that is available entirely online.

AstroApp supports all schools of Astrology: Modern, Hellenistic, Medieval, Vedic, Chinese, Tibetan, Mayan, Huber, Uranian, Cosmobiology, 13-Signs, Magic, Medical, Generalized Planetary Hours, Synastry, Mundane, AstroGeography, Financial and more.

AstroApp upgrades are frequent, automatic and always FREE!

AstroApp will run anywhere: on Mac, Win, Linux; on SmartTVs; as a mobile app on all Tablets and Smartphones **(Android, iOS, Win).**

AstroApp is fully customizable and is available in 5 Editions and 10 languages.

AstroApp is also available as a **Facebook** app.

AstroApp.com

www.ingramcontent.com/pod-product-compliance
Lightning Source LLC
Chambersburg PA
CBHW050620300426
44112CB00012B/1587